WAY DOWN
YONDER IN THE
INDIAN NATION

Oil Man:
The Story of Frank Phillips
and the Birth of Phillips Petroleum
(1988)

Route 66:
The Mother Road
(1990)

Pretty Boy:
The Life and Times
of Charles Arthur Floyd
(1992)

WRITING
FROM
AMERICA'S
HEARTLAND

ST. MARTIN'S PRESS NEW YORK

WAY DOWN YONDER IN THE INDIAN NATION

MICHAEL WALLIS

The publisher gratefully acknowledges permission to reprint the following:

"Oil Man" from *Oil Man: The Story of Frank Phillips and the Birth of Phillips Petroleum*, Doubleday, 1988; "Route 66" from *Route 66: The Mother Road*, St. Martin's Press, 1990; "Pretty Boy" from *Pretty Boy: The Life and Times of Charles Arthur Floyd*, St. Martin's Press, 1992; "Thunderbirds: The Fighting 45th," which appeared as "These Colors Don't Run" in *Oklahoma Today* in 1985; "A Golden Time in the West," which appeared as "Mennonites: A Search for the Golden Time in the West" in *American West* in 1981; "Okie Deco," which appeared in *Oklahoma Today* in 1988; "Texhoma: The Lives and Times of a Border Town," which appeared in *Oklahoma Today* in 1985; "The Way Things Used to Be," which appeared as "Riding Herd on the West" in *Oklahoma Today* in 1985; "Freckles," which appeared in *Oklahoma Today* in 1985; "That Old House: Woody Guthrie's Home in Oklahoma," which appeared in a different form in *American West* in 1982; "The Mystic Blend of Fire, Smoke, and Meat," which appeared as "Sniffing Out the Best 'Q' " in *Oklahoma Today* in 1982; "An All-American Spiritual Warrior," which appeared in *Sooners Illustrated* in 1990 and as "Football's Unrepentant Rebel" in *Oklahoma Today* in 1992; "Oklahoma's Most Haunted," which appeared in *Oklahoma Today* in 1990; and "Hail to the Chief," which appeared in a different form in *Phillip Morris* in 1989; Quotation by Woody Guthrie on page 20, copyright © 1947 (renewed) by Woody Guthrie Publications Inc. All rights reserved. Used by permission; and "So Long, It's Been Good to Know Yuh" ("Dusty Old Dust"). Words and music by Woody Guthrie. TRO—copyright © 1940 (renewed), 1950 (renewed), and 1963 (renewed) Folkways Music Publishers, Inc., New York, N.Y.

Library of Congress Cataloging-in-Publication Data

Wallis, Michael
    Way down yonder in the Indian nation : writings from America's heartland / Michael Wallis.
        p.   cm.
    ISBN 0-312-09410-8
    1. Oklahoma—Social life and customs.   I. Title.
F701.W35   1993
976.6—dc20   93-14838
                                                          CIP

Design by Maura Fadden Rosenthal

First Edition: June 1993
10 9 8 7 6 5 4 3 2 1

To Suzanne Fitzgerald Wallis,
the woman who shares my journey

To Angie Debo,
the distinguished historian, teacher, author,
and editor,
an inspiration to so many others,
and an Oklahoma pioneer
who deserves nothing less than sainthood

CONTENTS

ACKNOWLEDGMENTS   XI
INTRODUCTION   XV

1. SEARCHING FOR HIDDEN RHYTHMS IN
    TWILIGHT LAND   1
2. THAT OLD HOUSE: WOODY GUTHRIE'S HOME
    IN OKLAHOMA   19
3. ROUTE 66: THE MOTHER ROAD   29
4. THE MYSTIC BLEND OF FIRE, SMOKE, AND MEAT   59
5. THUNDERBIRDS: THE FIGHTING 45TH   73
6. A GOLDEN TIME IN THE WEST   89
7. OIL MAN   99
8. OKIE DECO   125
9. TEXHOMA: THE LIVES AND TIMES OF A
    BORDER TOWN   137
10. THE WAY THINGS USED TO BE   149
11. PRETTY BOY   157
12. AN ALL-AMERICAN SPIRITUAL WARRIOR   177
13. OKLAHOMA'S MOST HAUNTED   195
14. FRECKLES   207
15. HAIL TO THE CHIEF   217
16. THE REAL WILD WEST   229

PHOTOGRAPHIC CREDITS   252
ABOUT THE AUTHOR   253

ACKNOWLEDGMENTS

During the process of putting this book together, the generous encouragement and understanding of my wife, Suzanne Fitzgerald Wallis, and our friends Dixie Haas and Scott Dooley helped me more than they will ever know. I am forever grateful to them for all of their love, suggestions, and patience.

Scott was always there when I needed to test the waters. I appreciate his critical ear. Mostly, I prize his friendship.

Dixie acted as my primary researcher, assistant, sounding board, guide, and much more. When I think of Dixie, words like *diligent*, *unselfish*, and *hard-working* come to mind. A talented writer in her own right, she is a literary angel of the highest order.

Suzanne has never failed me. I know she never will. She remains a constant source of inspiration. It was my good fortune to marry the most talented person in the world. Every day I thank my lucky stars.

I am forever grateful to Robert Weil, my editor at St. Martin's Press and a man who shares my love for the history, folklore, and culture of this country, especially the American West. Bob is bright, candid, and resourceful. Also, he goes over and above the call of editorial duty in my behalf. He is a good friend.

Others who deserve hearty thanks at St. Martin's are Becky Koh, the best editorial assistant in the Flatiron Building, and Michael Accordino, the skillful artist who breathed life into the book's cover design. I also appreciate the hard work of Stephanie

Schwartz, production editor; Andrea Connolly, copy editor; and the gifted Maura Fadden Rosenthal, interior designer.

My gratitude and special thanks to Michael Carlisle, my talented and astute literary agent and vice president of the William Morris Agency.

Many kudos and much appreciation to the highly skillful women of The Wallis Group—Kathryn Sanford, Nancy Edwards, Kim Bailey Schaefer, and Donna Cross. When it comes to creative marketing and promotion, there are none better.

My gratitude to two other important people in my life who helped more than they know with this book's birth: One of them is Allen Strider, an Oklahoma native who began as a reader of my books and has become one of my best pals. And also Dr. Lydia Wyckoff, a woman whose own life is a magical blend of England and Osage, as well as someone whom I cherish.

Many thanks for editorial and photographic assistance go to Terrence Moore, Suzi Moore, Tom Luker, Guy Logsdon, and Lynn Howard.

And, as always, my lasting appreciation to two creatures who do their damndest to keep a bit of fantasy in my hectic life. Beatrice and Molly have no feline equals when it comes to teaching mortals the fine art of daydreaming.

OKLAHOMA HILLS

Words and music by Woody Guthrie and Jack Guthrie

Many months have come and gone
since I wandered from my home,
In those Oklahoma Hills where I was born.
Tho' a page of life has turned,
and a lesson I have learned,
Yet I feel in those hills I still belong.

'Way down yonder in the Indian Nation,
I rode my pony on the reservation,
In those Oklahoma Hills where I was born.
'Way down yonder in the Indian Nation,
A cowboy's life is my occupation,
In those Oklahoma Hills where I was born.

But as I sit here today
Many miles I am away
From the place I rode my pony thru the draw.
Where the oak and blackjack trees
kiss the playful prairie breeze,
In those Oklahoma Hills where I was born.

'Way down yonder in the Indian Nation,
I rode my pony on the reservation,
In those Oklahoma Hills where I was born.
'Way down yonder in the Indian Nation,
A cowboy's life is my occupation,
In those Oklahoma Hills where I was born.

Now as I turn life a page
to a land of great Osage,
In those Oklahoma Hills where I was born.
Where the black oil rolls and flows
and the snow-white cotton grows,
In those Oklahoma Hills where I was born.

'Way down yonder in the Indian Nation,
I rode my pony on the reservation,
In those Oklahoma Hills where I was born.
'Way down yonder in the Indian Nation,
A cowboy's life is my occupation,
In those Oklahoma Hills where I was born.

INTRODUCTION

I discovered Oklahoma—in truth, uncovered Oklahoma—in 1980. It was the summer. June to be precise, and it was hot as blazes.

At the time, I made my home in Miami, Florida. I had been there for a year, working as a magazine journalist and living in a sturdy cottage made of Dade County pine. Outside my door were a pool, tennis courts, and avocado and grapefruit trees. People said my address was in the best of both worlds—between Coconut Grove and Coral Gables. Trouble was, I never felt like I really and truly lived in Miami. Like others there, I looked at myself as a transient with a packed bag waiting in the corner. I was always wondering about life elsewhere, in the places I knew from before, places where it snowed at Christmas and folks didn't pack pistols to go to a PTA meeting at their kids' school.

In Miami, I stayed busy sending in my stories and dispatches from the field to several domestic and foreign magazines. The nation seemed to hunger for news from south Florida—the scene of another exodus of Cuban refugees, as well as a favorite port for Caribbean drug smugglers. Florida appeared to be the "hard news" capital of the country. I told my friends back in the Southwest that I felt like I was living in Casablanca. Every day brought a new adventure as I followed the exploits of "cocaine cowboys" and the crime fighters who pursued them.

When the opportunity came for me to leave Florida for a

swing through Arizona, New Mexico, Oklahoma, and Texas, I almost turned it down. At first I thought that I couldn't abandon my post just because an old pal wanted me to cruise around with him to gather material for travel stories. I had more than enough material for stories within a few miles of my cottage. The threat of riots loomed over the city that summer, while endless streams of immigrants poured into the state. Not to mention the surging crime wave.

Fortunately, I reconsidered. I thought about my friend—Terrence Moore—and his proposal. Not only would I again have the chance to work with this superior photographer, but the notion of a whirlwind trip through four states promised a much-needed break from the rigors of news reporting. The journey might be the ideal tonic. I picked up my packed bag and caught a plane. It was one of the best decisions I ever made.

Our circuit began in Tucson and took us to points in New Mexico, on to several stops in Oklahoma, then south to Texas, and finally back to Arizona. We had set up a number of appointments for story interviews and photo sessions. This single journey promised to yield a half dozen superb feature stories for as many magazines. We had assignments from editors in hand. Several of the sights and many of the people we encountered along the way were memorable. Much of the time we traveled through country we both knew very well, so we saw old friends and familiar scenery.

But when Terrence's automobile glided across the Texas border and we entered Oklahoma, I was in for a real surprise. I thought I knew what Oklahoma was all about. After all, I had lived in Missouri, Texas, and New Mexico—three of the six states that share a border with Oklahoma. I had driven across the state countless times, usually going somewhere else.

This time it was different. This time I was forced to deal with Oklahoma up close. I absorbed the experience of new towns, cities, and, most important of all, new people. We covered a lot of real estate on that trip through the Sooner State. We were grateful to have a constant serenade thanks to the songs of the Eagles, Merle Haggard, and one of Oklahoma's truest treasures—Woody Guthrie. We found comfort with occasional pit stops for ice, chilled beer, and Eskimo Pies, but also through conversations with boys pumping gasoline, waitresses, and old cowboys.

We stuck to the back roads, using the busier interstates only when we were forced to make time. We drove through wheat fields, across ranch lands, and along rivers and lakes. We were up and down Oklahoma's favorite highway and America's Main Street—Route 66. We went to Elk City, Weatherford, Clinton, Okemah, Boley, Oklahoma City, Tulsa, Muskogee, Bartlesville, Atoka, Durant, and scores of other small towns and cities. We met Socialists, rednecks, rodeo stars, and Native Americans whose quiet eloquence spoke volumes. We saw Art Deco palaces, the best fireworks stand in the world, a landlocked submarine, and tallgrass prairie so beautiful it left us in tears. As I would later write, we came to Oklahoma expecting to find bland hamburger. Instead we discovered a rich chili made of filet mignon and loaded with spice. It was a damn good trip. One of our best.

Within two years I finally managed to marry a woman I should have married years before. We moved to Oklahoma. We are still here. I have written countless stories chronicling this place and published several books about the land and its people.

Enclosed within the covers of this book are some of my favorite spoonfuls of Oklahoma. I hope you relish them as much as I savor the time I spent putting them together for you.

Michael Wallis
Tulsa, Oklahoma
February 1993

1

SEARCHING FOR HIDDEN RHYTHMS IN TWILIGHT LAND

The lands [of the planet] wait for those who can discern their rhythms.

—Vine Victor Deloria, Jr.

Oklahoma is tallgrass prairie and ever-lasting mountains. It is secret patches of ancient earth tromped smooth and hard by generations of dancing feet. It is the cycle of song and heroic deed. It is calloused hands. It is the aroma of rich crude oil fused with the scent of sweat and sacred smoke. It is the progeny of an oil-field whore wed to a deacon; the sire of a cow pony bred with a racehorse. It is a stampede, a pie supper, a revival. It is a wildcat gusher coming in. It is a million-dollar deal cemented with a handshake.

Oklahoma is dark rivers snaking through red, furrowed soil; lakes rimmed with stone bluffs. It is the ghosts of proud Native Americans, crusading Socialists, ambitious cattle kings, extravagant oil tycoons, wily bandits. It is impetuous and it is wise. A land of opportunists, resilient pioneers, and vanquished souls, the state is a crazy quilt of contradictions and controversies, travails and triumphs. It has been exploited and abused, cherished and fought over. It is a puzzling place.

Forever, Oklahoma is American through and through.

It is difficult for most folks to comprehend what Oklahoma is all about. Mention the name and all sorts of images, mostly pure cliché, flitter in people's minds. They are hard-pressed to even acknowledge that Oklahoma actually has telephone service and paved streets, let alone traffic lights and flush toilets. These people would be more inclined to believe that on a daily basis Oklahomans are forced to reckon with outlaw ambushes, cantankerous rattlesnakes, and beds of quicksand. Some only need to hear "Oklahoma," and thoughts of cowboys and Indians, oil derricks, evangelists, dusty plains, and overflowing football stadiums come to mind. Just say "Oklahoma" to someone, then step back and wait for the reaction. Most responses are predictable. Many are negative.

Sometimes they picture John Steinbeck's fictional Joad family. They envision paltry Dust Bowl "Okies" dodging windswept tumbleweeds as they flee their parched tenant farm in a rattletrap jalopy crowned with a mattress and crammed with tattered belongings and faded dreams. It's a grim and enduring impression, as haunting as one of Woody Guthrie's ballads, as indelible as a Dorothea Lange or Russell Lee photograph.

Still others confess that Oklahoma causes them to conjure up notions of "good ol' boys" cruising in their pickup trucks, complete with gun rack, six-pack, and, of course, a National Rifle Association membership decal prominently displayed on the window. Typically, those with this particular image in mind steadfastly believe that Oklahoma's louts behave every bit as sexist, racist, and homophobic as other surviving Neanderthals scattered across the country.

Then there are those individuals who imagine Oklahoma as the primary stomping ground for behemothlike athletes—the kind with thick necks and puny IQs who fuel themselves on whole sides of beef seasoned with liberal doses of steroids. Football, the public has been led to believe, and with ample reason, is much more than a contact sport in Oklahoma. To a whole host of adoring disciples, football is considered an extension of every citizen's God-given rights. Some of them even relate to it as they do to their religion. For that reason, it has been said that the football field is simply another place of worship for considerable numbers of rabid Oklahoma sports fans.

And, while on the subject of religion, there is the classic perception of Oklahoma as a haven for legions of puritanical religious fundamentalists and social conservatives—the types who thrive on intolerance, censorship, and public posturing. The types who enjoy nothing more than a barbecue over a heap of banned books set ablaze. Or, perhaps the name Oklahoma sparks thoughts of those oily televangelists whose main concerns are Bible thumping, preaching in tongues over the diseased, and bilking old ladies with blue-tinted hair out of their pension checks.

Surely, all of these Oklahoma stereotypes possess a grain of truth. An examination of the record quickly proves that.

Tens of thousands of Oklahoma farm families, exactly like the Joads in Steinbeck's *The Grapes of Wrath,* made their sad exit during the terrible 1930s. The Great Depression took its toll just as the rains stopped, causing the earth to dry up and blow away. That is when, it is often said with tongue in cheek, Bakersfield, California, became the third-largest city in Oklahoma after Oklahoma City and Tulsa.

Anywhere inside the state's borders it's also relatively easy to locate an exemplary redneck complete with narrow mind, "gimme cap," and a cheek or lip bulging with tobacco. The macho "Old West" man's man—the John Wayne variety—is alive and well in Oklahoma. The state has never experienced a shortage of false patriots and manly men who go through life secretly burdened with every insecurity in the book.

And, as far as ultra-right-wingers go, oftentimes it seems that every religious zealot and political conservative drawing breath resides within the borders of Oklahoma, frequently referred to as the buckle on an ever-expanding Bible Belt. Wearing personal religious beliefs on one's sleeve in public is de rigueur in all quarters of the state, as it is in other parts of the nation. Curiously, many of those obsessed with uttering their prayers at public rallies prior to sports events have already reached a euphoric state by swigging beer. The concoction of religion, politics, patriotism, and football is as unhealthy and dangerous as a combination of alcohol and gunpowder.

Not a locale much associated with intellectual enlightenment or social and spiritual forbearance, despite much historical evidence to the contrary, Oklahoma seems to be a metaphor for the kind of hypocrisy found in Dallas, Virginia Beach, and other bastions of self-righteousness that thrive in the born-again hamlets and cities of the South and Southwest.

Unfortunately, Oklahoma remains susceptible to a full array of less-than-flattering axioms, derisive snickers, and snide commentary.

But in reality, and in the state's defense, Oklahoma doesn't deserve such a hackneyed image. Much of it is unwarranted. Many of the unfavorable stereotypes are either no longer appropriate or applicable, or else they generally overshadow and cloud a more tenable view of the state. As is often the case, the chief stereotypes are much more complicated than they appear on the surface. Some are nothing but misconceptions and distortions that have never been corrected.

Ironically, a great deal of the adverse image problem Oklahoma suffers from actually begins at home. Oklahomans do not have a proper sense of themselves or their state's history. Critical eras from the past, such as the Dust Bowl years, have been blurred or forgotten or, even worse, shunned because they seem to cast a poor light on the land and its people. There is a wholesale denial of history. At times it seems to be a conspiracy.

That is certainly not the case just south of Oklahoma, across the Red River in that sprawling state of mind named Texas. Lone Star State citizens are confident when it comes to their homeland. Make that smug. They relish their state's colorful past and accept its history, whether bitter or sweet. Walk into either a funky beer joint in Odessa or, at the opposite extreme, a fancy restaurant in Dallas and the folks there without hesitation will boast that they're damn proud to be Texans. No inferiority complexes in Texas.

On a smaller scale in the other states bordering Oklahoma, the same seems to be true. Certainly Arkansas has made positive steps in the right direction, such as launching successful economic development measures and nurturing its natural and historical resources in order to overcome any "poor Arkie" or "Dogpatch" image. For the most part, the residents of Missouri, New Mexico, Kansas, and Colorado appear confident in themselves and are cognizant of their heritage.

But for many years there has persisted this kind of second-class-citizen attitude in Oklahoma. It endures. Despite the riches and limelight brought the state by the once-phenomenal oil and gas industry and many other notable achievements, a feeling of being poor country cousins to the rest of the nation, especially the state's regional neighbors, thrives throughout Oklahoma. Money, the old adage goes, cannot buy respectability. State government hasn't been much help. For many years, stamped on motor vehicle license plates was the rather insipid motto, "Oklahoma is OK." Not "Spectacular," not "Diverse," but only "OK." Mediocrity at its best.

This apparent deficiency when it comes to appreciating the true value of the state's rich history is further strengthened because Oklahoma has never really been defined as a place. One journalist described the state as "a large flat piece of ground covered with oil wells, wheat fields, and a crop of rangy individuals." Even the people who live there have never been quite sure what Oklahoma is all about. To say the state suffers from a lack of identity is an understatement. With rare exceptions, the media and political and civic leaders historically have done little or nothing to help shape Oklahoma's image and identity. If Oklahomans have no sense of their state's history or place, how can others?

In the mid-1980s, an Oklahoma City advertising agency commissioned an informal national survey to find out how others perceived the state. Surprisingly, instead of encountering the typical stereotypes, those conducting the survey found few of the respondents connected Oklahoma with oil, cowboys and Indians, or even the Dust Bowl. Many of those polled claimed they had no impression at all of Oklahoma. Not only that, but most of the survey participants had real difficulty in pinpointing the state's location or in indicating any of Oklahoma's preeminent features. Some thought that Oklahoma was "near Texas" or "along Interstate 40," but not one person placed the state in the Southwest or the South—two of the regions that have had a profound impact on the state. Very flat, windy, and dusty were frequently the words used to describe Oklahoma. The survey also showed that few people associated Oklahoma with the Great Plains region.

The results of the survey informed state leaders that in some respects not much had changed, although in recent years many of the traditional stereotypes about Oklahoma seem to have re-emerged. Apparently people either have some vague notion of the state based on one of those conventional opinions or else, and perhaps worse, they don't have an inkling about Oklahoma. Ask any reasonably intelligent-looking person on the street in Buffalo, Seattle, or Tampa to provide the location of Oklahoma and, likely as not, after one or more of the clichés about the place registers in their mind, they are hard-pressed to give a precise answer. It's really not that difficult.

To find Oklahoma, simply start by looking toward the midsection of the nation. Oklahoma lies slightly south of the geographic center of the United States. A huge plateau, the state tilts down generally from northwest to southeast, ranging from about 5,000 feet above sea level at Black Mesa in the far northwestern corner of the Panhandle to the less-than-325-feet level in the southeastern corner on the Red River.

Oklahoma has common boundaries with six states—Colorado and Kansas on the north, Missouri and Arkansas on the east, Texas on the south, and Texas and New Mexico on the west. It is part of what is known as the Great Plains region. The state is shaped roughly like a meat cleaver or a saucepan, with the pan's bottom formed by the winding Red River and the conspicuous Panhandle—a treeless region, once known as "No Man's Land," that is only thirty-four miles wide and juts out to the west for 166 miles in length.

Surely geography is a major contributor to Oklahoma's identity problem. It is a state without any strong sense of place in national thinking. Perhaps that is the reason Rand McNally—the venerable geographer—even forgot to include Oklahoma in one edition of a U.S. atlas. Too many times, Oklahoma is simply described as being west of Arkansas, south of Kansas, and north of Texas. Because of Oklahoma's geographic location and patterns of development, some people identify it as a southern state while others assign a western-state status. Lots of other folks, including natives, ask if the state is midwestern or southwestern. What is it? Oklahoma, they finally decide, is just out there somewhere.

The fact remains, the total area of 69,919 square miles, or roughly 45 million acres, makes Oklahoma the eighteenth-largest state in geographical size in the United States. It is bigger than any state to the east aside from Minnesota and, with the exceptions of Hawaii and Washington, smaller than any of the states to the south, north, or west. Oklahoma is one-eighth the size of Alaska, and more than twice as big as all of New England.

Situated between 94 degrees 29 feet and 103 degrees west longitude and 33 degrees 41 feet and 37 degrees north latitude, Oklahoma's latitudinal location, coupled with its great size, had a noticeable influence on the cultural activities of its citizens. So did the land itself.

Contrary to popular belief, Oklahoma is far from treeless. A fourth of the state is covered with forest, representing 133 varieties of native trees. In central and eastern Oklahoma, blackjack and post oak are prevalent. These trees grow so closely together that the first travelers through the region found the going difficult. Later, during the heyday of the Chisholm, Shawnee, and Texas trails, it was a chore to drive herds of cattle through the cross timbers.

The terrain of Oklahoma is like its fabled weather. It changes completely as it crosses the state. It varies from the Great Salt Plains to verdant forests and unceasing seas of wheat. Oklahoma ranges from cypress bayous, pine forests, and woodlands filled with hardwoods—oak, honey locust, hickory, pecan, and syca-more—to the high plains and semiarid desert sprouting cactus, mesquite, sage, buffalo grass, salt cedar, and willow. Principal streams include the Arkansas, Cimarron, North Canadian, Cana-dian, Washita, Illinois, Verdigris, Grand, and Red rivers. There is also an abundance of lakes. Eastern Oklahoma has an even higher ratio of square miles to water surface than Minnesota, the state known for its many lakes. Oklahoma's not all flat, either. There are also plenty of mountains and hills—the Arbuckles, the Wichitas, the Kiamichis, the Winding Stairs, the Ouachitas, the Jackforks, the Cooksons.

The state is in the transition zone between the humid Mid-west and the drier Southwest, between the grasslands of the West and the forests of the East, between the low elevations of the coastal plains and the higher elevations of the Rocky Mountain foothills, and between the long growing season of the South and the shorter growing season of the North. It is in limbo. Some say the whole state, and not just the Panhandle, should be called No Man's Land.

To be sure, Oklahoma is a land of contrasts—social as well as natural. Within the state one can find cowboys and Native Americans, wild mustangs and thoroughbreds, dogtrot cabins and Art Deco palaces, rodeo and ballet, opera and country-western music, tuxedos and blue jeans, pickups and polo ponies, beer joints and country clubs, street preachers and pagans.

Oklahoma is the nation's great mixing bowl. It is a little bit of all six states that surround it plus much more. There are parts of Tennessee, Kentucky, Alabama, and Georgia in Oklahoma. Great swarms of white immigrants and countless numbers of Na-tive Americans came to what became Oklahoma from those and other southern states. Early oil barons and petroleum executives moved into Oklahoma from New York and Pennsylvania and points east. Perhaps that is why the upper-crust neighborhoods of Tulsa, with their manicured lawns and gardens and elegant residences, greatly resemble some of the exclusive enclaves in the eastern portion of the country.

Oklahoma is a microcosm of the nation. Yet it remains a land that has misplaced its sense of rhythm. It needs to be

MICHAEL WALLIS

rediscovered. As the venerable Dame Edith Sitwell put it: "Rhythm is one of the principal translators between dream and reality. Rhythm might be described as, to the world of sound, what light is to the world of sight. It shapes and gives new meaning."

Without any rhythm, there can be no balance. The invigorating rhythm of the land and its occupants needs only to be found and memorized again. Part of the rhythm comes from the cadence of oil-pump jacks, Native American drums, and jazz horns, as well as from the music, poetry, and language of history. Part of that distinctive Oklahoma rhythm is the voice of Will Rogers, the songs of Woody Guthrie, the words of Angie Debo, the fiddle of Bob Wills. Oklahoma's dubious yet stirring past is replete with lessons that apply today, lessons that not only help shatter some of the stereotypes about Oklahoma but help others from outside the state to take a closer look at their own locales and personal history.

Angie Debo, the beloved Oklahoma historian, stated it well in the very first paragraph in the preface of *Oklahoma, Footloose and Fancy-free*, her candid history of the state first published in 1949. Debo wrote: "Any state of the American Union deserves to be known and understood. But Oklahoma is more than just another state. It is a lens in which the long rays of time are focused into the brightest of light. In its magnifying clarity, dim facets of the American character stand more clearly revealed. For in Oklahoma all the experiences that went into the making of the nation have been speeded up. Here all the American traits have been intensified. The one who can interpret Oklahoma can grasp the meaning of America in the modern world."

In 1930, Edna Ferber even felt compelled to issue a warning to the readers of *Cimarron*, her epic novel about Oklahoma. Ferber wrote: "In many cases material entirely true was discarded as unfit for use because it was so melodramatic, so absurd as to be too strange for the realm of fiction. Anything can have happened in Oklahoma. Practically everything has."

To understand this inscrutable place, it is necessary to learn about the human side of Oklahoma's history. That means starting with the people who lived on the North American continent prior to the encroachment of any Europeans.

Long before the arrival of the explorers and trappers, the

cowboys and farmers, or the merchants and oil barons, distinct and important groups of indigenous people populated present-day Oklahoma. The earliest known inhabitants roamed the Panhandle twelve thousand years ago. Cave dwellers and mound builders later lived in many parts of the state, but disappeared in the mists of time and history.

Tribes of people, now Native Americans, were the first residents. For that reason, the state name is fitting since the word *Oklahoma* comes from the old Choctaw phrase meaning "red people."

Some of the early tribes include the Kiowa, Comanche, Cheyenne, Arapaho, Wichita, Lipan Apache, and Caddo. Many of them were wanderers who built their camps and fires wherever the buffalo were most numerous. Later, other tribes were driven into Oklahoma from their ancestral homes and hunting grounds in northern and central states. All of them—including the Osage, Quapaw, Catawba, Cayuga, Huron, Modoc, Mohawk, Oneida, Otoe, Pawnee, Ponca, Seneca, Yuchi, and many more—possessed their own complex life-styles and distinct heritages. These original Oklahomans—fifty-two tribal groups—are as dissimilar from each other as Europeans differ from Asians or Africans. More languages are spoken in Oklahoma today than on the entire European continent.

Legend has it that the Vikings were the first Caucasians to visit the area that ultimately became Oklahoma. These dauntless Norsemen supposedly preceded other white intruders by more than one thousand years. First mention of the future Oklahoma appears in the journals of Spanish explorers who traversed the vast North American plains with Francisco Vásquez de Coronado, Juan de Oñate, and Hernando de Soto in the mid-1500s. Early dispatches from these great military expeditions include descriptions of wild fruit, broad rivers, luxuriant grasslands, and nomadic tribes. In 1541, the Coronado band, searching for gold and riches, even left some graffiti behind. While camped at Castle Rock, alongside the Cimarron, on a trail much used from earlier times, one member of the conquistador's party carved his leader's name in a rock inside a small cave. Three centuries after Coronado and his ironclad men passed by, that same route became the Cimarron cutoff of the fabled Santa Fe Trail.

French explorers followed the Spaniards. In 1682, La Salle floated down the Mississippi and pushed overland to the West.

He claimed for France all the land drained by the mighty river. A few of his followers ventured up the Red River into Oklahoma and named the Poteau and Verdigris rivers. Other French explorers and traders in search of pelts soon entered the Oklahoma country by way of the Red and Arkansas rivers, and Jean Pierre Choteau established Salina, the first permanent white settlement in 1796.

France ruled Oklahoma, except the territory that became the Panhandle, as a part of the Louisiana Province from 1682 until 1762. Then that portion of the Louisiana Province was given back to Spain. The Spaniards had little luck in making the area pay off for them, so in 1800 the real estate passed back into French hands. Only three years later, Napoleon was more than ready to abandon his country's expensive North American empire. Louisiana was bought by the United States, and Oklahoma was made part of the Territory of Indiana, governed from Vincennes. By 1812 the Oklahoma region became part of the Territory of Missouri, and in 1819 it was transferred to the Territory of Arkansas.

From about the late 1820s until the early 1840s, sad processions of displaced Native Americans streamed westward from the Deep South. They surrendered their homes and farms to the whites and were forcibly uprooted as part of the federal government's oppressive "Indian Removal" process. The Cherokee, Seminole, Choctaw, Creek, and Chickasaw were designated as the "Five Civilized Tribes"—a detestable and pejorative expression still in common use. As a result of the Indian Removal Act of 1830, many other eastern tribes besides the Five Tribes lost their land and were removed to a huge parcel of land in the West.

The routes followed by the Five Tribes in their treks—down a path filled with death and suffering from tuberculosis, pneumonia, and even starvation—came to be known as the Trail of Tears. This infamous journey of sorrow and pain terminated in a wild land where the white government decided to dump all the relocated tribes. It was dubbed Indian Territory, most of present-day Oklahoma.

Under the terms of yet another treaty drafted by the federal government, the relocated Native Americans were to have this new homeland for "as long as grass shall grow and rivers run." More hollow words and empty promises.

In Indian Territory the tribes formed their own "nation,"

which was a protectorate of the United States. The Indian Nations had their own capitals, set of laws, legislatures, and courts. Schools and churches were built and farms were created. The Native Americans residing in Indian Territory were to be forever protected by laws that prevented whites from stealing their land. And so the Indian Nations prospered by themselves as the flood of the westward-expansion movement passed them by.

All of that changed with the advent of the Civil War. Many members of the Five Tribes were significant slave owners and most of the tribal members sided with the Confederacy. Some Indians wished to stay neutral during the conflict while still others fought with the Union. Bitter quarrels and bloodshed occurred among the tribes. After the war, the victorious Union punished the residents of Indian Territory. The government ruled that the Indians had lost all rights to their land because they fought with the South. Half of their assigned lands were taken and a large number of displaced northern Plains tribes, including the Caddoes, Comanches, Cheyennes, and Kiowas, were moved into the western half of Indian Territory. To maintain control, the federal government also erected a string of Army posts in the west, such as Fort Sill, built near Lawton in 1868.

A postwar cattle boom drew huge herds of Texas longhorns into "the Nations," where they fed on the rich bluestem grass while making their way up trails like the Chisholm to the new Kansas rail centers. A few whites were allowed to live in the Indian Nations, as long as they did not attempt to own the land or violate the codes established by the native peoples. But not all the whites were desirable. Hordes of poachers, bootleggers, prostitutes, and renegades also crept into Indian Territory. As unruly cow towns, such as Dodge City up in Kansas, ended their wild ways, Indian Territory became a haven for cattle rustlers, horse thieves, bank robbers, and common criminals, mainly because the legal system kept Native Americans from prosecuting whites in courts of law. As a result, Indian Territory was considered to be the most lawless area in the United States.

By the latter part of the nineteenth century, the regions surrounding Oklahoma's borders filled with fidgety white settlers casting increasingly covetous eyes on the broad ranges and open spaces of Indian Territory. A systematic movement, or "booming," started for the opening of certain parts of Oklahoma to white settlement. Kansan David L. Payne and other nervy trespassers known as "Boomers" began their invasion. Troops were used to force the squatters to leave. But each time the soldiers escorted the tenacious nesters back across the Kansas line, more of them slipped over the border. The Five Tribes protested, but little was done to discourage the violators.

Finally the federal government succumbed to the Boomers' demands and purchased an absolute title to nearly two million acres of land belonging to the Indians in the central portion of the territory. By this time Congress had already passed the Dawes Severalty Act, providing that all the Indians except members of the Five Tribes should be made to accept individual "allotments" of land and that the rest of the reservations should be opened to white homesteaders as soon as possible. President Benjamin Harrison, during his third week in office, issued a proclamation regarding the settlement of the so-called Unassigned Lands.

The stage was set for April 22, 1889, when the curtain went up. It was on that auspicious, some would argue infamous, date when more than fifty thousand men, women, and children gathered on the borders of the Unassigned Lands of Indian Territory. Government survey teams divided the two million acres into quarter sections for homesteads and set aside larger tracts for potential town sites. Federal land offices were quickly built so that homesteaders could file their entry claims. Troops tried to hold back the masses of anxious settlers eagerly poised on the starting line. Gangs of dishonest would-be settlers could not wait and sneaked into the area to grab up the choicest land. Most of them were later evicted because they could not prove that they were on the starting line at high noon, as required by law. These rogues would become known as "Sooners," a term that Oklahomans still prefer as a nickname for themselves and the University of Oklahoma's sports teams.

The starting signal of waving flags, bugle calls, and cavalry gunfire finally came, triggering one of the wildest land grabs, or as it is often put, "runs" in the annals of American history. Some came up from Texas, but most of the newcomers hailed from Kansas. Others poured in from Missouri and Arkansas. Wherever their origin, the majority crossed the ranches of the Cherokee

Outlet or else followed the Chisholm Trail and then spread out along the northern and western boundaries of the Unassigned Lands.

They came on swift cow ponies and ponderous plow horses, in wagons and buggies overflowing with belongings, aboard crowded trains, and even riding oxen or furiously pedaling bicycles through the clouds of dust. Years later, many who were there that sunny day recalled seeing four circus midgets astride a single horse. Whoever came and whatever their means of transportation, it was a mad dash to hammer into the prairie earth sharp-pointed sticks with their initials whittled on the sides in order to stake precious claims. Tent towns sprang up within a few hours. By sunset of that first day, Oklahoma City had a population of ten thousand and Guthrie boasted fifteen thousand residents. Yancey Cravat, the main character in Ferber's *Cimarron*, was on target and spoke for many when he declared: "Creation! Hell! That took six days. This was done in one. It was history made in an hour—and I helped make it."

Soon additional lands were opened for settlement. Within the next few years there were four more runs as more tribal land was taken by white immigrants. Most of these newcomers were dirt poor. They had lost their land in Texas or Kansas. Some were out-of-work laborers or blacklisted miners. Though tough as cowhide and resilient as coyotes, few of them were the prim and righteous pioneer types pictured and mythologized in the school history texts.

In 1890, Congress passed an organic act creating Oklahoma Territory in what is now western Oklahoma and providing for some self-government. The legislation made official the Choctaw name *Oklahoma*. Guthrie was proclaimed as the capital, and a gent from Indiana was appointed as the first territorial governor. Over in neighboring Indian Territory, the Dawes Commission, created by the federal government in 1893, negotiated with the Five Tribes for the division of all of their lands into individual allotments and the release of surplus lands for further white settlement. The Dawes Commission's work lasted a dozen years. By the time it finished, any and all plans for a Native American commonwealth were gone.

The largest of all the land runs came on September 16, 1893, when the government opened up more than six million acres of deluxe grazing land created decades before to provide the Cherokee tribe with an outlet to hunting grounds in the West following their removal to Indian territory. This land was called the Cherokee Outlet, but was popularly known as the Cherokee Strip. Estimates of those making this fabled run range from 100,000 to 150,000. Like the Run of '89, it, too, was a spectacle to be remembered. It was now certain that the land of the "red people" definitely belonged to the white man.

Even though the largest percentage of settlers in the Twin Territories hailed from Texas, Arkansas, Missouri, and Kansas, practically every region of the nation was represented. So were diverse nationalities. The land runs brought vast groups of foreign immigrants—German, Czech, Mexican, Russian, Italian, African, Jewish, and Greek settlers. All of them left their distinctive marks on the land.

Talk of the territories entering the Union was immediate and constant. But even back in 1891, before the Cherokee Strip opened up and the very first statehood convention was convened, opinion was split. A sizable coalition wanted two separate states, one for Oklahoma Territory and one for Indian Territory, while another faction advocated admission as a single state. It would take sixteen years before achievement of statehood.

The citizens of the Five Tribes and other residents from the eastern territory favored establishment of an independent state to be named for Sequoyah, the man who many decades before had developed an eighty-four-character Cherokee syllabary enabling his tribe to be the first to have a written language of its own. In 1905, a convention was held at Muskogee to consider a constitution for a "State of Sequoyah," but this effort was discounted by Congress, just as was Oklahoma Territory's campaign to set up a sovereign state.

At long last an Enabling Act was passed. This provided for the two territories to form the state of Oklahoma. Fifty-five delegates from each territory plus a pair from the Osage Nation, which was still in the process of allotment, were elected to draft a state Constitution. Of the 112 delegates, 99 were Democrats, 12 were Republicans, and one called himself an Independent. Most were young farmers and several were mixed-blood Native Americans.

William H. "Alfalfa Bill" Murray was picked as president of the constitutional convention. Murray, married to a refined Chickasaw woman, was a former schoolteacher from Texas who moved to Indian Territory to practice law. When he arrived in Tishomingo, capital of the Chickasaw Nation, he carried a carpetbag containing a well-worn copy of the U.S. Constitution. As was the situation with three of the other delegates, "Alfalfa Bill" (a nickname he earned from his experiments at growing alfalfa) one day would become the governor of the state he helped to create. He would also be remembered as one of the most colorful characters in Oklahoma history.

During the winter of 1906, the convention delegates wrote a reform constitution. The final draft contained many new ideas intended to return democracy to the citizens, such as initiative and referendum. By initiative, Oklahomans could propose laws. By referendum, they could vote on laws submitted to them by the state legislature, thus giving the people a direct voice in the government. There were also social reforms and a Prohibition clause that banned the sale of alcoholic beverages. The constitution was ratified by an overwhelming majority on September 17, 1907.

Then on November 16, 1907, President Theodore Roosevelt issued a proclamation declaring Oklahoma as the forty-sixth state of the Union. As soon as Roosevelt scrawled his signature on the document, officials in Washington telegraphed the news to Guthrie, where a crowd waited to celebrate and dine on succulent barbecue.

"We spoiled the best Territory in the world to make a state," cracked Will Rogers.

Many years later, Oklahoma historian Edward Everett Dale told the story of a Cherokee woman whose white husband asked her to go with him to the statehood festivities. She declined and he went alone. When the man came home, he gently reminded his wife that they no longer lived in the Cherokee Nation. "All of us are now citizens of the State of Oklahoma," he told her. The woman's eyes brimmed with tears. "It broke my heart," she said. "I went to bed and cried all night long. It seemed more than I could bear that the Cherokee Nation, my country and my people's country, was no more."

On that day tears flowed throughout all the old Indian Nations. Lots of tears. Silent weeping of vanquished people drowned out in the din of celebration. The deed was done. "The Nations" were in the past. It was time to get on with the business at hand.

The new state, like a precocious child, was impatient to step forward.

Oklahoma's long search for identity had begun. It continues to this day.

2

THAT OLD HOUSE: WOODY GUTHRIE'S HOME IN OKLAHOMA

Just a boy from Oklahoma on an endless one-night stand . . .

—Willis Alan Ramsey,
Boy from Oklahoma

 Okemah, a farming town in Oklahoma with an oil-boom memory, is an unlikely place for a poet to be born. But on July 14, 1912, a bona fide muse squalled alive there.

Since the baby's father was a staunch Democrat, it was decided that the third child of Charley and Nora Guthrie would be named after the reform-minded Democratic presidential candidate. Only twelve days before the baby's birth, Woodrow Wilson had received his party's nomination on the forty-sixth ballot. He was less than four months away from victory at the polls. So Woodrow Wilson Guthrie it had to be. Trouble was, hardly anyone ever used all those names the Guthries gave their baby. Instead, folks just called the boy Woody. That name seemed to fit him the best. Woody. Woody Guthrie.

Woody's birth on an oven-hot Bastille Day came just five years after Oklahoma joined the Union. Nobody living in Okemah could ever know the baby born there on that sweltering Sabbath would become a celebrated troubadour or that his haunting music—bred in ochre-red Depression dust—would wind up a national treasure.

"Just another of those little towns . . . where everybody knows everybody else," Woody once said of Okemah. On another occasion Guthrie wrote about the town where he resided until he "lit out" at the tender age of fifteen to become a wandering minstrel of social protest and the best-known balladeer of the Depression and Dust Bowl.

> Okemah was one of the singingest,
> square dancingest, drinkingest,
> yellingest, preachingest, walkingest,

talkingest, laughingest, cryingest,
shootingest, fist-fightingest, bleedingest,
gamblingest, gun-club-and-razor carryingest
of our ranch and farm towns because it blossomed
out into one of our first Oil Boom Towns.

In some ways Okemah, like the rest of rural east-central Oklahoma, has not changed too much from times of yore. The glory days of the oil patch are in the past and the town may not be quite as colorful as Woody once described it. But, small-town clichés still apply, and more than likely always will.

People get all the news of the day just by walking to the post office. They hold spelling bees and gospel sings, and the Canadian River provides endless fish fries and lots of material for winter stories and harmless lies. Saturday night was invented for square dancing, and the next morning damn near everybody goes to church. They worry over corn and cotton and pecans. They have long talks about their mung beans and hogs. The blooming of the azaleas makes the front page, and when the wheat is in and the football team is clicking, Okemahns sit back and wonder why anyone would want to live anyplace else.

Many people say that Okemah is a Creek name for "big man," the moniker chosen when the railroad town, the seat of Okfuskee County, was established in 1902. Others contend the town's name can be traced to an old Kickapoo Indian named Okemah. They claim the word means "high man" or "great chief." Then, there are yet a few others who maintain *Okemah* is an Indian word meaning "town on a hill." Nobody can figure that one out. One of the few hills around is the one on the edge of town, the one where the graveyard is located. No matter about the name or its origin. Okemah is just about as good as any handle for a little old Oklahoma town.

And, even if the name has nothing at all to do with hills, that doesn't diminish the importance of the graveyard. The townspeople make a point to honor all their dead. They still go out to the cemetery on Easter and Memorial Day, or a lot of times they go between church services and Sunday dinner. On certain occasions they bring jars of wildflowers, or else roses and irises and lilies from their yards. Sometimes they settle for plastic blossoms from Wal-Mart. On dates set aside for dead heroes, they take along little American flags to stick into the soft earth. They walk over the fresh-cut grass to pay their respects at the final resting places of their loved ones and neighbors.

One thing is certain, though. They never go out to the "bone orchard" for Woody. He has friends and kinfolk buried in the cemetery, and there is a marker that clearly says, "Guthrie," but Woody himself never came back to the place where he was born.

On October 3, 1967, Woody lost a thirteen-year battle with the degenerative brain disease Huntington's chorea and died at age fifty-five. He had talked about Okemah being his final resting place, but instead his friends took Woody's ashes and lovingly sprinkled them over the Atlantic Ocean near Long Island, New York. It seemed a suitable end for a rambling man.

Except for the memorial stone placed in the cemetery by family members, the sole public remembrance to Oklahoma's populist poet in the town of Okemah is a simple inscription. It was painted in bold letters in the early 1970s on one of the three water towers that, like the graveyard, are also situated on a hill, this one overlooking Interstate 40. One tower says HOT, one tower says COLD, and the third tank sports the words HOME OF WOODY GUTHRIE. That tribute was grudgingly permitted. Some of the 3,300 stalwart citizens who savor public displays of patriotism still spit hard and glower like truant officers every time they pass the tank and glance up to spy Guthrie's name. Those four words for Woody burn in their craw something fierce.

"I want his name stricken from the water tower," Bart Webb once told a reporter when some Guthrie fans gathered in Okemah to stage a long-overdue tribute to Woody. "It's un-American as hell to support a Communist. His name is a disgrace to this community." Webb, at the time a city council member and owner of a local funeral parlor, told the press he was especially distraught because of the participation of schoolchildren in the program. "I'm violently opposed to anything in his memory," said Webb. "Guthrie is still a rotten seed of Communism and to help sow his thoughts and work in our young schoolchildren's minds is wrong. They're trying to make him out to be a hero. He never was and never will be." Webb saw to it that posters declaring WOODY WAS NO HERO were tacked up at the American Legion hall and other spots around town.

Other Guthrie skeptics echoed Webb. "We shouldn't be holding him out as a national hero," said Allison Kelly, an Okemah banker. Kelly went so far as to suggest that Woody's

MICHAEL WALLIS

well-known song, "This Land Is Your Land," could be construed as a Communist ballad since some of the lyrics suggest communal ownership of property. Perhaps Mr. Kelly did not realize that the beloved Guthrie song had long before become a popular patriotic standard, frequently played at political rallies and Fourth of July celebrations. Some good Americans have suggested the song as an alternative national anthem.

Throughout the years, both before and after Woody's death, it became increasingly evident that certain people in God-fearing and conservative Okemah are not very proud of the native son, the man who left behind a musical legacy that includes at least one thousand ballads, such as the classic "Oklahoma Hills." These certain people in Okemah reject Guthrie because they believe he was not only a Communist but also an atheist, the most cardinal sin of all in the Bible Belt. These Guthrie detractors openly scorn the renowned folk singer and even spurned a proposal by Woody's late widow, Marjorie Guthrie, to help establish a Guthrie memorial and enlarge a children's section in the town library.

Woody's many supporters stress that there is no proof he ever officially joined the Communist Party. As far as believing in God, they say all a person has to do is really listen to Woody's songs and they will realize it's music fit for angels. Woody's advocates also point out that Woody served in the Merchant Marine and the Army Air Corps during World War II. They note that, although his name appeared on one of Senator Joe McCarthy's notorious Communist sympathizer lists, FBI files on Woody make no mention that J. Edgar Hoover's agents believed for a minute that Guthrie was a Communist or a danger to his country.

Besides, say members of the pro-Woody camp, the man should be remembered for the songs he wrote rather than his political beliefs. After all, Woody Guthrie was an important social commentator and a driving force in this nation's folk-music movement. He was also a champion for the disenfranchised and an inspiration to all who have heard his poetry and know about his personal struggle. Woody himself, as usual with tongue in cheek, said, "I ain't a Communist necessarily. But I been in the red all my life."

Guy Logsdon, a recognized authority on southwestern folk culture and music and a Guthrie scholar, likes to remind people— especially worrisome "rednecks"—that when the House Un-American Activities Committee was probing alleged Communists in the entertainment industry during McCarthy's witch-hunt, they were not interested enough in Guthrie to subpoena him to testify. Woody, according to Logsdon, was a classic Oklahoma populist in the best traditions of the populists who drafted the state's constitution. Woody focused his time and energy, as well as his musical talent, on political causes and in support of labor unions, migrant laborers, and victims of hard times.

Like many of his fellow Oklahomans, Woody distrusted most of the big-time politicians, bankers, and business tycoons. But that didn't make Guthrie a Communist. Not in the least. A good example from the man's own work to prove this point is Guthrie's ballad "Pretty Boy Floyd," the romantic rhapsody that reinforces the legendary side of Oklahoma's most infamous bank robber. Communists, explains Logsdon, tend to write stirring songs about workers' productivity quotas, not about bandits.

"Opposing Woody is the only way some people can get attention," said Logsdon. "Anyone who knew Woody Guthrie realizes that his personality did not support or fit any kind of organized belief. Woody was a rebel who didn't fit in. He was an absolute free spirit. He was an independent thinker. He was Oklahoma's most creative citizen. He was footloose and fancy-free. He was interested in the everyday working person having a good time. He was opposed to the exploitation of labor. Was he sympathetic to some of the things Communism espoused? Yes. And so was Ronald Reagan once."

Perhaps Logsdon was most on target in 1991 when he told a writer for *Oklahoma Today* that the people who object to Woody's leftist politics and unconventional life-style may just be a little bit frightened. "Fear is a lack of faith," said Logsdon, who married an Okemah woman. "If you have faith in your country, you're not afraid. People who were afraid of Woody had no faith in their country."

Yet Guthrie's foes in Okemah, mostly a vocal minority of nervous pseudo-patriots, won't be silenced. They argue that their native son had to be a dreaded Commie bastard since he penned a column, "Woody Sez," in the *Daily Worker* during the 1930s. They say he participated in Communist fund-raisers and also had more than a few pals with Communist ties, like the actor Will Geer.

That is why it came as no great surprise years ago when town fathers ordered Guthrie's old homestead torn down. The owner of the property fought and screamed about lost tourist revenue, but he was not popular with the establishment and rubbed Okemah's powers that be the wrong way. The local historical society said razing the house was a shame, but that did not make a dime's worth of difference. It's a health hazard, officials declared, and eventually down it went.

A few old-timers remembered the Guthries lived in a place known as the London house, because a family named London lived there for many years. Woody's father paid a thousand dollars for the frame residence built on sandstone rocks, with a cellar and attic, surrounded by mulberry trees. Woody's mother, who like her son also suffered from Huntington's chorea, with its characteristic unstable behavior and fits of depression, was known around town for doing strange things, such as setting her kids on fire. Nora Guthrie, who spent her last years living in an asylum, did not like the house and neither did Woody's brother and sister. "This old house is mean," his sister Clara declared. "This old dump," said his brother Roy.

Woody did not seem to mind the house. "I liked the high porch along the top story, for it was the highest porch in all of the whole town," he said.

Actually, the Guthries lived in several houses in Okemah. All of them were struck by tragedy. Before they moved into the London house, they lived in a seven-room place that burned to the foundation. The London house was clobbered by a cyclone. It somehow survived.

For many years the last of the Guthrie's houses sat desolate. Plans to restore it and make it a museum died. Vandals broke the windows and hammered down the doors. Some people visited the empty house to pay tribute to Woody. They left their names and messages tattooed with chalk and crayon on the battered walls.

Most of the graffiti was sweet. "Woody, just stopped by to say hi," said one caller. "Howdy Woody, I heard your music in the mountains and the meadows and in my heart," said another. One visitor wrote, "Woody, why did you have to be born in a sorry town like Okemah. We all know you're no communist. We all still love you." One intruder left the simple, "Thanks."

All the walls went down. For a long time only a scar remained in a city lot surrounded by brown winter weeds. There was some talk of selling scraps of lumber for souvenirs.

A few memories of Guthrie linger in Okemah. Every so often somebody finds Woody's initials in a cement wall where he left them as a kid. Old-timers recall the Guthries as a pathetic family burdened with tragedy and sorrow. "Hard luck seemed to sit on their shoulders regardless of their effort," said one old man.

"I do recall Woody," said Grace Croy, back in the early 1980s, when all the fuss was going on about the Guthrie house. "I recall him alone and walking with his harmonica. I have this impression of seeing Woody the boy always alone and thinking."

At the Dairy Boy drive-in, where burgers are juicy and malts are thick, the man fixing lunches quietly talked about Woody and the mess about the London house. "Part of a power struggle— a personality conflict," he said. "They say Woody was a Communist. Well, he might have been, but what of it? He's good enough for them to teach his songs to our children in school."

Reasonable heads have prevailed in Okemah. In the spring of 1989, hundreds gathered in the town to honor Woody and his music. There were no outbursts, no protests or picket lines. Arlo Guthrie, the son of Okemah's most famous citizen, put on a tribute concert to salute his father. "Thank you for being here," Arlo told the crowd of 750 persons from Texas, Arkansas, Missouri, Kansas, and, of course, Oklahoma. They filled the local Crystal Theatre and spilled out into the lobby. "I know that my dad thanks you also, very much, for this night. God bless you all." An old woman in the crowd that night beamed when she heard Woody's music riding out of the theater on the spring breeze. "It's about time all this has come to pass," said the old woman. "Woody has come home."

Since that memorable concert there have been other public salutes for Guthrie. Each July, a tribute to Woody is held in a city park on the Saturday closest to Guthrie's birthday. The tribute is sponsored by a group called WOODY, the Woody Guthrie Okemah Organization for Developing Youth, formed to introduce Okemah's young people to the man whom Robert F. Kennedy described as "one of the finest and most authentic artists our nation has ever produced."

It seems that most folks realize that Woody Guthrie left his legacy in songs, not a pile of boards from a bulldozed house. What's done is done. Woody's songs will live on as the best memorial of all. His benediction for the town of Okemah comes straight out of his music:

> So long, it's been good to know yuh;
> So long, it's been good to know yuh;
> So long, it's been good to know yuh,
> This dusty old dust is a-getting my home,
> I've got to be driftin' along.

3

ROUTE 66:
THE MOTHER ROAD

*For me, Oklahoma was always
the heart and soul of Route 66
country.*

—*Will Rogers, Jr.*

The man aimed his automobile down the old highway connecting Tulsa and Oklahoma City. He didn't consider taking the turnpike. Not for a moment. He would never do that. He was too old and time had become holy for him. Time was something he treasured. He knew the turnpike was a faster way to go, but it wouldn't make the best use of his time. The "free road," as some folks still called it, was the way to go. It was a road of character and memories, both bitter and sweet.

As he drove in and out of towns along the way and passed farms, fields, and crossed creeks, he saw that many things were still the same. The drive made the old man feel young again, but with the patience and honesty that come with age. Traveling the old road did that for him. It gave him the best of both worlds—past and present.

He paused for coffee and pie in Bristow, and near Little Deep Fork Creek, he pulled his car off the road and picked a handful of wild flowers. Their scent filled the car, and the old man remembered his wife and how she looked when she was a girl. He said her name out loud, just to hear it, and he hummed her favorite song as he drove down the road.

After he passed through Arcadia and Edmond, the busy traffic of Oklahoma City loomed ahead. He turned the car around and drove back to Tulsa. He stuck to the free road, and he hummed the song, and some others he could recall, most of the way back. He switched off the air conditioner and rolled down the windows. Summer air rushed through the car.

That night the old man ate a big supper at a cafe he liked, and he went to bed and dreamed—of being a boy in the Canadian River bottoms before he moved to the city, of his wedding day, and of other times that only returned to him in sleep. When he opened his eyes the next morning, the first thing the old man saw was the jar filled with flowers, wild flowers from the edge of the ghost road—from Route 66.

Nowhere is Route 66 more at home than in Oklahoma, where the pavement follows the contours of the land as though it had always been there. In Oklahoma, the West and East collide on Route 66, and the state becomes the crossroads for America's Main Street.

In a way, Route 66 was born in Oklahoma—home of Cyrus Avery, Lon Scott, Andy Payne, Jack Cutberth, Will Rogers, and so many others who inspired the growth of the highway. In 1926, when word of the new U.S. Route 66 got out, Oklahoma was celebrating its nineteenth anniversary as a state, and Woody Guthrie, then a scrawny fourteen-year-old, had already outgrown those Oklahoma hills where he was born.

Route 66 was big news in Oklahoma. All along the highway, which linked the industrial states of the East with the golden plains of the West, Oklahomans watched a new culture emerge complete with hitchhikers, Burma Shave signs, and neon lights. It took several more years to connect the bits and pieces, but before too long the highway reached across the land, racing through time and history, following old trails blazed by explorers and adventurers.

The path through Oklahoma emerged from the trails worn in the prairie, and slashed through tangles of blackjack and mesquite. The highway begins its descent into northeastern Oklahoma at the Kansas line and slashes southwest through old Indian Territory, past Tulsa and Oklahoma City, the state's two largest cities, and then proceeds westward to the Texas Panhandle.

In the 1930s, Route 66 became the road of desperation described so poignantly by John Steinbeck in *The Grapes of Wrath*. As the brutal Dust Bowl years arrived, many of those Oklahoma refugees, or Okies, struck out on Route 66 in single cars or caravans, carrying all their furniture, kids, hopes, and dreams with them.

Sometimes only humor kept folks sane. According to the common folk wisdom, a car with three mattresses strapped to its roof meant a family of rich Okies; two mattresses meant mediocre wealth; and a lone mattress meant the Okies inside were dirt poor. Some officials estimated that as many as a third of a million

Okies—or 15 percent of the population—fled the choking dust storms and took Route 66 to California.

Those tragic years of the Great Depression and the Dust Bowl left deep scars on the land and emotional wounds on the people along the highway. In the early 1930s, the rain stopped and did not come again for years. The timing was horrendous—the century's worst drought arrived to accompany the century's worst Depression. In 1925, wheat sold for $1.16 a bushel; in 1931, the price dropped to 33 cents. Banks foreclosed and families moved on.

Parts of Oklahoma, Kansas, Texas, New Mexico, and several midwestern states looked like the landscape of the moon. Years of drought and outdated farming methods turned the land into a desert of sand and pale dirt. The sky was a choking sea of dust. Giant dark dust clouds swept away the topsoil. Folks wrapped wet neckerchiefs around their faces and crammed newspapers and pages ripped from catalogs under the doors and around the windows to keep the powder-fine dust from seeping in. It did little good. Dust covered everything and coated the lungs of people and livestock. Some dust storms lasted seventy-two hours straight with no letup. Schools closed, and cars, trucks, and trains sat still. People died from dust pneumonia. Flocks of geese, blinded by the swirling storms, crashed to the ground. Cattle by the thousands died of thirst. Derricks were used no longer to drill for oil, but water. Route 66 became a road of safe passage to what the Dust Bowlers prayed would be a better way of life.

Steinbeck described the highway this way:

Highway 66 is the main migrant road. 66—the long concrete path across the country, waving gently up and down on the map, from the Mississippi to Bakersfield— over the red lands and the gray lands, twisting up into the mountains, crossing the Divide and down into the bright and terrible desert, and across the desert to the mountains again, and into the rich California valleys.

66 is the path of a people in flight, refugees from the dust and shrinking land, from the thunder of tractors and shrinking ownership, from the desert's slow northward invasion, from the twisting winds that howl up out of Texas, from the floods that bring no richness to the land

and steal what richness is there. From all of these the people are in flight, and they come into 66 from the tributary side roads, from the wagon tracks and the rutted country roads. 66 is the mother road, the road of flight.

For many Oklahomans, any memories of the Dust Bowl era—including Steinbeck's prose and Guthrie's ballads—are best forgotten. Many of them are apt to wince at the mere mention of the word *Okie*. To them, *Okie, Dust Bowl,* and *Route* 66 are phrases from the past. Interdispersal loops, cloverleafs, turnpikes, and interstates are much preferable.

"Everybody always talks about Okies—those folks who packed it all in and went on down the road," says an old farmer who left Oklahoma only long enough to serve a hitch in the army. "I'd like to know about the ones who stayed and spit in the dust and stuck it out. They were the tough ones. They were the real Oklahomans. Or the ones who did leave and built new lives. Some of them even came back. What about them? There's nothing wrong with being called an Okie. That should be a name of pride, not a brand of shame."

Besides serving as an escape route for the migrants, Route 66 in Oklahoma carried more than its fair share of vagabonds and poets, servicemen heading to and from war, truckloads of commerce, and, of course, an endless stream of tourists. It was this wave of tourists headed to the Painted Desert or the Grand Canyon that helped romanticize Route 66. They motored along listening to a series of warblers croon about "getting their kicks" on the highway. In the post–World War II years, Route 66 became the nation's most popular highway. It was the evocative symbol of freedom, fun, and escape. Americans took to it in droves.

The route was heavily traveled all year long, but the main season was summer when the schools let out. On some portions of Route 66 in Oklahoma during those busy summer months, traffic was so thick it was difficult to cross the road. Highway towns in Oklahoma thrived on the revenue.

At the height of its popularity, Route 66, especially in Oklahoma, signaled the age of the hamburger stand, filling station, and the motor court with refrigerated air. Tourists got no wake-up calls because there were no telephones in the cabins. But most desk clerks worth their salt had a stash of alarm clocks behind the counter to lend their customers. The tourists tried to stop at the cafes where they spied the trucks, knowing well that the legions of truckers hauling oranges and beefsteak always dined where the gravy was the tastiest and the biscuits were the lightest. These authentic cafes can still be found in Oklahoma. They still turn out homemade pies, thick hand-patted burgers, real milk shakes, and there's nothing instant, except the service.

In Oklahoma, there are still garish postcards to buy and joints where patrons are serenaded by jukebox tunes. There are still people who consider time important. They take time to chat with a trucker or waitress. Take time to watch a hawk sail across the summer sky. Take time to pull off the road for a skinny-dip in a shady creek.

Even though folks are singing new songs and driving new highways, and the old road has been nudged aside by the interstate, America's Main Street in Oklahoma continues as a vital frontage road, a business loop, an alternative for those people who aren't particularly anxious to go lickety-split. Remnants of the proud highway can be found from one end of the state to the other.

Route 66 also cuts directly through the prime marketing territory of the Phillips Petroleum Company, founded in 1917 by oil tycoon Frank Phillips. Coincidentally, almost every major midwestern city on the Phillips Petroleum marketing list happened to be located on the highway. Eager to find a suitable name for the new gasoline, Phillips finally settled the question of the company trademark on the eve of an executive committee meeting in Bartlesville, Oklahoma, in 1927. Returning to Bartlesville from Oklahoma City, John Kane, one of Phillips Petroleum's top executives, was in a company car driven by Salty Sawtell. The tank was filled with the company's new gasoline. As the men sped toward Tulsa on Route 66, Kane noticed how fast they were traveling.

"This car goes like sixty with our new gas," said Kane.

"Sixty nothing," answered Sawtell. "We're doing sixty-six!"

The men looked at each other and grinned. Going 66 on Route 66. That was the sign they were looking for. They already knew the new fuel was in the gravity range of 66, an especially high gravity mark. Now that they'd had this experience on the new Oklahoma highway, it seemed that 66 was destined to be the name. When Kane reported the news to Frank Phillips, it was all the colorful oil tycoon needed to hear. Before long Phillips 66 gasoline was selling across America. Although the original Phillips logo started out on disk-shaped signs, the company by 1930 was using the familiar six-pointed shield that resembled the national highway signs. The Phillips Petroleum shield has been altered somewhat during the years, but Phillips 66 signs still dot much of the old road and many of the interstates and turnpikes.

"Oklahoma is where it's at as far as Route 66 goes," says Terrence Moore, a southwestern photographer raised in a California orange grove right beside Route 66. "I've traveled and photographed the length of the old highway most of my life. I've found that Oklahoma is the central state on the route and the heart of the road. Then there are the connections—*The Grapes of Wrath*, Phillips 66, the Will Rogers name—that link the road geographically and historically to the state. But the main thing is that Route 66 in Oklahoma means you are in the West. Especially when you get past Oklahoma City and the sky opens up. Then you know you've arrived. That's a spiritual connection."

Out of his many trips down the Mother Road, one particularly sticks in Moore's mind. "I was a kid hitching to California and I found myself on Route 66 at El Reno, Oklahoma. I can recall that precise moment very well. I felt like I was really home. It was so simple. I only stood there for a moment, and then somebody stopped and I rode all the way into L.A. But that single moment, there in El Reno, has never left me. It was just me all alone on Route 66. That's an entirely different feeling than being on the interstate. When you're on 66 you're in another time, another place."

The long surviving stretches of Oklahoma's Route 66 recall those other times. The old road that remains takes people back to the days before freeways, shopping malls, and designer clothes. Out on the open highway, along the old route—the free road— are towns where the only men wearing neckties are bankers and undertakers. These are places where lunch is called dinner, and what city folks call dinner is supper. Towns where people sit on the front porch in the evening and have conversations. Where they put up screens on the windows in the springtime and leave their keys in the ignition overnight. Towns where the biggest fear is a renegade tornado. Towns that will always consider Route 66 to be the "Queen of Highways."

For those unhurried motorists who choose to visit these places and leave the turnpikes and interstates, traveling the old road can be a potent tonic. Part of the route passes through an area of Oklahoma visited by Washington Irving in 1832, when the territory was still a virgin wilderness and the early American essayist was gathering material for A *Tour of the Prairies.* Going east to west on Route 66 in Oklahoma, the towns and cities and forgotten crossroads have one thing in common besides the water tower covered with senior-class graffiti—they are all united by the Mother Road.

The old highway quietly enters the northeastern corner of Oklahoma, a region that was once the center of some of the richest lead and zinc mining in the nation. Originally, this main road that linked the Oklahoma-Kansas border to Oklahoma City was called State Highway 7. In 1926, the government changed the name to U.S. Route 66. Initially just a wagon trail, the road had been graded by teams of mules and paved in some sections in the early 1920s. Much of Route 66 through eastern Oklahoma was constructed by widening State Highway 7, or in some instances straightening out curves. By the early 1930s at least 85 percent of U.S. 66 in Oklahoma was concreted.

Four miles south of the Kansas border, the first Oklahoma town on U.S. 66 is Quapaw, named after the tribe which moved to Indian Territory in 1833. The town was founded in 1897 on land those Indians once owned. During the mining boom years around the turn of the century, many Indians became wealthy by leasing their allotments to the mining companies. Just six miles east of Quapaw on the bank of the Spring River is Devil's Promenade, a huge stone bluff where the Quapaws commemorated the return of Indian soldiers from the world wars, built council fires, and danced in elaborate costumes.

After Quapaw comes Commerce, a mining town that got its start in 1913. It is best remembered as the boyhood home of Yankee slugger Mickey Mantle, whose father worked as a shoveler for the Eagle-Picher Zinc and Lead Company.

"The Depression for us lasted longer than for most people," says Mantle. "During that time, we lived in Spavinaw, Oklahoma, and I think my dad was working for about fifty cents a week. His dad was a butcher, and that's the way we ate—from my grandfather. Later, my dad got a chance to move up to the lead mines in Commerce and Picher. We never realized we were poor, I don't think. You go back up there now and look at the places where we lived, and you can't believe it. It really looks like a slum."

Like most boys in that country, Mantle grew up climbing the giant piles of spent ore called chat, rooting for the St. Louis Cardinals, and playing pickup games of baseball on a cleared field near the town's abandoned mine shafts.

"We made our own ball parks," says Mantle, "and we made our own baseballs out of that black tape you put around water pipes. We always had gloves, and we could make our own bats from broomsticks or whatever. So we made our own entertainment. All we had to do was play ball."

Nowadays, Mickey Mantle Boulevard runs through Commerce, a town where there are still good cafes serving the public and local kids playing sandlot games before it gets too dark to see the ball.

Only three miles south of Commerce is Miami, pronounced My-am-ah in Oklahoma, and an important area trade center. Named for the small Indian tribe living on the site in the nineteenth century, Miami bears no resemblance to the more exotic Florida city of the same name. Some old motor courts and restaurants that serve broasted chicken endure, as does the remarkable Coleman Theater, a restored Route 66 treasure at the corner of First and Main in the center of Miami's downtown business district. A Spanish Colonial revival masterpiece covered with stucco and intricate terra-cotta gargoyles, the Coleman first opened its doors in 1929 and was immediately showcased as one of the most beautiful theaters in the Southwest. Will Rogers and many other notables made appearances at the Coleman, and everyone who grew up in Miami had an emotional attachment to the theater as well as to the highway that continues to serve as the city's main street.

As travelers leave Miami behind, they cross the Neosho River that flows into Oklahoma from Kansas and meanders southward for 164 miles until it joins the Arkansas River at Muskogee. Soon after travelers pass a tiny settlement named Narcissa, the once-thriving farm and railroad center of Afton appears on the highway. Founded in 1886, the town was named for Afton Aires, the daughter of a railroad surveyor who named the girl after the Afton River in his native Scotland.

In this part of Oklahoma, near Miami and Afton, there are good examples of the original one-lane concrete route with curbs.

The short piece of Route 66 from Miami to Afton was the last part of the old road to be paved in the state. The paved road was finished in the autumn of 1937 and was marked by a celebration, which included Governor E. W. Marland cutting a fancy silk ribbon. Many years before, when the runners in C. C. Pyle's famed Bunion Derby came streaking through town, a crowd of more than 2,500 gathered along the sides of Route 66 in Afton to cheer for Andy Payne, the Oklahoman who would ultimately win the contest. Afterward, onlookers could spoon down a bowl of fiery chili and crackers for fifteen cents, or slip into a pie shop for a slice with fresh coffee for two dimes.

Prices have changed in Afton. But after a heated game of horseshoes, hungry men can march right down to the Rocket Drive-In—across the highway from the Rest Haven Motel and just down a piece from the old Palmer Hotel—and eat their fill of pork tenderloin sandwiches, Rocket burgers, and deep-fried onion rings. Afton is also the closest town to the famous Afton Buffalo Ranch where, since 1953, tourists from across the country have stopped to see bison in their pens. There's a trading post, a restaurant serving barbecue sandwiches, fries, sundaes, and—for the courageous—buffalo burgers. A patch of grass called the "Dog's Restroom" is patrolled by noisy turkeys and peacocks. A small army of house cats lurks in the shadows of the buildings, waiting for tourists to pitch the last bite of their buffalo burger at a garbage barrel and miss.

A few miles down the highway comes Vinita, an old railroad town founded in 1871 and named for Vinnie Ream, the sculptor who created the life-size statue of Abraham Lincoln in the nation's capital. Vinita hosted a big celebration in August 1933, when the paving of Route 66 was completed in the area. Will Rogers, who attended secondary school in Vinita, telegraphed his friend Earl Walker, the cashier at First National Bank, with congratulations.

"Ain't it wonderful to go from Vinita to Chelsea and not have to go by Coffeyville or Muskogee?" Rogers wired. Vinita became the site of the Will Rogers Memorial Rodeo, held each August. The famous Oklahoman was planning to attend that very first rodeo in 1935, when he was killed with Wiley Post in a plane crash near Point Barrow, Alaska. Vinita was also one of Cy Avery's early homes before he moved to Tulsa and started pushing for the creation of Route 66.

West of Vinita, the old road passes through White Oak, and then Chelsea, where the first producing oil well in Oklahoma was completed in 1889, and once the home of Sallie McSpadden, sister of Will Rogers. Gene Autry, the famous Singing Cowboy, also worked at the Frisco depot in Chelsea for a time. Next there's Bushyhead, named for an old chief of the Cherokee Nation; Foyil, a farming hamlet close to Bunion Derby winner Andy Payne's family farm and also the site of "the world's largest totem pole," a ninety-foot-tall concrete monument built by Ed Galloway; Sequoyah, a coal-loading settlement on the railroad and now nothing more than a memory; and Claremore, the seat of Rogers County, named in honor of Clem Rogers, father of Will.

The town of Claremore was named for the Osage chief, Clermont or Clermos, and became a busy trading center. The old stage route from Vinita to Albuquerque passed through the settlement. A bloody battle between Osage and Cherokee warriors also took place near the town site, but many years later it was Will Rogers, born "halfway between Claremore and Oologah before there was a town at either place," who brought Claremore its fame. As Rogers liked to explain, he claimed Claremore over Oologah because "nobody but an Indian could pronounce Oologah."

Claremore was also the home of Lynn Riggs, the author of the play *Green Grow the Lilacs*, from which came the classic American musical *Oklahoma!* The simple love story set in early Oklahoma is based on Riggs's play, with music by Richard Rodgers and lyrics by Oscar Hammerstein. It premiered in 1943 and was one of the longest-running musicals in Broadway history.

Nonetheless, Will Rogers—at least his name and spirit—dominates the town of Claremore. Oklahoma honors its most famous citizen at the Will Rogers Memorial, located about a mile west of Route 66 on a twenty-acre site Rogers once owned. Rogers, his wife, Betty, and an infant son are buried at the memorial, and there are also collections of his personal belongings, keepsakes, and mementos. In the main entrance stands a duplicate of Jo Davidson's familiar bronze of the cowboy humorist. The original resides in the national Capitol.

Route 66 winds past the motels, restaurants, and highway businesses of Claremore. Back out into the countryside, it moves along the edges of pecan groves and across the Kerr-McClellan Arkansas River Navigation System. The old highway then crosses the twin steel bridges spanning the sluggish Verdigris River. On the other side of the crossing waits the town of Catoosa.

Just past the WELCOME TO CATOOSA sign on the highway is a once popular tourist stop that has fallen into decay. It was a swimming hole and the ideal spot on a scorching summer afternoon. There aren't any swimmers in sight anymore. Floating in the murky pond is a large fading blue whale. Sunbathers used to rest on its back, and kids dove from its big gaping mouth frozen in a perpetual smile. The wooden docks along the banks are slowly rotting and no one goes near the round picnic tables. A marooned ark surrounded by weeds bakes in the sun. Long ago, children's birthday groups and tourists armed with cameras came here to gawk at snakes and alligators housed in the Animal Reptile Kingdom (A.R.K.) and Catoosa Alligator Ranch. Now honeysuckle covers the vacant buildings and climbs the fence surrounding the property. Visitors are clearly no longer welcome. One sign says KEEP OUT OR EAT LEAD. Another sign puts it this way:

DANGER
DON'T MESS AROUND
DO NOT ENTER
KEEP OUT
YOU MAY BE
SHOT

Just across the road—called State Highway 66 along this stretch—are the remains of the Chief Wolf Robe Trading Post, which once sold its share of Indian crafts and silver jewelry. Chief Wolf Robe Hunt, a full-blooded Acoma Indian, was known as a skilled painter and silversmith. Between the old trading post building and the highway is a plaque that commemorates the former site of Fort Spunky, used during the Civil War, and a relay station on the old Star Mail route between St. Louis and California. After the Civil War, Catoosa was founded as a post office by John Gunter Schrimsher, an uncle of Will Rogers.

The name Catoosa comes from nearby Catoosa Hill just west of town. It is said that the word derives from an Indian expression meaning "Here live the People of the Light," and that the "People of the Light" gathered on the summit of the hill. Lookout Mountain, an old Indian vantage point, is also nearby. During the wild days of the cattle drives, Catoosa was a rip-roaring gathering place for cowboys who had delivered their stock to market and were anxious for a Saturday night celebration. Used as a shipping point, Catoosa in recent decades has become known for the nearby Port of Catoosa, perched on the 440-mile-long Arkansas River Navigation System. Past Catoosa, the old road blends with the interstate and rolls into the outskirts of Tulsa, the second largest city in the state. Before the interstate and turnpikes were built through Oklahoma, the old highway proceeded farther south of Catoosa. It then turned sharply west and ran straight into Tulsa on either Admiral Place or 11th Street, both of which were Route 66 loops through Tulsa at one time or another.

Travelers can still take those early business routes. They can go south out of Catoosa on 193rd East Avenue, past clusters of gas stations, auto-parts shops, trailer parks, and fast-food franchises. After crossing below the interstate, they have the option of turning west on either Admiral Place or 11th Street. As they move toward the city, both roads pass through mixed rural and industrial areas before entering business and residential districts.

Pauline Puroff remembers old Route 66 winding its way into Tulsa, particularly the hot July afternoon in 1932 when she and her husband, John, and their six-week-old son first arrived in the city. A Chicago native, Pauline quit her job wrapping candy bars at a downtown factory, and John, a Bulgarian immigrant, left the printing plant where he worked on Chicago's West Side after they received a letter from his parents asking the young couple to move to a plot of land they were farming outside Tulsa.

"We were going to become truck farmers," recalls Pauline. "I had no idea what our life would be like. I was a city girl and had never been near a farm. I didn't even know for sure where eggs came from. But the Depression was on and we felt we could better our lives."

They packed enough food to get by on and left Chicago on a crowded bus bound for Tulsa. The journey down Route 66 took several days. There was engine trouble in Missouri and the bus stayed as hot as an oven. It was tiring and uncomfortable and a frightening experience for a young mother with a baby. "When we finally got to the bus station in downtown Tulsa, my father-in-law met us and took us out to the farm," says Pauline. "The roads weren't even oiled—they were still pure dirt. I had gotten all dressed up to meet my in-laws. I put on a pretty new dress with white shoes and a hat trimmed with ribbon. When we got out to the farm my mother-in-law, who didn't speak any English, welcomed me with a custom they brought with them from the old country. She sifted flour all over my new hat and poured a cup of water on my shoes. I was ready to turn right around and go back up the highway."

But she didn't leave. Pauline and her husband stuck it out, despite the fact that the Dust Bowl years had just arrived. "It was tough at first, but we made it. There were plenty of hard times, but nothing's easy. We learned how to raise every type of vegetable imaginable, and we worked that farm for more than fifty years. We're still going strong. But I still think about that day when we came down old Highway 66 and saw Tulsa for the very first time."

There have been tremendous changes through the years. At Admiral Place and Mingo Road, vehicles speed around a traffic circle where Cy Avery's popular gas station once stood. Avery probably twists a good deal in his grave, especially if he can see what's happened to his beloved highway in his own city. Route 66 through Tulsa had been pawed over and in long stretches is just plain seedy. Latter-day city fathers did not see the value of preserving the better architecture and businesses along the city routes. Tulsa had been a major Route 66 booster. But like some other key points on the highway, including Oklahoma City and Amarillo, Tulsa for the most part turned its back on the old road and the businesses that made a living from highway traffic. Tulsa sold out for the fast lanes of the interstate.

Today, the Admiral Place section of Route 66 is lined with strip shopping centers, fast-food establishments, and auto body and welding shops. Among the franchise joints remain a few Route 66–style eateries, including Hank's Hamburgers ("Since 1949"), Ike's Chili House, Family Diner ("Home Cooked Meals"), Wing's Hamburgers, and the East Side Cafe, open seven days a week for chicken and steak dinners.

Route 66 jogs back and forth on several downtown streets until it gets back to 11th, an avenue that still hints of the glory days when Tulsa was known as "The Oil Capital of the World." Many Route 66 motels and cafes fell victim to the interstate or the expressways that crisscross the city. When I-44 around Tulsa was completed, bigger and newer hotels, motels, and restaurants were built. Bigger and newer perhaps, but hardly any of them were any better than what had existed on the old highway.

Like the Admiral Place survivors, a few old motels and restaurants also remain on the 11th Street stretch of Route 66. But most are vacant or else a shadow of what they once were in the days before interstate madness swept the country. Several of the surviving motels, which used to cater to families, later had to resort to water beds and risqué movies in order to attract patrons. Some are used by transients, prostitutes, and drifters whose whole lives are spent in motels offering weekly rates.

Hardly anyone remembers the Pierce Pennant Terminal, the city's earliest motel and a Route 66 prize from the 1920s. The neon-lit sign of a cowboy mounted on a rearing stallion at the Will Rogers Motor Court, another 11th Street favorite, also disappeared along with the entire complex. Only a grassy lot and few pine trees remain. But next door, McCollum's Restaurant is still cooking. More than one Route 66 traveler has paused for a meal at McCollum's. Inside are booths and a lunch counter, glass cases stocked with several species of pie, a genuine malt and shake mixer, and a crew of highly capable waitresses who fill glasses from sweating pitchers of ice water before customers have a chance to open their menus.

Just up the highway, next door to the Oklahoma Academy of Hair Styling, another fine cafe named the Golden Drumstick was leveled and replaced with a plastic convenience store. But across the street, on a retaining wall that surrounds a school playground, the old restaurant appears in a mural. So does the distinctive U.S. 66 shield. Someone remembered and cared.

Unfortunately, not enough folks cared about the exquisite Will Rogers Theatre, just a few blocks away on 11th Street. A Streamline Art Deco gem with a marquée wrapped around a pencillike tower and the words WILL ROGERS spelled out vertically in bold neon letters, this theater entertained thousands during its lifetime on the Mother Road. A mob of Tulsans and Oklahoma visitors crammed into the lobby when it opened, in 1941, with *Mr. and Mrs. Smith*, a Carole Lombard film. Prices were twenty cents and four mils for adults and a dime and two mils for kids. The theater closed in 1977, on the forty-second anniversary of

Will Rogers's death, and a nearby church took over the property. First the church used the old theater marquee to advertise its services; then it tore down the Route 66 landmark and replaced it with a black asphalt parking lot.

Continuing on 11th Street, travelers pass a fine antique and collectible shop named the Browsery, the Oklahoma School of Poodle Grooming, and Skelly Stadium, located on the edge of the University of Tulsa campus. Students, families, and Tulsa visitors stop for stick-to-the-ribs meals at the Metro Diner, a glitzy neon throwback to the old road days. The Metro was built long after the decertification of Route 66, but the interior walls are crowded with vintage signs and memorabilia. The young men and women slinging plate lunches and mammoth slices of cream pie on the tables recall the energetic waitresses from the good old days.

Route 66 hasn't been entirely forgotten in Tulsa. Another re-created old highway beanery is the Route 66 Diner, just down the street from the Metro and across the street from the Casa Loma Barber Shop. The diner lies on the other side of the large Bama Pie Ltd. Bakery, where for many years commercial pies have been baked inside a big brick building decorated with plaques offering inspirational quotes from Woodrow Wilson, Abraham Lincoln, and Lawrence Welk. The 66 Diner, owned by Sherry and Debbie Higgs, uses the old highway shield for its sign and is in a building that dates back to 1935. Most of the people scarfing down burgers and fried spuds at the counter are locals, not travelers. None of the orders is written down, and the fry cook can flip four eggs at a time without breaking a yolk. A huge bean pot is always simmering on the stove alongside a pot of black-eyed peas. The mashed potatoes are real and even have lumps, and the French toast is made with freshly baked whole wheat bread. The aroma of hotcakes, omelets, blueberry muffins, and rising hamburger buns fills the diner. Lunch specials include smoked brisket, meat loaf, and the popular Route 66 Diner's Philly Chicken. Nobody leaves *this* place hungry. The same is true at the Pancake Place, El Rancho Grande, and Mark & Mary's Good Food—all on 11th Street, all as Route 66 in style and substance as they can be.

On the road through Tulsa, 11th Street passes several important Art Deco buildings, including the Warehouse Market built in 1929 on the site of the old McNulty ball park, where such sports greats as Babe Ruth, Red Grange, and Jack Dempsey thrilled the crowds. The stadium also served as a shelter for black families during the city's shameful 1921 race riot. Eight years later, just as Route 66 was getting started, a developer transformed the park into a public market and erected the huge Deco building. A tower with brilliant polychrome terra-cotta ornaments acted as a beacon to attract people to the market. The Depression closed the place, but a few years later it reopened as the Club Lido, where swingers danced to the music of Cab Calloway, Benny Goodman, Duke Ellington, and other touring performers. In 1938, it became the Warehouse Market and operated as a grocery store until 1978 when the building began its fall into limbo.

After passing the market building, the old city route flirts with the shadows of the famous Boston Avenue Methodist Church—an elegant Art Deco spire pointing like a finger toward heaven. Within minutes, travelers cross the Arkansas River on a concrete span built next to the 11th Street bridge, originally erected in 1916, and now a blocked-off structure that serves as a shelter for the homeless who sleep beneath the old bridge.

On the other side, the route becomes Southwest Boulevard all the way through West Tulsa. This side of the Arkansas is a part of the city often overlooked, especially by some "proper" Tulsans who consider the west bank the wrong side of town. They say the west side is where you go looking for trouble. Some tales are true. For many years, the west side was as raw as Oklahoma crude. The area earned a reputation for being bare-knuckled and always thirsty. In truth, the west side has cooled its hot temper and is home for generations of hard-working families who would not dream of living anywhere else.

"We keep the city honest," says a gnarled old-timer winking over a mug of coffee in a Southwest Boulevard cafe. "Without the west bank of the Arkansas and what happened here, good ol' Tulsa would be just another podunk town that people pass through on their way to someplace else." The old man's reference is to the oil discoveries at Red Fork, a west bank community, and site of one of the biggest oil finds back in 1901. Red Fork really helped put Tulsa on the map. Then, a few years later, an even richer oil discovery was made at Glenn Pool.

That was all long ago. The oil dried up and so has much of the oil-related business on the west bank. The Park Plaza Court, a 66 relic on Southwest Boulevard for a half century, turned into a haven for low-income families and the disenfranchised. It was finally torn down in the late 1980s. Up the highway, only a short distance from where the Park Plaza stood, the ghostly 66 Motel has seen better times despite "reasonable rates." But there's no need to despair. The best part of Route 66 in Oklahoma lies ahead. Travelers can switch on KVOO, the radio station that started down the road in Bristow with the call letters KRFU. During the Roaring Twenties, people started calling the station the "Voice of Oklahoma" and the call letters were changed to match that impressive name. In 1927, KVOO moved to Tulsa, and ever since, listeners have been treated to the music of Bob Wills and His Texas Playboys, Gene Autry, Hank Williams, and a legion of other country-western greats. Car radios can still get a good workout all the way to Oklahoma City as fingers twist the knobs back and forth picking up the strains of "Take Me Back to Tulsa" and "San Antonio Rose" or the Cardinals' doubleheader on another station.

Soon after leaving Tulsa, the old road works its way back into the country and heads for the little towns that will always be strong Route 66 havens. Along the old road between Tulsa and Oklahoma City stand ROUTE 66 MEMORIAL HIGHWAY signs. The two-lane is still well traveled and resurfaced through Sapulpa, Chandler, Luther, and the many other towns. In *A Guide Book to Highway 66*, Jack Rittenhouse describes this portion of the old highway.

> This section of your trip takes you from Tulsa to Oklahoma City. The route is through rolling countryside— once the haunt of Indians, later the territory of cowmen and "badmen," but now devoted principally to oil and agriculture. Part of your route is through a section of the famous "Cherokee Strip." On weekends the traffic is somewhat heavier near Oklahoma City. The road is good, but the shoulders are soggy in wet weather. In the smaller towns, brick streets are often bumpy.

That description, written in 1946, remains accurate. Watch the soft shoulders and mind the bumps. Oklahoma City traffic is still a bear. For the traveler with some time to spare, a ride down Route 66 to Oklahoma City can be a side trip to a bygone era that can't be found anywhere else. No part of the long journey down the old highway provides the traveler with more kicks than this particular run. It is narrow and crooked and sometimes tedious, especially when a motorist gets trapped behind a time-warped farmer poking along in his pickup in one of the tiny towns. But for those who opt for the free road, it's worth every minute.

As the old highway winds through the countryside, the Frankoma Pottery Plant appears on the side of the road just before the town of Sapulpa. Founded on a shoestring in 1933 by John Frank, a young ceramics instructor at the University of Oklahoma, Frankoma Pottery moved to Sapulpa in 1938. Frank had received his formal training at Chicago Art Institute, located at the exact spot where Route 66 begins its westward trek across the nation. That was in 1926, the year the highway was unveiled. The following year, Frank moved to Oklahoma and began his teaching career. In 1938, just after Frank and his wife, Grace Lee, moved to Sapulpa, a fire destroyed the plant. They started to rebuild, but when World War II arrived, the Franks could not get workers or materials for their pottery business. All production was halted as the family waited out the war. As soon as peace returned to the world, Frank fired up the kilns and started a training program for ex-GIs interested in learning the pottery trade. Tourists started traveling down Route 66 in greater numbers than ever before and Frankoma's business soared. Decades later, the pottery plant was charred by yet another terrible fire, but bounced right back.

Frank died in 1973. The plant remains a family operation and still turns out native clayware—dishes, vases, pitchers, tiles, ashtrays, flower bowls, and planters—sold throughout the Southwest. "People are interested in seeing pottery made, and they never get tired of seeing the new things that can be made from the earth," wrote Frank before his death. "It is for this reason that Frankoma Pottery is located on the main artery highway, so that passing tourists can stop by and see it made, and browse around enjoying the beautiful things we make from Oklahoma clays."

One of Frankoma's biggest fans is Norma Lee Hall, the woman who runs Norma's Cafe, a short distance away in Sapulpa, just past the big Liberty Glass Plant and across the street from the graveyard that also sits on Route 66. Norma wouldn't think of using anything but Frankoma dishes for her faithful customers. On the front window a sign proclaims, WOW! BREAKFAST 99¢. Inside, Norma bustles about setting tables with her pottery dishes and pouring coffee into diners' pottery cups. Hearty patrons go for her famous Tower of Power—scrambled eggs, bacon, cheese, and the works piled on Texas toast. But the breakfast special for under a dollar is hard to pass up. The price has not changed in years. Norma's Cafe has been serving good road food since the '50s. Opal Glenn, the stoic woman cracking eggs and flipping pancakes in the steamy kitchen, has been a cook at Norma's most of her life and keeps getting better with age. At Norma's, almost everything is made from scratch. The chili, Irish stew, and smothered steak are worth dying for, and the ham and beans with corn bread can make a grown man weep with joy.

"The fast-food restaurants took away a lot of our business," says Norma during a rare pause between pumping quarters into the jukebox, dusting off the bowling trophies, and delivering a slice of chocolate pie to her granddaughter. "We got all of 'em—McDonald's, Burger King, Arby's, Hardee's—anything you want except good food. The turnpike and the fast-food places really hurt us. Used to be we'd be open twenty-four hours a day. Anymore we stay open till about three in the afternoon. That just about catches everybody. But in those days before the turnpike was built, were we ever busy. Then one evening that ol' turnpike opened and the next morning we woke up and it was an entirely new world for us. Still, we have our regulars who come through these parts every year on vacations. They still stop. They have a few more gray hairs and some wrinkles but we remember them."

Next door to the cafe is an old service station and truck stop, the domain of Norma's husband, Bob Hall. "We called it the Diamond Truck Stop, and I ran it for thirty-six years and then retired," says Bob. "We had fifteen truck companies trading here and it took twenty-seven men working twenty-four hours a day to get the job done. I sold many a canvas water bag to hang on a bumper to some tourist headed out to California. Those were exciting times. Truckers knew they could always stop here for fuel and good food. Now the trucks have mostly left us for the turnpike."

Hall keeps old photographs he took of the truckers who were his regulars, standing by their rigs. Most of the photos are faded or have discolored with age. Hall wouldn't part with them for a sack of gold. "All of these men are dead. They were good fellas. They'd come back on vacations and bring their families to see us. One of them lived right up Route 66 in Tulsa and he died out on the highway. Had a heart attack. His family didn't have any pictures of him so they came out here and I got the negative and made them a photo."

Route 66 goes right through the heart of Sapulpa. Like so many Oklahoma towns, Sapulpa was named for an Indian who settled in these parts. At one time a hangout for such notorious gents as the James boys, the Dalton gang, and the Youngers, the town also became a rendezvous for cattlemen, railroaders, and roustabouts who worked in the nearby Glenn Pool field.

A few miles outside town sit some forlorn motor court units— all made of the native rust-colored flat stones that look like patches on a giraffe. The old road goes below a concrete railroad overpass tattooed with fading lovers' initials and remembrances. "Kenny Loves Linda—Baby on the Way," and "Kenny, I'll Be Back in October—Don't Forget Me!!" The road rolls on through more little towns. There's Kellyville, remembered with some notoriety for Oklahoma's worst rail disaster—the 1917 head-on collision of two Frisco trains. Kellyville was also where the state's first, and mercifully only, ski resort, complete with tons of artificial snow, was supposed to be built in the early 1970s. As one travel writer diplomatically put it, "The scheme was stillborn."

The highway crosses Little Polecat Creek and then Polecat Creek, scoots over the turnpike, and runs right into Bristow, a former Creek Nation trading post that developed into an oil-patch town. As the highway bridges Catfish Creek and snakes toward Depew, another farm town laid out next to the Frisco tracks, the earth begins to change to the ochre color of western Oklahoma. Soon all the soil will be that famous iron red. In these parts, the locals drive slowly and wave at each other as they pass on the road. They take great pride in their roses and peonies, and raise irises the color of root beer and butterscotch.

The little towns and place names keep coming. There's Stroud, a burg that prospered by peddling illicit whiskey from its nine busy taverns until 1907, when statehood brought respectability. Later, the discovery of oil gave the town a more dependable income. The path through Stroud is brick covered, the Rock Cafe serves up big portions of stew, and "Old 66 Antiques" can't keep anything in stock that has "66" on it, especially the cherished highway shields. Next comes Davenport, home of Dan's Bar-B-Que, owned and operated by a retired Route 66 trucker, and then Chandler, "Pecan Capital of the World." In the city cemetery is the grave of Bill Tilghman, a famous frontier lawman from territorial days who died in what became known as the last "Old West–style" gun battle in Oklahoma. That took place in the oil town of Cromwell in 1924, only two years before Route 66 was officially opened.

The Lincoln Motel in Chandler, recommended in the Rittenhouse guidebook, is as neat and comfortable as it was when it opened in 1939. In front of each of the twenty cabins flutters a small American flag. After devouring a slab of pork ribs at PJ's Bar-B-Que, travelers can return to the Lincoln, case into a canary-yellow metal lawn chair, and watch the evening traffic whiz past.

About ten miles down the highway from Chandler is Wellston, the first permanent white settlement in Lincoln County and a former trading post on the Kickapoo Reservation. Wellston is where Harold Stephens hung his cap all his life. When he turned seventy, Stephens retired as the town blacksmith, a trade he had religiously practiced every day since 1939 when he opened his shop less than a mile off Route 66.

"My dad came to Oklahoma in 1899 and brought his blacksmith tools with him," recalls Stephens. "I used those tools myself. His shop was over there, 'bout where that mimosa tree stands." Stephens, who spent his life hammering on farm machinery and fixing Route 66 vehicles, could remember when the old road was thick with passing traffic. "Sure were lots of folks going down ol' 66, headed for God knows where. I'd get some of their cars in my shop when they'd break down. But then things got real slow. The traffic wasn't nearly the same. Guess I didn't make a whole lot of money from that work on the highway, but I got a bunch of friends. That's all I ever wanted anyway."

Eight miles west of Wellston, the village of Luther lies south of Route 66, not far from the Little Brothers Store, where locals use the pay phone and buy gasoline, cold beer, cans of snuff, and hunting and fishing licenses. A state marker explains that nearby was the eastern boundary for the fabled Land Run of 1889, when the prairies and hills of the two-million-acre tract of land to the west were opened up to white settlers who poured in and overnight erected tent cities and staked their claims. Moving west, on the other side of Soldier Creek, is another historical monument. This one is for Washington Irving, who in 1832 hunted wild horses in this area and shot a buffalo on the banks of Coffee Creek just south of the highway. The town of Arcadia, once a fair-sized settlement, lies just ahead.

Arcadia was established during the 1889 land run, and during the peak years of the old highway was a thriving Route 66 pit stop. In one of the old deserted motor courts, Bob Taylor established a barbecue joint and smokehouse. "I can sell about a hundred pounds of ribs, brisket, ham, hot links, and sausage on a good day," says Taylor as he wipes his hands on a white apron already crusty from sauce and pork grease. "Folks still travel down this old road from Tulsa and from Oklahoma City."

Out back, beneath towering pecan trees, the old motor court cabins—some made of logs shipped from Missouri—are filled with cobwebs and misplaced memories. Harvey Ruble, born in 1907 on a farm on Coon Creek where the land run started, built the motor court in the late 1930s. He has lived along the highway ever since except when he worked in the shipyards and served a hitch in the navy. "I wouldn't go to bed at night until I had every cabin rented out," says Ruble. "I'd get five-fifty a night for a room and think I was a rich man." Harvey lives in a small house next door to his old motor court. His wife is dead, but he keeps her clothes hanging in the closet. Photographs of kinfolk, including Harvey in his sailor suit, are displayed in the front room. A sassy Pomeranian pup named Buffy, given to Harvey by a state trooper, keeps the old man company. "Those years when this was the main route across the land were truly great," sighs Harvey. "There were afternoons when I actually couldn't get across that two-lane highway because there were so many autos and trucks. A man had to make a mad dash. Now there are times you could eat a picnic lunch in the middle of the road and never have to move."

Arcadia is also the home of the famed Round Barn, built in 1898 and listed on the National Register of Historic Places. The barn, sheathed in native bur oak, was a landmark before Route 66 was even being dreamed of by Cy Avery and his cohorts. Locals claim that when the barn was new, a person could stand near a wall and hear a pin, dropped on the other side of the building, hit the floor. The acoustics were good enough for generations of revelers who danced many nights away while fiddle players serenaded the harvest moon.

The old highway leaves Arcadia, Harvey Ruble, and the

Round Barn behind, and moves on to Edmond, where Wiley Post is buried. In Edmond, a berserk postal employee massacred fourteen of his co-workers in 1986. The skyline of Oklahoma City looms through the haze on the horizon. State Highway 66 tends to get lost in the shuffle at Oklahoma City—the hub of the interstate network in Oklahoma. Three major highways—I-44, I-40, and I-35—all cross in Oklahoma City. The complex of busy thoroughfares is impossible to avoid. There are several options for driving through the city, where much of the interstate is built directly over the old road.

Oklahoma's largest city and the state capital, "O.K.C." or "The City," as locals are fond of saying, looks like a pawed-over oil-field floozy but with a touch of elegance. The city's greatest resource is the resilient Oklahomans who live there and have survived the Dust Bowl, depressions, and oil booms and busts. Through it all, they have kept a sense of humor and optimism. Many parts of the sprawling city look tired and pale, and most vestiges of America's Main Street have been stripped away. Still, next to the Cowboy Hall of Fame, which sits atop Persimmon Hill, crowds flock to the Oklahoma County Line, a barbecue restaurant that overlooks what was once Route 66. Built in 1918 and known for many years as the Kentucky Club, the colorful roadhouse was reputed to be a favorite hangout for the infamous Pretty Boy Floyd. The bootleggers, gamblers, and painted ladies are gone, replaced by famished crowds anxious to "dine at the line." Primed by a cocktail or two, they tangle with enormous beef ribs, bowls heaping with cobbler à la mode, and glasses of iced tea the size of small buckets, garnished with stalks of fresh mint. In the evening shadows, a traveler sometimes even remembers to ask about the old highway and lifts a glass in tribute to the Mother Road.

At Oklahoma City, I-40—another interstate replacement for Route 66—takes over. After battling through the Oklahoma City streets, travelers who wish to stick to the old route can find sections left throughout western Oklahoma, all the way to the Texas line. Service roads and spur bypasses hook through town after town. As is true along the entire length of the highway, motorists can always find pieces of Route 66 if they take the time to look.

In its prime, Route 66—both city and bypass routes—rejoined at the northwest corner of Oklahoma City and then proceeded through Bethany—the town that is home to the Nazarene religious sect. Here, billboards along the road advise, THE FEAR OF THE LORD IS THE BEGINNING OF WISDOM. After Bethany, old-road travelers cross a steel bridge over the North Canadian River, drive past Lake Overholser, and then barrel due west through Yukon, El Reno, Bridgeport, Hydro, Weatherford, Clinton, Canute, Elk City, Sayre, Erick, and finally reach Texola, a sun-baked town that still savors its past and looks the Texas Panhandle straight in the eye.

A short distance past Oklahoma City and Bethany, big white grain elevators let travelers know that the highway town of Yukon is coming up. A bedroom suburb of Oklahoma City, the town was founded in 1891 and apparently took its name from the Alaskan river. Winter wheat was once the mainstay of Yukon's economy, but that changed through the years. Housing developments and shopping centers cover much of the rich farmland, and residents commute to jobs in the big city to the east. But as the highway proceeds toward El Reno and the other stalwart towns guarding small sections of Route 66, westerners realize they're finally at home. As photographer Terrence Moore put it once when describing his hitchhiking experience at El Reno, "You know you've arrived." What remains of the old highway in western Oklahoma may not be as pristine as the unbroken stretch between Tulsa and Oklahoma City, but the bits and pieces of pavement through the western part of the state still provide plenty of magic.

El Reno, not far from the south bank of the North Canadian River and named for the nearby fort, has always been a Route 66 booster. Through the years, the *El Reno American* published stories about the coming of U.S. Route 66 and reporters covered the highway rallies where Cy Avery delivered impassioned speeches. On the edge of the old road through El Reno are definite traces of highway culture such as old motels and cafes.

W. H. Boyd, retired from the Rock Island Railroad, lives on Route 66, just two miles west of downtown El Reno. He was born in Paradise, Texas, but moved to Oklahoma and built his home on the old highway. He painted it bright pink with sky-blue trim and set out wagon wheels, windmills, and flamingos in the yard.

"That drive-in picture show across the street is out of business and things slowed some over the years since the interstate was built," says Boyd. "When the town got bypassed, there were definite changes. But my oh my, there used to be traffic passing here—right by my front door."

General Phil Sheridan and his troopers once rode through this area in search of Cheyenne and Arapaho warriors. The grave of Jesse Chisholm, of cattle trail fame, is located a few miles north of Route 66. The Chisholm Trail crossed the old highway at the point where El Reno stands, while a branch of the trail bisected the highway near the present site of Weatherford. The Dodge City Trail crossed 66 at Elk City. Now Route 66 is the youngest of all these ghost roads.

Past El Reno, the old highway at one time went toward Geary and then on to Bridgeport, just off the route on the south shore of the Canadian River. As its name implies, river bridges were always important to the town. The flood of 1914 destroyed the Rock Island Bridge, but the best-known Bridgeport span was a suspension toll bridge opened in 1921 as the last link in the Postal Highway through the state. When U.S. 66 was established five years later, lobbying efforts were started to make the crossing a free bridge, which was finally accomplished in 1930. Within a few years, however, a new steel and concrete bridge was opened a few miles downstream. U.S. 66 was rerouted, and the town of Bridgeport, now bypassed, began to fade. When I-40 came along in the 1960s, Bridgeport's isolation was complete.

Pressing westward, the path into Hydro (home of Lucille Hamons, who still sells gas and snacks at her service station as she has since 1941), Weatherford, and Clinton is mostly on interstate access roads. Clinton is one of the staunchest Route 66 towns. People in Clinton will not ever let go of their highway. Pop Hicks Restaurant, known far and wide as a Route 66 institution, serves home-cooked meals and acts as an unofficial town meeting place. At 66 Auto Salvage yard, just across the highway from the Rio Siesta Motel, two growling Dobermans with chain collars stand guard over sturdy Mack trucks, their stainless steel bulldog hood ornaments gleaming in the relentless summer sun.

Clinton was the home base for Jack Cutberth, "Mr. 66." His widow, Gladys, hands out sage advice to Route 66 fans who seek her counsel as they drive through town. Sometimes, Gladys Cutberth treats herself to supper at the Tradewinds Restaurant across from the Western Trails Museum on Highway 66. Printed on the menu are these reminders: "God without man is still

God. Man without God is nothing" and "Where there is an open mind, there will always be a frontier." Best bets at the Tradewinds are the Big Red (ham steak, a pair of fresh eggs, hash browns, and toast) or the Okie Special (charbroiled beef patty with potato salad, sliced tomatoes, and a mug of U.S. Senate bean soup). Both are road meals that can fuel a driver all the way to Amarillo.

West of Clinton, the highway starts its gentle southwest descent toward the Texas Panhandle through lands studded with yucca and prickly pear. There is a stretch of Route 66 at Canute, a small farming community settled in 1901 and named for the ancient Norse king. On the old road at the eastern edge of town is the Catholic cemetery, known for its hillside sepulcher and the bronze life-size figure of Christ on the cross looking down at the two kneeling Marys below.

The Oklahoma soil is its deepest red at this point. The land is rolling and hilly west of Canute as the road heads toward Elk City, originally named Busch, in honor of Adolphus Busch, the St. Louis beer baron. In 1931, Elk City hosted a crowd of more than thirty thousand—all Route 66 boosters—when the U.S. Highway 66 Association held its annual convention in the city, complete with a western-style parade, rodeo, and buffalo barbecue. Thirty wagon loads of Cheyenne and Arapaho Indians arrived and set up a model village, staged war dances, and stayed to watch Charles H. Tompkins, former mayor of El Reno, succeed Cyrus Avery as president of the association. Some of the celebrants predicted Route 66 would never be replaced. They vowed to protect the fabled highway forever. They didn't keep their word. The highway was eventually replaced by a superslab and Elk City was passed by.

Near the front door of a Texaco service station on the old highway in the midst of Elk City, a gorilla mannequin waves its hairy arm at the passing traffic. Up the street a few blocks, Lloy Cook keeps watch over Route 66 from his hubcap shop. "I was born in 1915, and have been in business on 66 since 1939," says Cook. "It was paved then, but I recall when it wasn't and parts of the highway were only sand. I went into the car business in 1929—buying and selling used cars—and quit in 1972. Now I have this little place here on the highway and I sell hubcaps. I started counting how many I had one time but I had to stop." Car buffs from as far away as Chicago and St. Louis stop at Cook's tiny shop to buy hubcaps for vintage Corvettes, Thunderbirds, Mustangs, and Studebakers. "I hated to see that interstate come and the old highway go. I sure did make a lot of money off Route 66."

On the far western edge of Elk City, past a forsaken drive-in theater and oil-field businesses that have seen better days, remains what is left of Queenan's Indian Trading Post, built by Reese and Wanda Queenan in 1948. For many years the Queenans offered tourists a selection of Indian pottery, beadwork, jewelry, and rugs, and also sold supplies to Indians who lived in the region. Although her husband died in 1962, Wanda stayed on and kept the trading post open. But when the interstate came and the oil patch went sour, business at the trading post suffered. Wanda stopped buying and sold out her remaining stock.

"We didn't get rich, but this trading post was something we really loved," says Wanda. "It was great fun out here on Route 66."

A solitary buffalo head remains mounted on a trading post wall and the empty shelves collect dust. Outside, a mimosa tree and some wind-whipped Chinese elms provide shade and there's still a huge Indian figure standing with hands on hips. A Delaware Indian welded together old barrels and chains in the early 1950s and made the giant kachina. There's a certain irony that the towering metal totem was fashioned from odd pieces from the oil field, the industry that once kept the wheels of commerce lubricated in these parts. But Wanda Queenan still lives behind the trading post and listens to the relentless wind howling up out of Texas and the sound of passing cars and trucks that continue to use the old highway but no longer stop.

A dozen miles down Route 66 is Sayre, established in 1902 and known as "The Cradle of the Quarter Horse." The north fork of the Red River flows along the southern outskirts of Sayre, and Jess Willard, former world champion prizefighter, once ran a rooming house in town. After Sayre, the old road tracks through weed-covered sand dunes and then, just a few miles past the agricultural community of Erick, comes Texola—the last Oklahoma town before Route 66 reaches the Texas border.

Texola is a mile off the interstate. This was the home of Longhorn Trading Post, built in the 1930s and one of the earliest restaurants along Route 66. Texola has dwindled to nothing but weeds and abandoned buildings. A sign on the fringes of town says THERE'S NO PLACE LIKE TEXOLA. Another sign offers BEER, OIL, SODA POP, RESTROOMS, EATS, ICE. All the essentials. Off in the distance, dogs bark eerily and the sky fills with a million Panhandle stars. The Lone Star State beckons.

To the east—all the way back up the long twisty Oklahoma highway—through Elk City, Clinton, Oklahoma City, Chandler, Sapulpa, Tulsa, Claremore, and Quapaw—the people who find time holy sleep like babies. They know the Mother Road is there. Old and proud and free.

4

THE MYSTIC BLEND OF FIRE, SMOKE, AND MEAT

Barbecue is more than a meal;
it's a way of life.

—Greg Johnson and
Vince Staten,
Real Barbecue

 Oklahoma twilight. The landscape softens as time hovers between day and night. A steady flow of Friday traffic on Highway 97 heads for turnpikes that connect to points east and west. Ball games are starting, fishing holes beckon, grass needs cutting. Another workweek has ended.

Outside Ethel's 97 Bar-B-Q, midway between Sand Springs and Sapulpa, hickory smoke scents the air like country incense, and lightning bugs blink awake. Half-breed dogs, feeling noble as royal hounds, stretch out in the dusty grass to rest after a day spent doing much of nothing. The dogs dream of rabbit hunts and chases through the weeds. They pay no mind to the car that pulls off the highway and stops a few feet from Ethel's door.

Inside, there's no doubt about the time. The jukebox is silent, the pinball is quiet, and the pool table sits as still as a graveyard. It's clearly time to eat. A sign tacked to the wall warns: NO CURSING OR VULGAR LANGUAGE ALLOWED PERIOD. But nobody's cussing. There's hardly any talk at the tables crowded in the tiny room where diners have their work cut out for them. They're there to tangle with pork ribs, juicy brisket, spicy links, and the trimmings—coleslaw, baked beans, white bread.

Not a head looks up or turns when the newest arrival takes a seat at the counter. One of the Friday-night regulars at Ethel's, a bus driver from Tulsa is still in uniform after a day spent hauling people up and down city streets. He has no need to consult the menu stained with barbecue sauce. This man knows what he wants. He didn't come for quiche or blackened redfish. Those kinds of things aren't served at Ethel's. Folks who come here are in the market for meat. The man takes a deep sip from a can of icy beer, wipes a sleeve across his mouth, and runs his tongue over his lips. He knows he's just moments away from the rib dinner he's thought about for days. When the tray loaded with steaming ribs, beans, and slaw is put before him, the man breaks into a grin and digs in. He grabs the biggest rib and tears off a good-sized hunk with a gentle bite. The flavor of the succulent meat is exquisite. He doesn't even think about reaching for the sauce. No need. This meat stands on its own.

Six napkins and twenty minutes later, it's all over. Only a pile of bones is left on the tray. If he were a cat, the bus driver would purr. He licks his fingers clean, sticks a toothpick in his mouth, settles the account, and heads out ready to face the world once more. He realizes he's the luckiest bus driver in Oklahoma. The word *ambrosia* isn't in his vocabulary, or that's what he'd call the dinner he just devoured. Instead, he winks at the girl who takes his money and drawls out loud to no one in particular, "Good barbecue." That says it all. Those are the words any Oklahoma pit master worth his or her weight in rib bones longs to hear.

"I cook up good sauce and use good meat—the best meat I can get," says Virginia Smith, the woman whose magic touch earns Ethel's consistently high marks amongst Oklahoma barbecue aficionados. "If you want regular customers, you have to buy the best meat you can."

Virginia ought to know. She and her husband and cohort, Floyd, learned all about barbecue from the late Ethel Tucker, the woman who founded the business and who taught them how to prepare the kind of mouth-watering "Q" that keeps people coming back.

"Ethel was in bad health and she wanted to sell the place," explains Virginia. "Floyd was working in a machine shop at the time, and we decided to have a go at it. We took over years ago. Ethel coached me and taught me how to cook the meat."

Although their mentor, Ethel, is dead, the Smiths can count on her husband, Jack—a relentless critic—to come out occasionally to taste the meat they serve and see if it's up to Ethel's high standards.

"We believe in keeping good fires in our pit," says Floyd, a Gore native who enjoys his cigars and listens to as many Cardinal games as he can between bouts of stoking the pit out back with armloads of green hickory. "You have to maintain a pretty good fire and then cook your dry spices right into the meat, but never under any circumstances do we put sauce on while it's cooking."

Floyd and Virginia live next door, and on weekends Floyd runs a popular flea market that draws big crowds, including those who savor beef, pork, and ham sandwiches or mixed plates. Four of the Smiths' five children and several grandchildren help out at Ethel's, and Virginia has high hopes that they will take over someday.

"One of my girls knows how to cook the sauce now and the rest are learning."

When dusk turns to evening and the moon rises like a big wheel of cheddar, the dogs outside slink off in the shadows and Floyd snaps on a ribbon of pink neon light to serve as a beacon for travelers who might have a craving for some beef or pork or chicken or maybe smoked bologna. Meanwhile, Virginia keeps chopping meat for her regulars and any passing strangers lured by the lights and the seductive aroma.

"Barry Switzer came in here, and he liked it so much he took a bunch of barbecue with him," says Virginia. "Ethel told me how to cook the meat and how to fix my sauces. I learned how to put those special touches in the hot barbecue sauce. None of it was written down. I got it all up here," she says touching her finger to her temple. "Ethel taught me well. Real well."

Thank God for Ethel Tucker. And thanks, too, for all the other professors of the pit and the scores of cooks who remain dedicated to upholding the high standards that have made barbecue in Oklahoma a way of life, and in some parts practically a religion.

There are countless barbecue restaurants (better known as joints) ranging from Altus to Miami, Hugo to Boise City. Still, contrary to popular belief, barbecue wasn't invented in Oklahoma. And, no, Texas cannot brag that the Lone Star State cooked up the first serving of piping hot barbecue. Nor can Kansas City or Memphis or the other great BBQ haunts in the South and Midwest.

The best culinary experts claim the first "barbecue" resulted when a Paleolithic lightning bolt charred some luckless creature, providing a family of cave dwellers with a delectable lunch. There are no records of sliced onions, jalapeños, or white bread being served with that first barbecue feast. Nonetheless, grilling over an open fire was the earliest method of cooking meat. Archaeologists probing digs that date back as far as 25,000 B.C. have uncovered evidence of primitive humans roasting game in pits. In many instances a trough, dug in the ground and lined with stones, held a fire over which the skewered carcass was rotated.

"Like all great ideas," explain Greg Johnson and Vince Staten in their *Real Barbecue* book, "barbecue came out close to perfect from the start. And unlike the wheel, which was another good idea, man has had the sense to leave barbecue pretty much alone." Indeed. Civilization has certainly done its level best to corrupt the wheel, but barbecue remains that same mystic blend of fire, smoke, and meat.

It's clear that long before Columbus set sail on his celebrated voyage of discovery, Native Americans (mostly in what is today the southeastern United States, as well as on the Caribbean Islands and in some parts of Mexico and Latin America) had devised a method of preserving meat by smoking it on wooden platforms elevated over fires. Probably those early BBQ chefs were kin to the Native American tribes who later settled in Oklahoma. At least that's what several proud Okie cooks like to boast.

The origin of the word *barbecue* remains the subject of heated debate and is shrouded in thick clouds of pit smoke. Historians argue over whether the name comes from the Spanish word *barbacoa*, for the elevated cooking frame on which meat is cooked, or from a French phrase *barbe à queue*, which refers to roasting a pig whole from *barbe* (chin) to *queue* (tail). What is known is that preservation of meat was important to the Caribbean Indians and natives of the southern East Coast because the humid climate brought on spoilage almost as quickly as a hunter could dress his quarry. Smoking and preserving meat on the trusty *barbacoa* was a practical necessity, not just a method of improving taste.

Shifra Stein, another noted BBQ author and a sworn fan of Kansas City–style barbecue, believes one of the earliest American-English adaptations of the word *barbacoa* was *barbacude*, which evolved into several different spellings and ultimately became *barbecue*. Shifra, who makes occasional forays into Oklahoma to chomp ribs and munch mounds of brisket, explains that as cooking developed in the southern part of the United States, so did barbecue.

In the South, barbecue became a popular dish to offer at everything from political rallies to plantation socials. It finally culminated in today's open-pit barbecues of the Carolinas and smokehouses of Virginia and moved across the country where the closed-pit barbecues of Kansas City, Texas, and, of course, Oklahoma appeared.

Barbecue was cowboy grub in the great American West. On the plains, prairies, and open range, barbecue quickly became a staple that helped quell desperate men's souls, as well as fuel hungry posses and wranglers. Cowpokes herding their longhorns through "the Nations" en route to Abilene and Kansas City craved something more than beans and biscuits. A roasted beef or smoked wild turkey was ideal for breaking the monotony of a long cattle drive.

Today, whether it's called barbecue or the popular nicknames BBQ and Bar-B-Que, the fact remains this time-tested dish is one of Oklahoma's cherished entrées and is firmly embedded in the state's soul. Simply put, all good Okies are addicted to the stuff.

In the deep South, many barbecue lovers go whole hog and insist honest-to-goodness barbecue doesn't involve beef at all but should come straight from the pig. Texans serve all sorts of meat but seem to prefer beef. They're especially fond of brisket, a solid, tough cut from the underside of the forequarters. But Oklahoma—influenced by Texas and the South—has the best of all worlds and serves up both barbecued pork and beef, as well as links, ham, chicken, and, in some parts of eastern Oklahoma, especially Tulsa, that all-American sausage known as bologna.

The best Oklahoma barbecue relies on a combination of slow cooking and the continuous wood smoking of meats over a hickory-wood fire until a crusty well-doneness is achieved. It takes patience and hard work to produce top-notch barbecue.

"Smoke it slow and cook it low" is the watchword for most Oklahoma pitmen. Hickory wood is favored since it yields a unique sweet, smoky flavor. Of course, tangy sauces are essential, but they're also the subject of controversy. Some swear sauce is needed to baste the meat during cooking; most don't want any sauce around unless it's a condiment on the table. Nobody is willing to discuss the details of sauce recipes. Almost everyone agrees that no matter if it's a mess of ribs or a twelve-pound chunk of fat-capped beef brisket, the sauce doesn't mean a thing unless the best meat money can buy is searing on the pit.

There are few arguments about side dishes. For openers there are sour pickles, Bermuda onions, fluffy white bread, and, sometimes, hot peppers. Accompanying the meat are potato salad, beans, and coleslaw. The meal can be washed down with scalding coffee, iced tea, pop, or beer. Hard liquor or milk doesn't really go with barbecue and neither do plates and silverware unless someone is trying to "put on the dog." Disposable is the name of the game. Plastic forks and paper-covered trays are standard at most respectable Oklahoma BBQ joints.

Don't expect to locate good barbecue joints by looking in the Yellow Pages. Many of the best BBQ pits won't be found there. If you want the best "Q," ask the locals. They'll tell you where to go. Also, check out the names. If the owner is proud enough of what he serves to use his own name for the joint, that's always a good sign. Another tip— Once the BBQ joint is located, don't be put off if you cruise by and find the place looks run down. Many times that's another indication that the food served is outstanding. If a barbecue joint is too spiffy, don't stay. Chances are strong that the meat won't be nearly as tasty as the place down the back road. Naturally, there are always exceptions to the rule, but atmosphere counts.

The very best way to find the truly great Oklahoma barbecue is to get out on the road and conduct taste tests. Lots of them. Because there're more people and certainly more wood in eastern Oklahoma, there appear to be more barbecue pits in that part of the state. But there are BBQ joints in every county from the Panhandle to the Red River. There's no better way to spend time than to go on a barbecue-sampling binge. Go anytime of year. The good pits are always cooking. It's a quest that will never end.

Here are descriptions of some of the best to help get you started.

It's appropriate that the state's unofficial emperor of barbecue can be found in Muskogee, the cradle of Oklahoma history. The city may have been immortalized in Merle Haggard's song and is recognized as a haven for azaleas as well as the USS *Batfish* (the World War II submarine marooned at the port), but where would Muskogee be without Slick's?

For decades Slick's has turned out some of the most delicious all-around barbecue in the nation. "I'd give up an eye or an organ to be able to belly up for an order of ribs at Slick's," laments an Oklahoma native who currently resides out of state.

A lean and quiet man, Slick was born just nine miles west of Muskogee in Taft, a predominantly black community that developed because of the large number of former slaves granted tribal memberships by the Creek Nation after the Civil War. His true name is Alonzo Smith, but he earned the moniker *Slick* when he was a seven-year-old marble ace whose "slick shootin' " didn't go unnoticed by his pals. Slick started cooking barbecue in Muskogee right after World War II, and he's been at his current location on the north side of town for years. He has two pits out back, velvet paintings on the wall, attractive girls to serve diners, and a list of regular customers that would make a dozen ordinary BBQ cooks jealous.

"All I do is cook my meat over hickory," allows Slick as he rings up another sale on his cash register. "I sell a lot of ribs and brisket. I sell to everybody—movie stars, working people, lawyers, preachers. They all seem to like my food."

Slick might be the current patriarch of Oklahoma barbecue, but there are plenty of other worthy contenders for the crown.

Certainly the folks around Sallisaw would cast their votes for Hubert Holman. He and his wife, Betty, operate Wild Horse Mountain Bar-B-Q, just a couple of miles south of town on U.S. 59. The Holmans' barbecue is so tempting that choppers carrying soldiers from area Army posts have been known to land nearby to pick up generous carryout orders of pork ribs.

Holman, who like many cooks turns to cigars out of self-defense to counter the pit smoke, prepares his barbecue out back in a big steel pit protected by a roof. Peacocks and roosters prance outside the joint, and there's an old pop machine that dispenses only beer—when it's working. Besides fine barbecue and cold beer, customers go for the sauce at Wild Horse Mountain and also rave over the beans. Business is so good that the Holmans shut down for vacation last Fourth of July. "It's nothing for us to run out of meat by early afternoon," says Betty. "People sure seem to like what we serve."

Speaking of liking, for years out on the Great Plains, generations of townspeople and Fort Sill GIs have fed well on the barbecued ribs, beef, links, and pork turned out by the pair of John & Cook's Bar-B-Que locations in Lawton. John Weatherd and Lamar Cook, the gents who founded the business in 1938, are gone—but the tradition continues.

"Lamar was my father, and he died in 1982," explains Corrie Certain, proprietress of John & Cook's No. 2. "My Uncle John passed away eleven years before my dad. The business stayed in our family."

Corrie's brother, L. C. Cook, runs John & Cook's No. 1, and between the two siblings, southwestern Oklahomans don't need to worry about getting a barbecue "fix" as long as they can make it to Lawton.

"There just aren't many barbecue places out in this part of the state," explains Corrie. "They come and go. The overhead and cost of hauling good wood for the pit gets to them. We're lucky. My brother has a good source for wood, but sometimes he has to go as much as a hundred miles."

Corrie learned the business at her dad's and uncle's sides and uses the brick pit her father built with his own hands. "Barbecuing just comes natural to me," she smiles. Her four children—Troy, Lonzo, Carrie, and Torrey—work with her and make sure the customers get plenty to eat, especially the popular (and "finger lickin' good") rib tips. "We're always busy. During the holidays we custom-smoke wild turkey, wild pigs, and buffalo. I've shipped ribs and beef as far as Seattle."

By far and away the best barbecue in the state can be sampled in Oklahoma City and Tulsa and the territory surrounding the state's two largest metro areas.

In Oklahoma City some of the highest-rated BBQ comes from Leo's two locations. Staten and Johnson, authors of *Real Barbecue,* not only included Leo's in their book but sent owner Leo Smith a special letter which declared: "We travelled 40,000 miles and ate at more than 700 barbecue restaurants during 1987, and we think you do barbecue right."

Leo learned how to cook barbecue when he was eleven years old at Ben's Barbecue in Tulsa, the domain of his illustrious uncle, Ben Stevenson. "My Uncle Ben taught me everything he knew," says Leo. "I was the one who brought smoked bologna from Tulsa and introduced it in Oklahoma City," claims the jovial maestro of the pit. "My uncle also helped me with my sauces, but I was getting weary just going back and forth to Tulsa, so I finally asked him before he died if he'd give me the recipe. He said he had never flown so if I'd bring him down in an airplane he'd give it to me. I did just that, but he wouldn't write the recipe down. I had to memorize it." When Leo's sister, Joyce Gillam, set up her barbecue business in San Diego, she got the same treatment. "I helped her all I could, but she had to memorize that recipe. We're taking no chances."

Leo puts stock in a slow-burning hickory fire and claims the secret to good barbecue is "not to rush it—we cook our beef eighteen hours." His patience shows. Leo also cautions that sauce should always be used sparingly. "Real barbecue eaters don't even need sauce. You should put it on the side if you like and just dip every once in a while."

After consuming some of his tender brisket or thick-sliced bologna, be sure to sample Leo's Homemade Banana Strawberry Cake. It's heaven-sent. But then so is Leo himself. Besides sponsoring golf tournaments for needy children, every year without fail this angel in an apron feeds barbecue to as many as three thousand homeless people in a downtown park. "I've got to give back something. I've been a lucky man."

Luck is an essential ingredient in every good barbecuer's recipe for success. Luck and lots of hard work. That's what it took for Gene Caldwell, owner of the Oklahoma County Line, to get folks flocking to his popular barbecue restaurant near the Cowboy Hall of Fame in Oklahoma City.

"When we bought this old building and started up back in 1980, it had been vacant for a while," says Caldwell, a native of Lubbock who started learning the BBQ trade when he was seventeen. "It was hard times at first. We had trouble attracting help and customers. But that's all changed."

Did it ever. These days (and nights) it's tough to find an empty chair in what has to be not only one of the tastiest but probably the largest barbecue restaurants in the state. Along with his wife, Sharon, who acts as manager, and a staff of seventy-five, Caldwell serves more than five hundred barbecue platters daily.

Many Oklahoma County Line devotees waiting for a table find solace in the spacious bar overlooking old Route 66. "There are trapdoors in every one of the booths off the main dining floor," smiles Caldwell. "They came in handy whenever there was a gambling raid and patrons needed to dump the chips and cards." The trapdoors are no longer used. These days there's nothing to get rid of, unless it's the piles of enormous beef and pork rib bones left by contented patrons who come from all over

Oklahoma to "dine at the Line." All comers get the same royal treatment—loaves of hot homemade bread to go with huge portions of scrumptious barbecue, smoked duck, pork loin, or prime rib. The cobbler and ice cream—all created on the premises—can't be beat. Nobody leaves the Line hungry.

A raft of truly great barbecue cooks has been stomping out hunger in Tulsa for years. BBQ is serious business in Tulsa, and the north side of the city alone has produced some of the finest barbecue chefs in the nation. Joints such as Latimer's, Reese's, Ben's, Reed's, and Al's were all part of Tulsa's BBQ heritage.

One northside product who is fast becoming a modern Tulsa institution is Elmer Thompson, a wizard of the pit who established Elmer's BBQ in the upscale Brookside area in 1983. Elmer, with the help of his wife, George, son Tony, and a crew of ten, has earned the respect of veteran BBQ cooks and eaters alike.

"Barbecue is a true delicacy," says Elmer. "You have to eat it with your hands. It's greasy. It's sticky. It's something purely American. There's nothing like it in the world."

Elmer (whose catchy slogan is "Elmers—it be bad!") put in a long apprenticeship cooking "Q" for Ezell Reese, a noted north Tulsa pitman. Elmer learned his lessons well.

"A person has got to be able to really taste the meat," explains Elmer. "The sauce is important, but treat it like syrup on pancakes. Don't overdo. I can tell if a person knows barbecue if they pick up a rib and taste it before they add sauce. You need to be able to taste the smoke. And as far as cooking, the fire is important. I prefer green hickory for a slow burn. The pit is important, too. You have to know your pit and know the hot and cold spots."

Elmer puts in long hours to ensure that customers who crowd into his place get their money's worth. But for Elmer and most of the other top barbecue cooks, the bottom line isn't just monetary reward.

"I feel kind of like ol' Slick does about this business. Slick enjoys seeing people eat his food. That's me, too. To watch someone come here and eat my barbecue fills me up just like I was sitting there eating it myself. You see, when you cook barbecue you have to have that desire to see people enjoy the meat. When a customer gets up with a smile, then I feel terrific."

North of Tulsa and just west of Skiatook on Highway 20, out where Tulsa and Osage counties collide, dwells a spunky woman who feels terrific just about all the time. And well she should. In less than a year Becky Brewer became known as one of the finest barbecue chefs to pick up a meat cleaver. Just ask the folks who congregate at her Big Buck's Barbecue to gorge on ribs and sliced beef.

"I like a good mild-to-hot hickory fire, and then I just set back and smoke that brisket and those ribs until they're ready," says Becky, a Tulsa native who drove a cement truck for four years before the BBQ bug bit. "I always liked camping and cooking out. When I heard about the contest and the cash prize for whoever shot the biggest buck in the state, I decided to give it a try." There were more than four thousand entries, but on a cool November morning, Becky took aim and dropped a buck that dressed out to 215 pounds. She won $3,000 in prize money and used it to grubstake a portable barbecue pit and concession stand.

"I hauled that thing to rattlesnake hunts, rodeos, and fairs and finally saved enough money to build this place." She proudly mounted the prize-winning buck's head on a wall.

Fellow hunters, anglers, cowboys, and families eager for tasty treats come to Big Buck's to feast on barbecue (note: sliced onions and jalapeños on every plate without having to ask) and peach cobbler, and to sip cold beer or sun tea. Becky makes time for her pride and joy—daughter Kala Marie Cale—and to go bass fishing every chance she gets. Then she has her team of jumping mules, which she likes to ride and show off in community parades.

But on most afternoons, when stomachs are starting to rumble and thoughts turn to the next hot meal, Becky, with her honey-colored hair and china-blue eyes, will more than likely be tossing hickory in the pit, cutting healthy slabs of brisket or swapping a fish yarn with a satisfied customer.

It just doesn't get any better than that.

All across Oklahoma are worthy barbecue joints. On old Route 66 alone, between Tulsa and Oklahoma City, pit stops beckon at PJ's Bar-B-Que in Chandler, Dan's Bar-B-Que in Davenport, and Bob's Bar-B-Que in Arcadia, site of the historic Round Barn. Elsewhere, there's Bad Brad's Bar-B-Que in Pawhuska, Ben's Bar-B-Que in Wewoka, Ass Kickin' Bar-B-Que near Locust Grove, and Robert's Bar-B-Que between Broken Arrow and Coweta.

In Ponca City, the popular Chick and Millie's Blue Moon and Head Country Bar-B-Que are proven hunger busters. Among the Tulsa favorites are Pete's Famous Bar-B-Que, J. B. Wilson's

Bar-B-Q, and Martin's Bar-B-Q. The Bar-B-Q Place and Dink's Bar-B-Q serve diners in Bartlesville, and there's a Knotty Pine Bar-B-Q in both Broken Arrow and Sand Springs.

Most any of these revered joints are a far sight less than elegant. And, as every true barbecue fan knows, any one of them is reason enough to make your home in Oklahoma.

5

THUNDERBIRDS: THE FIGHTING 45TH

Old soldiers never die;
They only fade away.

—*British Army song*

 In Oklahoma City, surrounded by chrome and glass buildings, is a monolith that serves as a monument to uncommon warriors from ordinary places.

Here the stark prairie sun is shaded by the shadows of time, and memories are sacred. People come to this place to remember moments of combat not meant for human eyes but for the gods of war, and they pause to honor the dead heroes who appeased those gods.

Often older men, veterans of World War II and Korea, go to the memorial. They come on their lunch hours or on their way through town or when there's a reunion of old soldiers. They stand serene as priests and gaze at the simple inscription chiseled in the granite: *45th Infantry Division.* Some of them smile as they brush their fingers across the cold stone. Some weep. A few even salute.

This monument to all of the men, in both peace and war, who served in the fabled 45th Infantry Division is topped by the figure of a Thunderbird. It's an important symbol, and it comforts those who pause to silently recite prayers.

In Indian mythology, some tribes feared the Thunderbird, but many southwestern Indians believed the great creature brought good luck. They said thunder came from the movement of its powerful wings and that the arrows grasped in its talons were hurled earthward as lightning. Some believed the Thunderbird could even flash lightning from its eyes and mouth. All knew that the Thunderbird brought them life-sustaining rain.

Certain Indians told the story of an underwater panther with supernatural power. This "great lynx" lurked in streams and lakes and was terrifying because it dragged people into its submerged den. But luckily the water monster was terrified of thunder, the noise made by the Thunderbird when it protected the Indians. A quilled Thunderbird design brought the wearer success in war and protection from the revenge of the mythical panther.

It was the Thunderbird that became the insignia of the 45th, a striking emblem that distinguished this division from all other units. With hundreds of Indians serving in its ranks as the 45th set out across the Atlantic to battle Nazi Germany, it was entirely appropriate that this symbol of luck and protection—a golden bird with outstretched wings against a red background—adorned each shoulder patch.

Each side of the square patch represented the four states— Oklahoma, Colorado, Arizona, and New Mexico—that had originally given men to the division, and the old Spanish colors stood for the Hispanic heritage of those states. But most prominent was the golden bird, and it was from that figure that the 45th took its nickname—the Thunderbird Division.

A plaque at the 45th Infantry Division Monument bears the words of General H. J. D. Meyers, taken from his farewell address to the division as it was deactivated on December 7, 1945, at Camp Bowie, Texas:

> Whatever destiny may hold in store for our great country, and however long that country's military history may continue, readers in the future will search long before finding a chapter more brilliant than that written by the quill that was dipped in the blood of the Thunderbirds.

The 45th Infantry Division. The Fighting 45th. The Thunderbirds.

No matter what they were called, this remarkable division, comprised largely of Oklahoma National Guardsmen, sodbusters, city dudes, clerks, bank tellers, schoolteachers, and others from every station of life, left a brilliant record of achievement as citizen soldiers.

From the early twenties, when the 45th was organized, the division served state and nation for more than forty-five years before being reduced to brigade status in 1968.

It was never a glamorous outfit. It was pure infantry. Doughboys. GIs. Dogfaces. Grunts. Standard-issue citizen turned combat soldier. Bricklayers and college students who came to know the tragedy and destruction, as well as the dull routine, of war. Troops who day after day listened to thundering guns, roaring planes, the staccato of rifle and machine-gun fire and exploding shells and grenades. Working stiffs from Muskogee and Tahlequah, fresh-faced kids from Atoka and Guymon who learned to live and die in a world of mud and rain, trench foot and blisters, barbed wire and foxholes, mine fields and snipers. Chili pickers, sheepherders, cowboys from both drugstore and ranch filled the ranks of the Thunderbirds.

They joined the marching armies, watched ancient cities ablaze, and almost became accustomed to the smell of death.

Cato, the Roman philosopher, said that an agricultural population always produces "the bravest men, the most valiant soldiers, and a class of citizens the least given of all to evil designs." He must have been thinking of Oklahoma farm boys.

Most of the accounts of the division are from the 45th's participation in World War II and Korea. Official records for the earlier years are sketchy.

The division's battle record at Anzio, in Sicily, on "Old Baldy," at Monterhouse, and at all the other battlegrounds of Western Europe and Korea are legend. But the roots of the "Fighting 45th" go much deeper.

The story of Oklahoma's citizen soldier began long before territorial days. The colonial militias back east were just thinking about forming by the time the Great Plains Indians had their own group of "soldiers" to defend the tribes, and later Indian militias were founded by the Five Tribes in Indian Territory. These "lighthorsemen," as some were known, were the first citizen soldiers in what is now Oklahoma.

In 1890, when Oklahoma Territory was organized, the legislature quickly formed a territorial militia. Five years later it became the Oklahoma Territory National Guard, consisting of cavalry troops, artillery batteries, and, last but never least, infantry companies.

Because the legislature did not appropriate funds for the volunteers, the recruits not only offered their service, but also were expected to provide their own clothing, food, and, if handy, guns.

Many of these militia volunteers were some of the first to see action in 1898 when the Spanish-American War erupted. Congress passed legislation allowing National Guard units to serve as state units in the Army. The first U.S. Volunteer Cavalry was mustered from Arizona Territory, New Mexico Territory, Oklahoma Territory, and Indian Territory. Recruited by Colonel Leonard Wood and later commanded by Lieutenant Colonel Theodore Roosevelt, the troop was called the Rough Riders because of its cowboy background.

Troop D from Oklahoma Territory and Troops L and M from Indian Territory trained at San Antonio, Texas, before joining the Army in Florida, where preparations were under way to invade Cuba. Once on the Caribbean island, the Oklahoma troops wasted no time. The Rough Riders' most famous exploit during their four-month stint in Cuba was the charge up San Juan Hill.

The cavalry regiment from Oklahoma Territory serving with the Rough Riders suffered 128 casualties—23 killed and 105 wounded during the short but furious war. Following the brief interlude with the Spanish, the territorial legislature expanded its support of the local troops.

Then on November 16, 1907, with statehood, the Oklahoma National Guard was born. Between 1907 and the entry of the United States into World War I, the Oklahoma National Guard was called upon to help the new state with growing pains and in times of trouble, such as the Crazy Snake Rebellion of 1909. Colonel (later Major General) Roy Hoffman led a detachment of the guard to Okmulgee and McIntosh counties to quell a disturbance in the old Creek Indian Nation.

In the spring of 1916, the Oklahoma Guard was pressed into federal service to chase Pancho Villa and his bandit-soldiers on the Mexican border. Along with other state militia units, the Oklahomans served as part of a federalized force until relations with Mexico improved and the border force could return home in 1917.

The lessons learned on the border were soon put to good use. Less than one month after being mustered out, the Oklahomans were federalized again. This time the mission was more challenging and the stakes higher. It was the war to end all wars—World War I. The Yanks were coming, and that included a division of Okies with fixed bayonets and rifles at the ready.

Merged with the Texas National Guard, Oklahoma's citizen soldiers became part of the 36th National Guard Division and served with distinction in Europe. Another group of draftees from Oklahoma and Texas formed yet another division that also served on the western front.

Following World War I there were sweeping changes in the military organizations of the United States. On August 27,

1923—as a result of those changes—Oklahoma's most illustrious military unit, the 45th Infantry Division, was formed with troops from Oklahoma, Colorado, New Mexico, and Arizona. Division headquarters for the 45th was Oklahoma City.

During the Roaring Twenties, and the Depression and Dust Bowl years of the thirties, soldiers from the 45th earned their wages and stripes. They halted riots and protected lives and property during strikes and civil disturbances, and in 1921, when the infamous Tulsa race riot erupted, fed by irresponsible reports from a local newspaper, National Guard units turned out to secure and maintain order in the city. Those companies of the Oklahoma National Guard in Tulsa were members of the newly organized 45th, whose rookie troopers would be veteran officers and noncommissioned officers less than twenty years later when another world war rocked the earth.

In other actions in the years between the world wars, the Oklahoma Guard was used to preserve order in Okmulgee and Henryetta when the Ku Klux Klan reared its ugly masked head and martial law was declared. During Governor William A. "Alfalfa Bill" Murray's term, from 1931 to 1935, the National Guard was called out thirty-four times in what has been described as "an unprecedented display of gubernatorial power."

During this period the 45th Division was mostly occupied with weekly drills, summer camps, and calls to state service in times of disaster. National Guard armories were constructed across the state, and a feeling of pride developed between civilians and guardsmen.

In *Citizen Soldiers*, the detailed history of the Oklahoma National Guard, author Kenny Franks describes those early Thunderbird years:

> The officers and senior NCOs were usually local civic or business leaders, and the enlisted men were mostly always residents of the community. The closeness between the guardsmen and the local citizenry became one of the great strengths of the National Guard in Oklahoma. Again and again, in times of civil unrest, natural disasters, and man-made catastrophes, the National Guard stepped in to control the situation. Local residents depended upon the guardsmen in time of emergencies, and in return they wholeheartedly supported their guard unit. The same feeling of camaraderie existed in the units,

with each man and officer feeling a special loyalty to his unit and to the men with whom he served.

This close relationship of citizen soldier to community, country, and comrades was to pay off in big dividends. The 45th's intensive training during peacetime would prove invaluable. In September 1940, the 45th was activated for what would be the ultimate test of will and courage. The dark clouds of World War II were building, and the Thunderbirds were asked to meet the challenge of this terrible conflict.

This would be the war that would kill more people, affect more lives, cost more money, damage more property, and cause more far-reaching changes than any other war in history. The 45th Infantry Division put in 511 combat days in World War II and gave up thousands of lives—Thunderbirds killed and wounded at scores of battles and assaults. Eight valiant Thunderbirds earned the Congressional Medal of Honor and scores of unit citations were presented for valor at the Battle of the Caves at Anzio and for distinguished service in actions at Padiglione and Salerno in Italy, Fremefontaine in France, and at Bobenthal and Nuremberg in Germany.

Just the 45th's timetable from mobilization in 1940 to war's end in 1945 leaves an impressive legacy:

Activated, Fort Sill	Sept. 1940
Camp Barkley, Abilene	Feb. 1941
Fort Devens, Mass.	April 1942
Pine Camp, N.Y.	Nov. 1942
Camp Pickett, Va.	April 1943
Landed in Africa	May 1943
Landed in Sicily	July 1943
Landed at Salerno	Sept. 1943
Anzio Beachhead	Jan. 1944
Rome Occupation	June 1944
South France Invasion	August 1944
Belfort Gap Battle	Sept. 1944
Munich/V-E Day	June 6, 1945

The 45th Infantry Division—the proud Thunderbirds—loosed a terrible and swift thunder and lightning all its own against enemy forces in Sicily, at Salerno and Anzio, at Saint

Maxine and Alsace, at the Rhine River and finally at Munich, in the heartland of Nazi Germany.

German Field Marshal Albert Kesselring, whose troops engaged in bitter fighting against victorious Thunderbirds, said: "The 45th is one of the two best American divisions I have encountered." Lieutenant General George S. Patton Jr., a man remembered best for his harsh words and not compliments, had this to say about the 45th: "Born at sea, baptised in blood, your fame shall never die. Your division is one of the best, if not the best division in the history of American armies."

Appropriately, not a general but a dogface serves as the most eloquent spokesman for the 45th. In fact, his pictures still speak louder than anyone's words. Bill Mauldin, the acclaimed journalist and Pulitzer Prize–winner acknowledged as the greatest cartoonist of World War II, was a Thunderbird.

A New Mexico native, Mauldin grew up on an Arizona ranch and enlisted in the 45th Infantry Division about the time he started shaving. Mauldin's famous GI cartoon characters—Joe and Willie—came to symbolize the common American foot soldier who daily faced the terror and misery of war.

Ernie Pyle, in *Brave Men*, said of Bill Mauldin: "Mauldin's cartoons aren't about training camp life, which is most familiar to people at home. They are about the men in the line—the tiny percentage of our vast Army who are actually up there doing the dying. His cartoons are about the war."

Mauldin said he depicted the infantrymen because he knew what their life was like and understood their gripes. "They don't get fancy pay, they know their food is the worst in the army because you can't whip up a lemon pie or even hot soup at the front, and they know how much of the burden they bear."

Although he went on to serve with other outfits, Mauldin never forgot his beloved 45th. "During the three years I spent in the 45th Division, I was convinced that it was not only the best Division in the Army, but that it *was* the Army," said Mauldin.

There are thousands of Joes and Willies who know what Mauldin said is true. The 45th was tough to beat.

Each year the old soldiers—members of the 45th Infantry Division Association—meet in Oklahoma City. They bring their wives and memories and take over a hotel. The parking lot is lined with sedans and campers bearing decals that display the

American flag and the gold-and-red Thunderbird emblem and the words *These Colors Don't Run.*

The old vets hold their meeting and memorial services and take shuttle buses to the 45th museum to look at the original Mauldin cartoons, the battle flags, and the cases holding their uniforms and weapons. There's always a dinner-dance and lots of speakers and a toast for all the Thunderbirds who never came home.

Without a doubt, the core of the organization are those units comprised of veterans of World War II and Korea. Most of them are paunched and a bit stooped and have either lost their hair or watched it turn gray. But when they get together and embrace each other and look into the eyes of old buddies they soldiered with to hell and back, the years melt away. They're kids again. They're back on a ship waiting to hit the beach, or they're sloshing down a muddy road in Italy or maybe they're at a USO dancing to "Sentimental Journey."

They may have come home from the war and ended up a judge or a doctor, a carpenter or a cop. They may be living in splendor at a country club or barely getting by on Social Security. It doesn't matter. Not at this reunion. For a couple of days the slate's wiped clean. They're all 45th. To a man they're Thunderbirds. Nobody can ever take that from them.

The Thunderbirds live across the nation, but many still call Oklahoma home. Here are a few:

PENDLETON WOODS

Arkansas born and bred, Pen Woods went off to kick Nazi tails with the 94th Infantry Division. "I did just fine for a time, and then I finally ran into a bit of trouble. I was on a recon patrol behind the Siegfried Line, and we were cut off. There were nine of us, and it was six days before the Battle of the Bulge." Pen was taken prisoner, but five months later Russian artillery toppled the prison camp fences. "It was April 20, 1945—Hitler's birthday— and we got away. It took five days of hard work, but we reached American lines. I guess we just had the determination and adrenalin." After the war, Pen earned a degree from the University of Arkansas and a commission as a second lieutenant. He moved to Oklahoma City ("I am a bona fide adopted Okie"), and in the spring of 1949 he joined the 45th. ("I was just in time for Korea.") After putting in thirty years as an officer—the maximum allowed—Pen retired his commission, but he decided he couldn't leave the 45th—not just yet. "So I just resigned my officer's commission as a colonel, and the very next day I became an enlisted man again and went on the division books as a sergeant. I ended up as an enlisted man on both ends of my career. Nobody knew just what to call me. Officers I had served with called me 'Pen,' and the older sergeants called me 'Pen,' but some of the junior people called me 'Sergeant' and sometimes 'Colonel,' and most of the older enlisted guys all called me 'Colonel.' There was even one who called me 'Colonel Sergeant.' " Pen served a total of forty-one years and one month. Today he continues to serve—as president of the 12,000-member 45th Infantry Division Association.

WILLIAM R. MOORE

"Shorty" Moore, as his friends call him, was born in Yale, Oklahoma, in 1905, a couple of years before the close of territorial days. He moved to Oklahoma City when he was a kid, went to barber college, and cut hair until the late 1970s. Shorty, who calls himself "a damned ol' bachelor," was drafted at the start of World War II, but because of his diminutive stature and his age, he was quickly informed that he was eligible to be excused from all military service. "No way," he says. "I didn't want out. I liked it in the Army. I really liked the 45th and wanted to go. And, let me tell you, I did it too. I stuck it out and went all the way with my Thunderbirds. I was in till the war ended and it was all over and done." Shorty worked on the ambulances and as a litter bearer at the front lines. Afterwards he came back to Oklahoma City and cut some more hair. In the eyes of his fellow Thunderbirds, Shorty Moore is a mighty big man.

BILL WILLETT

In 1939, just about the time Hitler's shock troops stormed into Poland, seventeen-year-old Bill, barely out of high school in

Oklahoma City, enlisted as a Thunderbird. "There were sure lots of Oklahomans in the division," he says. "Lots of Indians, like the regiment from up at Pawnee. All damn fine soldiers." During the war, Bill, an automotive mechanic, progressed from private to tech sergeant, and after the war he stayed in the guard and jumped from master sergeant to warrant officer in 1950, when he was mobilized again for Korea. Bill retired from the 45th in 1979 after thirty-nine years and fifteen days of service. "The very worst part of my time had to be the war. Watching friends die is not pleasant. You see ol' boys from back home get it. It was always tough to see a dead person—a corpse—but when they had our Thunderbird patch on their shoulder, well, it was real bad. I never ever got used to it."

ARTHUR PETERS

Born in Edmond, Art Peters joined the guard in 1928 so he could pull down the seventy-five cents they paid for weekly drills. When the pay went to a buck during the Depression, things looked even brighter. Art worked as a body man, plumber, and concrete finisher and put in a fourteen-month hitch vaccinating buffaloes at a Civilian Conservation Corps camp in the Wichita Mountains. He also invested thirty-four years of his life in the guard, including years of combat in World War II and Korea. Three of Art's brothers also served in the 45th, and Art himself rose from buck private to sergeant major. But in his heart, Art Peters was always a mess sergeant: "When I joined up we cooked over open fires just like cowboys, and was it ever sorry chow. Now the Army has dietitians and serves the best food there is. It's gone from beans to filet mignon." Art's biggest claim to fame was near the end of the war when the Thunderbirds swarmed into Germany and Art and some pals took possession of none other than Adolf Hitler's private apartment in Munich. "There we were in Hitler's place. I picked up a book and stretched out," recalls Art. Margaret Bourke-White, the *Life* magazine photographer, happened to be in the neighborhood, and she quickly snapped a photograph of the relaxing Oklahoman. In the May 14, 1945, issue of *Life*, the folks back home got a good look at a native son. There was Sergeant Art Peters lounging on the Führer's couch, reading *Mein Kampf.*

This soldier, and a general to boot, was one of the decision makers responsible for changing the Thunderbird shoulder patch to its present design. "The original Indian sign of the Thunderbird we wore actually looked like a counterclockwise Nazi swastika. Right before the war some of our enlisted men came back from an Army school in New Jersey, and while they were there they saw some of the Nazi swastikas. There was some real confusion and some problems. They looked too much like our old patch. We decided to change and change quick. . . . It got down between the .45-caliber pistol—the ol' thumb buster—or the new Thunderbird design. We went with the Thunderbird. It was the best." General Routh joined the guard in Edmond in 1930. Like so many, he worked his way up the chain of command. During World War II, he was a lieutenant colonel and the 45th Division finance officer. "I paid Thunderbirds from Fort Sill to Munich." During the Korean War, by then a full colonel, Routh was the Eighth Army's finance officer. He retired in 1965 as a brigadier general. "One of my clearest memories of the old 45th was when we landed in Sicily during the war. I had more than two million in Army payroll with me. It was July 10, 1943. They landed me and all my people on one beach and then they landed all my money—the entire payroll—at a different beach. We finally found the safe in the drink! It was underwater. Let me tell you, I had money laid out all over Sicily drying in the sun. Then we took over a town, counted out the money, and every dime was accounted for. We paid the troops on time."

JAMES O. SMITH

Anybody from Hickory Ridge who married his high-school sweetheart and played football in Okemah when Woody Guthrie was the team's water boy has got to be pure Okie. That's J.O. Smith. Born in 1910, J.O. enlisted in the 45th Division in 1929. "I went in a private and worked my way right on up to first sergeant," he says. "I was just belligerent enough and I could holler loud and knew close-order drill. Made a hell of a top sergeant." When the 45th was mobilized in 1940, J.O. was commissioned a second lieutenant, and by the time the division reached Sicily, company commander. "Sicily was the 45th's baptism of fire. The sea swells coming at us were terrific, and when we hit those beaches the Germans had us scattered all over the place. Lots of men died. Lots of men were wounded. But we made it, by God. We had initiative, and we knew we had to do some real bold fighting. Nobody was going to do it for us. So we got it all together and got the job done. Just a bunch of hard-core Okies." J.O. went on to command the 180th Infantry Regiment of the 45th during the Korean War. He also watched with pride as three of his sons served in the 45th. (Two became colonels and one was wounded in Korea.) "I raised my boys up in the 45th," says J.O.

▼▼▼

Every year at the reunion of the 45th, there are fewer of the old soldiers. More and more of them fade away. But every once in a while someone turns up who is all but forgotten. When that happens, there is a real celebration.

For instance, there's the story of Corporal Sylvester Jagodowski. The veterans of Battery "C," 171st Field Artillery Battalion of the 45th, call him their "Miracle Boy." The name fits.

Jagodowski, from Holyoke, Massachusetts, was transferred from the 28th Infantry Division to the 45th and assigned to Battery "C," commanded by Captain Joe Bosa, of Pauls Valley, Oklahoma. Jag, as the Oklahomans called him, joined the outfit while they were still stateside at Camp Pickett, Virginia, and making final preparations for their embarkation to North Africa and Europe.

After the Sicily campaign and Salerno, the 45th and Battery "C" turned their sights on Anzio, the small Italian town thirty-three miles south of Rome where the ancient emperors Caligula and Nero were born.

British and American forces landed at Anzio to divert the German forces from the Cassino area where the Allied advance on Rome had been halted. It ended up a hellacious battle, and despite fierce German attacks, the beachhead was held until contact was made with the U.S. Fifth Army. Unfortunately, Jagodowski and many other fine Thunderbirds never saw the battle's end.

"Old Jag was up in the forward observation post with our

lieutenant and another GI," recalls Arthur Masten, a Chandler native who joined the National Guard in 1937. "We were in the process of trying to break out, and the fighting was fierce and the machine-gun fire heavy. Jagodowski apparently spotted one of the machine guns and he turned to tell the lieutenant when he took a direct hit in the mouth. It shattered his jaw, took out all of Jag's teeth and his left eye, and the fragments went into his brain." As his outfit advanced, Jagodowski was left behind with the rest of the dead and was reported "killed in action."

But, unknown to his grieving friends in Battery "C," Jagodowski was not dead. Miraculously, he had survived.

"A couple of weeks later we found out that he was just barely alive but that he had made it and was in a Naples hospital," recalls Masten. "Some of our guys—George Claus, Stanley Stepinski, and George Young—jumped in a Jeep and went to see him. They never thought he'd leave that hospital. I guess none of us did."

But again Jagodowski proved them all wrong. Thanks to skilled medical teams and the devotion of his wife, Helen, the severely wounded soldier survived and returned home. He was hospitalized for three years, living mostly on a liquid diet. He endured nineteen head operations alone, had steel plates inserted in his skull three times, and had to learn to speak and walk all over again.

And finally, at the last 45th Division reunion, the "Miracle Boy" returned.

When Jag and Helen, his wife of forty-two years, walked into the hotel suite where the vets of Battery "C" were gathered, there wasn't a dry eye in the room.

"It's truly a miracle," said one man. "We hadn't seen him since 1944. I never thought we'd see him again."

Jagodowski remembers little of that day at Anzio when his life was changed.

"All I knew is that I lived. I made it while a lot of others didn't. And I'm proud of the 45th—of my brothers. We're not just friends—we're family. I'll never forget them."

If he can, Jagodowski—the 45th's "Miracle Boy"—wants to retrace the route he and his fellow Thunderbirds took so many years past. He wants to return to North Africa and Sicily. He wants to go back to Anzio.

"I want to go back before I die. I want to walk there. I want to go back and kneel and pray."

As he speaks, Jagodowski gently fingers a 45th Division patch. He looks at the brightly colored insignia and the mythical bird that has always brought protection and luck to the men of the 45th. Then he looks up at the others and he smiles.

6

A GOLDEN TIME
IN THE WEST

In the evening a strange thing happened: the twenty families became one family, the children were the children of all. The loss of home became one loss, and the golden time in the West was one dream.

—*John Steinbeck,*
The Grapes of Wrath

 High noon in Oklahoma and the five hundred acres of wheat marching across the lowlands toward the chocolate waters of the Canadian River are suntanned and ripe. A sultry July rain has prompted the old ladies in town, who smell of lilac sachet, to retreat to shady porches for iced tea spiked with stalks of fresh mint. But in the country, where America's groceries are grown, mature crops beckon. There is time only to fuel on meat-and-potato lunches and wring out sweat-slick bandannas.

Ed Friesen, a wheat farmer, splashes his Chevy pickup through puddles pocking the dirt road and surveys waving fields of grain. Cutting time is at hand, and he plots the harvest. The wheat was planted in the autumn, and all winter Friesen has worried over his fields. Spring rains quenched the black soil standing in deep layers, thanks to the Canadian, a river rising in the snowy pastures of the Sangre de Cristo Mountains of northern New Mexico that races across Texas and central Oklahoma until it becomes one with the Arkansas.

Friesen has known for months that he's raised a bumper crop. He felt it in his bones at New Year's, and the feeling grew stronger in April when the heavens erupted and thunder punctuated the spring. A farmer all his life, Friesen has grown crops in three countries. He learned to plow in Canada on his father's lush Manitoba farm. As a young man, he worked the fields sheltered by the rugged Sierra Madre in the sprawling Mexican state of Chihuahua. Now, Friesen is graining America, and his third Oklahoma crop is the best yet.

Ed Friesen is a Mennonite, one of approximately 600,000 members of a Protestant denomination founded in 1525 in Zurich, Switzerland. The name was derived from Menno Simons, a Dutch priest who renounced the Catholic faith and cast his lot

MICHAEL WALLIS

with the humble Anabaptists. The original Mennonites considered themselves true heirs of the Reformation. Their doctrine was characterized by separation of church and state, freedom of conscience, adult baptism, and the practice of nonresistance and love.

Mennonites are easy to like. Yet generations of these pious people have been persecuted for their religious convictions. In the sixteenth and seventeenth centuries, persecution in a number of European countries brought imprisonment, martyrdom, or deportation to members of this sect. In 1683, the first Mennonite settlement in America was founded at Germantown, Pennsylvania, by Mennonites fleeing Europe to seek free practice of their religion. This group was noted for its early stand against slavery in the British colonies. After some years, Mennonite communities were established in other parts of the United States, in Canada, Mexico, and South America.

Centuries of suffering, coupled with continuous migration, have tempered the Mennonites and given them inner strength to tap when rains don't come and crops wither. Their lives are entwined with their religion. Being a Mennonite is as natural as tilling the earth, a condition that permits gentleness and sanity in a world of violence and insanity. Insular people, Mennonites do not seek public office or fight wars. Murder, suicide, and armed robbery are unheard-of in their culture. They shun television and most modern gadgets, but many own cars and trucks and operate the latest in farm machinery. The use of alcohol, tobacco, and drugs is forbidden. Mennonites don't play the stock market, but they can be shrewd in business. Their lives are far from utopian, just simpler than most. If a Mennonite marriage is troubled, divorce isn't a consideration. Pain and turmoil are to be endured. They never visit psychiatrists, and a Mennonite with an ulcer is rare.

Most Mennonites are farmers or skilled laborers. They are not as rigid as their distant cousins the austere Amish. Mennonites don't proselytize, but they have been known to travel hundreds of miles, with no thought of recompense, to help people stricken by catastrophe. Their sect ranks as one of the true "peace churches" even though historically, Mennonites divide over doctrinal interpretations. It is not uncommon to find several branches of the denomination in one colony, each with its own church and school. Mennonites such as Friesen and his family, who have lived in Canada, Mexico, and the United States, speak English,

Spanish, and Low German or Dutch, the church's mother tongue. Church services and sometimes school subjects are presented in German. Mennonites aren't averse to hard work; they thrive on it. As the seasons pass, they battle drought and floods, wind and ice, boll weevils and wheat worms. The Roman poet Virgil observed that "Love conquers all things." That's an appropriate Mennonite motto. Perhaps a line from the Koran says it best: "God is with those who persevere."

Perseverance may mark the Mennonites, yet they embrace the nomadic life-style of their ancestors that enables them to uproot whole communities if it's apparent such a move will benefit the colony. This zest for movement sparked an important rendezvous in Canada in 1977. Elders from some of the Canadian Mennonite communities, as well as leaders from an offshoot colony established by Canadian Mennonites in Chihuahua, Mexico, in 1922, met to discuss the future. The Canadian Mennonites were tired of the cold winters and wanted to find a place with longer growing seasons. Members of the Mexican colony, located in a remote part of Chihuahua about three hundred miles south of El Paso, Texas, complained of harassment by their Mexican neighbors. Although the Mennonite dairy business was successful, and it produced some of the best cheese in the country, the Mennonites realized that government restrictions prevented further growth in Mexico.

The hunt for greener pastures turned to the United States. Scouts from the Mexican and Canadian colonies visited potential community sites in Missouri, Arkansas, and Oklahoma. The majority of the Mennonites, listening to the advice of their elders, passed up those lands and continued their search for a land of milk and honey, a quest that ended in west Texas. But a part of the Mennonite migration, about eighty souls, decided that the old Tucker Ranch—a tract along the Canadian River—between Tulsa and Oklahoma City suited their needs.

Oklahoma seemed an unlikely place for a band of Mennonites to settle. A land of paradox, Oklahoma provided refuge for the Cherokee Kid, the Daltons and the Doolins, Belle Starr, and "Pretty Boy" Floyd. Indian ghosts stalk the countryside, and unpleasant memories of the Dust Bowl linger. But the Mennonites weren't after manna, just a place to raise their children and their crops. Fifteen families, including Ed Friesen, his wife, and their five children, shelled out a total of $750,000 for 1,500 acres of Okfuskee County bordered by the all-black community of Boley and the town of Okemah, where Depression poet Woody Guthrie was born. The Mennonites rolled up their sleeves, built modest homes on the hills, and planted crops in the Oklahoma soil.

"Guided by our faith in God, we want to become self-dependent, self-sustaining, and self-supporting," explained George Plett, a Mennonite elder. "We wanted to come to Oklahoma because the United States is definitely preferable for our children. There was no future left in Mexico, and it was time to move on." Plett and the others knew the struggle would be difficult. "We want to help build this country and not be a burden to it," said Plett in his thick German accent. "We want to do our part, and I believe we can. I just hope and pray we are given the chance."

Five hundred miles to the southwest at Seminole, Texas, on the edge of the oil-rich Permian Basin, the other Mennonites from the Canadian and Mexican exodus found their place in the sun. The land is so flat in west Texas, folks say you can see a pretty girl or a sucker coming for ten miles. Somebody must have spotted the Mennonites coming a long way off. Their hopes quickly soured. The larger Texas contingent—580 men, women, and children—was already split into a half-dozen branches of the church. Problems accumulated for them as thickly as tumbleweeds piling on range fences. Their spiritual leader, Bishop Henry Reimer, after rejecting the Oklahoma land, convinced his sizable flock to sink $1.7 million into the 6,400-acre Seven-O Ranch, nineteen miles outside Seminole. Reimer was assured by local realtors that simply by buying land in this country, the Mennonites would automatically gain United States citizenship. The smaller group in Oklahoma was under the same impression.

The Texas Mennonites sold their farms and homes in Mexico and Canada, put their life savings in a communal pot, and made a down payment of $455,000, or $264 an acre (about $70 over the going price) for the ten sections of arid land where they hoped to raise cotton and build new lives. Seminole, "the city with a future," looked like an ideal place. It was off the beaten path, the surrounding country yielded big cotton harvests, and the climate offered long and prosperous growing seasons. The seven thousand townspeople, mostly hardworking, religious people themselves, offered no threats and for the most part welcomed the Mennonites. On weekdays in Seminole, everyone worked hard, and on weekends they cheered the high school athletic teams and worshiped at one of the twenty churches within the city limits.

But the Mennonites soon became painfully aware that they had been allowed to enter the United States only as visitors, not immigrants. Their visas permitted them to stay just sixty days, and there were further restrictions concerning employment and the notion that the newcomers might take away jobs from American citizens. The same immigration statutes also hung over the heads of the Oklahoma Mennonites, but because they were fewer in number and more unified, they escaped the brunt of the government's attention that fell on their Texas kin. When the U.S. Immigration and Naturalization Service (INS) officials sounded threats of deportation, some of the Mennonites in Seminole returned to Mexico, and others stopped farming and looked for jobs in town.

A temporary reprieve was won in September 1977, when INS extended the deportation deadline to let farmers gather their crops. It was a bitter harvest. Near the close of the extension period, a second chance came when legislators from Texas and Oklahoma introduced a bill in Congress that would make the entire membership in both colonies permanent residents of the United States. "These are hardworking, peaceable, God-fearing people who have immigrated to the United States in search of a better way of life," said Texas senator Lloyd Bentsen. "These good and decent people had been led to believe that by purchasing land in our country they would be allowed to remain as citizens." The legislation perished when the 95th Congress adjourned without taking any action on the proposed measure. New legislation was drafted and placed in the legislative hopper, but for many months the Mennonites of Texas and Oklahoma lived in limbo, waiting uneasily for more help, offering their ceaseless prayers.

"It makes me mad as hell," said Bob Clark, a local businessman and former Seminole mayor. "It just doesn't make sense to me that a law-abiding people like the Mennonites would come here on tourist visas and settle down and start farming. They were getting some bad advice or someone was deceiving them." Public support continued to build on their behalf, especially in Texas where local oil-field-equipment firms and farmers became hooked on reliable Mennonite labor. Public opinion was outraged when news stories broke telling of U.S. plans to admit several thousand Vietnamese refugees, many of whom would be dependent on welfare. Hundreds of letters supporting the Mennonites flooded the offices of President Jimmy Carter, congressmen, and state officials.

Still more problems plagued the Mennonites. They learned that they held water rights on only a little more than one-third of their Texas land. "We didn't know until we were out drilling wells, getting the fields ready for another crop," said colony member Frank Wiebe. "Then a man from one of the oil companies showed up and showed us a contract and told us they owned the water rights and that we could not drill wells on the land." The results were disastrous for the corn and cotton crops.

The crop failure and looming deportation sentence caused many Mennonites to stop making payments on the Seven-O Ranch. As expected, the colony was finally forced to forfeit the communal farm in April 1979 at a public auction on the courthouse steps in Seminole. The business was swift and routine, and in the end the land's original owner simply foreclosed on the note and reclaimed the spread.

"We really can't believe much anymore," said Peter Harder after the land auction. Harder had been a successful beef rancher at the Mennonite settlements in Mexico and Belize but gave up his holdings in order to go to Seminole and invest in a ramshackle motel. "We don't want to go back," said Harder. "We want to make new lives here. There's nothing left to go back to. I just don't know what to do. I will wait and pray. I cannot complain about what has happened, but there is so much to lose."

When the reality of life in America became apparent, the faith of steadfast Mennonites, such as Harder, was challenged. Disillusioned with the church hierarchy, many Mennonites stopped attending Sunday services. But for the most part they held fast, reaching into that well of inner strength for confidence. As luck and God would have it, the tide at last began to turn in their favor. With the help of church lions like Andrew Plett, an ordained Mennonite minister with two decades of service to his credit, the Seminole colony began mending splintered feelings and working together again.

Plett is a man intoxicated with God. The brother of George Plett, the Oklahoma elder, the Reverend Mr. Plett was sent by the church from Manitoba to Texas in November 1977. His job was not only to save his people from deportation but to halt any religious decay in the community. A minister in the more liberal Evangelical Mennonite Church, Plett considered his charge a mission of mercy. "I am where the Lord wants me to be," declared Plett. "This is an awful tragedy that's happened here. But there is hope. The hope that is here just needs to be uncovered. It needs to be opened up like the soil is opened up for planting. I am here to do that. I want to stir up the hope and make the people aware." Plett established a school and conducted church services in an abandoned warehouse while his church was being constructed. He helped draft letters to politicians asking them to use their influence to win citizenship for the Mennonites. He saw to it that the colony had proper legal counsel. Plett restored confidence among the parishioners who had begun to abandon hope. Mennonites took jobs as oil-field workers, welders, and carpenters. Others hired out to established farms and ranches in the region, and a few operated small businesses of their own.

"Let me tell you about Mennonites," said Mark Harris, a Texan who hired as many Mennonites as possible to get his oil-field-equipment business launched. "These people are terrific workers—nothing like them anywhere. I lay out a work plan and that's it. I can forget about it and not worry. I know they will carry it out and get the job done. I never have to check on them or tell them another thing. They just go out and work, and work hard. They are something else."

Each Sunday, as the Mennonites' hopes built, Andrew Plett led his growing congregation in a cappella song and fervent prayer. He urged them to remember the biblical heroes who withstood countless trials for the goals they valued. He recited a list of Mennonites who had perished for their beliefs. More than two and a half years after their struggle began, the reward came at last for the Mennonites of the Texas and Oklahoma colonies. On October 19, 1980, President Carter signed legislation making the Mennonites—a total of 653 in both states—permanent residents of the United States. "God has been good to us, and the reward is sweet and plentiful," said Andrew Plett, smiling.

Soon every seat in Plett's church (and most of those in other Mennonite churches of Seminole) was occupied. More than one hundred children were enrolled in the Mennonite school. Mark Harris's fledgling oil-field-equipment firm became Seminole-Mennonite Industries, providing wages for thirty Mennonite households. Several Mennonite women started their own seamstress business and had more work than they could handle.

And in the Oklahoma wheat lands on the Canadian River, there was more rejoicing. "Our prayers were surely answered," said George Plett. "Our dreams have come true. This is our land now. We are part of this country." On summer Sundays at the new Mennonite church, the Reverend John Plett (no relation to George or Andrew), the community minister who also provides fresh butter and milk, drones on in German monotones. The adults quietly swap Scripture verses, and the well-scrubbed youngsters glance out the windows, patiently awaiting their escape into the sunshine.

After services, there is time for food and fellowship. Carloads of Mennonite teenagers drive through the country visiting shut-ins and stopping at the nursing home near Boley to sing hymns for the elderly black residents. The old people tap their toes and canes as young Mennonites serenade with their brand of gospel music.

At the Ed Friesen home—a long and tidy trailer house on a hilltop beneath huge oaks—Sunday afternoon is devoted to family and friends. Henry Dueck, another farmer, and his wife, Mary, with a few of their seven children, are sharing a chicken dinner with the Friesens. The Duecks were married in Mexico in 1957. Their children range in age from toddlers to young adults. Henry and Ed wear white shirts buttoned to the neck. They sit and discuss the harvest and grain prices. Outside, thirty head of cattle graze in high clover.

In the sparse kitchen, Betty Friesen and Mary Dueck put the finishing touches on the feast. Besides roasted chicken there will be slaw and fresh bread and plates of potatoes. For dessert Mary has provided a bowl of *pluma moos*, a traditional Mennonite treat made with fresh fruit, sugar, and cinnamon. Mary is a beautiful woman. She has never been to a hairdresser, never touched a tube of lipstick. Her striking beauty comes from within. She has the grace of a wise mother superior. "I sometimes long for our old home in Mexico," she says. "I remember how lovely it was there. . . . It is beautiful here. If you look hard you can see beauty wherever you are."

And beyond the garden—past the church and the house of the Reverend Mr. Plett, where his daughters slice *sierra verde* cheese shipped from the Mexican colony and dream of marriage, past the home of Cornelius Dueck and the hog pens and barn of George Plett, stand the great fields of wheat. Mennonite wheat. In those fields Ed Friesen can be found. It is his place, his land; it is where he belongs. In those timeless fields of wheat Ed Friesen counts his blessings and celebrates his golden time in the West.

7

OIL MAN

The memory is a living thing—it too is in transit. But during its moment, all that is remembered joins, and lives—the old and the young, the past and the present, the living and the dead.

—Eudora Welty,
One Writer's Beginnings

Frank Phillips sits in his favorite chair on the front porch and listens to the sweet song of a mockingbird. It's the same bird he's heard all day—singing from the chimney before sunup and ever since from the oaks in front of the lodge.

The oak leaves are new and tender and the geranium blooms in the flower boxes on the porch railing are fiery red. All around the big log lodge, sunlight—the color of honey—flows through the leaves and melts on the ground. A faint slice of moon that's hung around for days peeks through the tree branches like a ghost waiting for nightfall.

Frank's cane is hooked on the chair back, and on a small table are kitchen matches, a glass of water that's sat untouched for hours, and an ashtray. Dressed in a dark business suit and bow tie, Frank watches summer close in on his ranch in the Osage. The rosy flush of spring is about to vanish.

Potatoes and gravy and a slice of beef he poked at during Sunday lunch soon take effect and Frank's eyelids grow heavy. After a few minutes of dozing he jerks awake, listens to the mockingbird some more, and manages to smoke most of the cigar before he nods off again. Soon he's back asleep. His Japanese valet, Dan Mitani, comes out on the porch and takes the cigar from between Frank's fingers and puts it in the ashtray. The old man stays deep in his dreams. The sleep has made him young again and he's on the prowl for crude oil in the everlasting hills of Oklahoma.

He's back in the oil patch with his brothers and they're building an immense empire by risking big money on their big notions. He's watching gusher after gusher come to life—a series of wildcat eruptions that showers the prairie with rich Oklahoma crude. He's hitting the first real wild boom in a land where Indians are rich, outlaws are respected, and oil is in abundance.

In his dream, Frank sees oil derricks covering the land, and then just as the oil rumbles from the earth once again and explodes in a great black plume into the sky, he cries out and wakes himself. At first, he's not sure where he is, but then he sees the shimmering lake and, beyond, the rolling hills where his herd of buffalo feeds on tender spring grass.

Dan returns and with him the newest nurse who's been hired to care for Frank. The nurse is a pleasant young man, and he and Dan hover about to make sure Frank is comfortable. They brush the cigar ashes from the skirt of his suit coat and Dan offers to bring a fresh glass of water, but Frank waves him off.

Behind the lodge, Frank's museum, filled with Wild West art and treasures, has closed for the afternoon, and Sabbath visitors return to their cars. A few straggle down the hill to look at Clyde Lake and catch a glimpse of Uncle Frank Phillips, hoping he'll happen to be out on his porch for some afternoon air.

One family stops just short of where Frank is sitting. The young wife holds the hand of her three-year-old daughter and the child peers around her mother's legs at the old man sitting on the porch. The husband is a Phillips Petroleum employee, as was his father, and he nods out of respect to Frank. When Frank sees that the man is holding a baby, he reaches out his hand and the young man gives the baby to Dan, who carefully places the child in Frank's arms.

Frank holds the little girl for a few moments. He laughs and gently tickles the baby and then she is passed back to her father. Not a word is spoken. The family and Frank just smile at each other. After a few seconds the family leaves and Frank returns to his dreams.

His mind slips back in time: It's years before at Woolaroc lodge and Frank sees Indian and cowboy fires scattered over the hills as guests arrive the night before one of his Cow Thieves Reunions. He sees the proud Osage chiefs, wrapped in their colorful blankets, and the Indian dancers walking beside Pawnee Bill and Zack Miller and the other guests. He spies Grif Graham in his best red shirt and a new ten-gallon hat; over at the edge of the crowd is Henry Wells and a few of the old-time desperadoes passing around a bottle of bootleg whiskey.

There are tables piled with barbecued buffalo and everyone is talking and dancing and fiddles are playing. Frank believes the music never sounded better.

It's one of his best dreams and he sees every guest that ever came through the ranch gates. It's as though all the parties and picnics he hosted through the years have combined into one fantastic blowout. The parade of guests goes on and on. There's Tom Mix, Herbert Hoover, Harry Truman, Perle Mesta, Rudy Vallee, Edna Ferber, Aimee Semple McPherson, Ernie Pyle, Will Rogers, Cardinal Spellman, and all the rest. He hears a humming sound and he looks up and sees Wiley Post circling in his airplane, and above him is Art Goebel in his plane and he's writing out Frank's name in huge white letters made of smoke.

Then the scene shifts from the ranch and Frank is back in Bartlesville at his fine town house on Cherokee Avenue, and he sees his family—his brothers and sisters and his son and foster daughters. And he sees Jane—his own Lady Jane—and she's moving through the rooms chatting with friends and family and making sure everyone's glass is filled. She's holding a cigarette in her own jaunty way just like always and Frank hears her deep throaty laugh. In his sleep the old man smiles and laughs out loud.

Inside the lodge, beneath the huge chandeliers and the lifeless animal heads staring from the walls, Dan hears the laughter and comes back out on the porch just as Frank awakens once more. Dan sits on the porch step and the two men talk about the disappearing spring and of the summer holiday Frank is planning to take in Atlantic City.

Dan tells him that Fern Butler telephoned during the afternoon to see how Frank is feeling. At the mention of her name Frank can picture his secret lover in his mind. He sees her bustling through the New York office and in her soft lounging pajamas at her apartment. Finally, he sees Fern astride Woolaroc, the spirited horse Frank sent her from the Osage. It's a pleasing image.

By now the afternoon is almost gone. Shadows stretch across the porch and Frank looks beyond the dark lake to the hills, but he can no longer see the buffalo grazing. Soon the oaks become silhouettes and the discussions of thousands of insects fill the night air.

Frank and Dan stay in their places for a few more moments, comfortable in their own silence, content with their own thoughts, at ease with themselves and the evening. Neither of them notices that at last the mockingbird has stopped its song.

MICHAEL WALLIS

"A Wonder Well," screamed the headline in the *Washington County Sentinel*. Although, in truth, the well more than likely was good for at least 1,000 barrels a day, the newspaper stories boosted the output to more than 3,500 barrels a day. No matter—there was more than enough production to earn the Lewcinda's well the enviable claim of "biggest oiler in local field." The whole town celebrated.

"After drilling six dry holes on Lot 185 in the Osage, Frank Phillips, president and owner of Lewcinda Oil Company, yesterday startled the local oil fraternity by bringing in the biggest well yet brought in around Bartlesville," said the *Sentinel* story. "There are no other completed wells in this section of the Osage, for the territory has always been considered dangerous."

In the Bartlesville *Morning Examiner*, another reporter—who liked using the word "immense"—was obviously impressed with the amazing Mr. Phillips. This story claimed the new discovery would "open up a pool of immense richness." The newspaper account went on to explain that Frank Phillips had "a 'hunch' that the well would be a big one," and predicted that its discovery "may mean some immense development in that portion of the Osage country and will mean an immense sum of money coming into Bartlesville."

Crowds of townspeople went out to the Lewcinda well on Lot 185 and found that everything the newspaper reports said was true. The five gravity-flow lines were carrying excess oil to earthen tanks and a gasoline pump was working overtime trying to force the remainder of the oil to the surface line in the prairie.

Later that same spring, the other shoe dropped on the proposed bank venture. Just when the oak leaves were in full bud in the Osage Hills, Woodrow Wilson—in his second term as president—convinced Congress to declare war on Germany. Plans were made to send tens of thousands of American doughboys overseas. "The world must be made safe for democracy," Wilson told Congress. George M. Cohan put it another way: "The Yanks are coming." And come they did, in every imaginable motorized vehicle in existence. Just as Frank had figured, the market for oil and gas exploded. The buried treasure the Lewcinda drilling crews tapped on Lot 185 was part of the thousands of barrels of oil that helped stoke the fires of war.

There were more oil and gas wells drilled by the Lewcinda crews during the spring and summer of 1917. Most showed an initial production of anywhere between 30 to 150 barrels a day, and No. 16 came in at 1,200 barrels per day.

By this time, the banking-chain plan was totally discarded. Frank and his brother L.E. decided to keep their bank in Bartlesville and consolidate their remaining oil properties into the Lewcinda Oil & Gas Company. They also set about expanding the firm's holdings. Soon Lewcinda was valued at more than $1 million. Frank and L.E. owned almost the entire interest. Money was rolling in, and the prospects looked even better. With the war in Europe going full throttle, the price of oil skyrocketed from less than forty cents a barrel to more than a dollar a barrel.

Frank and L.E. realized they were fortunate to own their own bank to help underwrite many of their oil-field operations. But they also knew that because the industry was on the brink of major change due to continuous technological developments, the cost of competing required major capital investment. This financing could be found only in the large financial centers back East.

Frank became more certain that the time was right to organize a public company, sell stock, retain a good share of it, and keep right on going. There were no limits. All they needed was a name.

Through the early years in Bartlesville, the Phillipses had formed many private oil companies, each with its own identity. They named them for their wives, their parents, a revered ancestor, and even a favorite town from back in Iowa. Now that they were going to form a public company, another name would be needed. It would have to be a name of distinction that could instantly tell the world what kind of business Frank and his brother L.E. were running.

Frank had a name in mind right along. He thought it was straight to the point and no-nonsense. He tried it on Jane and John. They liked it. He tried it on his best hands from Lewcinda. They liked it, too. He wrote the name out and looked at it. He repeated the words out loud. Frank liked the way it looked and sounded. It was the one name that said it all.

"Phillips Petroleum Company."

It was a natural.

▼▼▼

Frank Phillips could be as predictable as Christmas. But there were times when he was a total enigma and puzzling as a cat's cradle. He was like that all of his life—a stream flowing deep and straight but with sudden twists and turns and rapids. When Frank was a young barbershop owner he was bald, yet he sold tonic to make hair grow. The barber-turned-banker-turned-oil-tycoon built an empire that included a huge network of gas stations and refineries, all of which had a profound impact on the automobile, yet Frank never learned to drive.

Frank was a self-proclaimed tough guy and a shrewd corporate captain who some competitors believed had ice water in his veins, yet he was often a compassionate man who would worry over injured employees or sick animals out at the ranch, and not rest until he knew they were out of danger or on the mend. He was a stern disciplinarian, with a temper hot as a branding iron, who would fire a worker on the spot for the slightest infraction, yet a forgiving employer apt to hire the same worker back by the end of the day. He was an expert at delivering off-the-cuff speeches and a masterful communicator able to win over just about any audience he faced, yet a father who never really learned how to express himself with his only son.

Frank Phillips was a riddle waiting to be solved. A complete contradiction.

The main incongruity in his life became evident out at the ranch. That's where it became public. A few family members and associates picked up on this personal quirk earlier in Frank's career, soon after he and L.E. opened their first bank. Others noticed it when Frank went out into the oil patch. It had to do with outlaws. Real, honest-to-goodness desperadoes—the kind who packed shooting irons and wore masks and made their living robbing banks and trains and stealing horses and cattle. The Henry Wells variety.

When it came to outlaws—especially the ones like Wells who frequented the Osage and found refuge in the nooks and crannies near the F.P. Ranch—the ramrod-stiff banker and conservative businessman side of Frank Phillips melted like a cube of sugar in a cup of hot jamoke. He was the descendant of a Pilgrim father and counted many preachers and God-fearing souls in his family tree, but Frank would just as soon hunker down and swap lies with a pack of rascals from Okesa as endure a meeting in some fancy conference room with a bunch of spruced-up and slicked-down executives. To Frank, outlaws were like the wild mustangs, the longhorns, and the buffalo that lived on his ranch—all were symbols of the Old West.

Outlaws absolutely fascinated Frank. He loved their look and swagger, enjoyed their company, listened to their tales, banked their money, and loaned them some if they asked for it.

After his ranch operations were under control and the lodge was built, Frank even devised a way to salute the old-time outlaws as well as the cowhands and the Indians of the Osage. For several years, starting in 1927, Frank hosted an annual party for them at his ranch. Some called it a picnic, others a barbecue. Frank gave the affair a more flamboyant name and touch. He organized the hard-core regulars—genuine cowpokes and tough guys from the area—into an association and summoned them to the F.P. Ranch each year. He called these annual blowouts the Cow Thieves and Outlaws Reunion. Nothing before or since ever quite compared.

Frank soon found there were plenty of experts around willing to offer advice about how he should stage his colorful gatherings. Only a few were worth listening to and Frank did just that.

Gordon W. Lillie, better known as Pawnee Bill, was a close friend and was willing to share his experiences from Indian Territory days, as well as pointers he picked up on the road when he was touring with his Wild West circus. Lillie had combined his show with Buffalo Bill's, and was an expert at putting on unrivaled western-style spectaculars. Lillie's wife, a former Philadelphia socialite who could ride like a wild Indian and became the "Champion Lady Horseback Rifle Shot of the World," also befriended Frank and Jane, and after the Lillies retired in 1913 the two couples visited at each other's homes. Frank brought them out to Woolaroc after it opened in the mid-1920s, and Pawnee Bill hosted the Phillipses at his mansion, which he built atop Blue Hawk Peak on his buffalo ranch near the town of Pawnee. Frank learned firsthand from Pawnee Bill, one of the masters of cowboy and Indian pageantry and a man who had actually been Buffalo Bill's partner, how to throw a genuine Wild West shindig. It was invaluable counsel.

Another big influence on Frank's outlaw wingdings were the Miller brothers, who sponsored rip-roaring rodeos at their 101 Ranch and, starting in 1924, also came up with a new style of racing that developed into an annual event during every Labor Day roundup.

It was an altogether different type of racing and it didn't involve sleek cow ponies. Instead, they were tongue-in-cheek contests before audiences of hooting and hollering cowboys and

ranch visitors, in what the Millers called the "Terrapin Derby"—
or, for the unwashed, turtle races.

For only a two-dollar entry fee a guest at the 101 could go to
the terrapin pit and make a selection from the hundreds of turtles
rounded up on the range by the Millers' cowboys. All the money
went for prizes, and "Foghorn" Clancy, known from the Osage
Hills to the Rio Grande for his loud voice, announced each race.

By 1925 the second derby drew 1,679 entries, and the next
year there were 2,373, including one owned by Frank, which
didn't win, place, or show. The entry numbers were painted on
the turtles' shells and some of the better-known contestants were
even named. There was "Jenny Lind," "Bridesmaid," "Marie
Antoinette," "Easter Bells," and "Star of the Night."

Old cowboys who made up a group known as the Cherokee
Strip Cowpunchers Association met for reunions at the 101 about
the same time as the annual roundup and the derby. The old-
timers liked to gather on a bluff on the south side of the Salt Fork
River known as "Cowboy Hill" and they'd sing old trail songs
and recall the stories of cattle drives, Indian fights, and stringing
up rustlers.

After the derby, Frank and the other guests mixed with the
old cowboys and ate suppers of barbecued meat, cider, and biscuits, served out under the stars. The days and nights at the
101 Ranch left an impression on Frank, and he remembered his
experiences there when he began planning for his outlaw bashes
at the F.P. Ranch.

Grif Graham, the former sheriff who served as Frank's first
ranch manager, was the driving force behind the Cow Thieves
and Outlaws Reunions—annual affairs intended to salute those
survivors from the territorial days "when men were men and
women were respected."

Although, as the name implied, the idea was to get together
as many cow thieves and outlaws as possible, there were usually
a good many law-abiding citizens in attendance, including ex-
sheriffs, ranchers, and others.

When the first reunion was held at the ranch in 1927, only
about one hundred guests showed up. Within a couple of years
there were more than five hundred in the Cow Thieves and
Outlaws Association and, counting members' families and other
guests, the attendance swelled to more than twelve hundred when
the fourth annual reunion took place.

From the start, the reunions were colorful affairs attended by a variety of locals—old trail riders, horse traders, Indians, U.S. marshals—and usually a sprinkling of Frank's personal guests, including a few of the Phillips directors and others he was trying to impress.

"Cowboys, real cowboys, old riders of the plains in the days when the cattle business was the only business and every man had to ride his stuff and throw a wicked rope to hold his job, gathered at the Phillips ranch Thursday for an all-day barbecue and picnic as guests of Frank Phillips," said a newspaper account of the first reunion.

A kangaroo court was in session throughout the day and a mock trial was held, with one of the guests playing the role of "Hanging Judge" Parker of Fort Smith, the famed jurist who had tried to tame Indian Territory during the tail end of the nineteenth century. Several guests were fined on a variety of trumped-up "charges" in order to collect fifty-five dollars to buy Frank a fancy Stetson hat with an inscription in the band: "With the compliments of Cow Thieves and Outlaws Reunion. F.P. Ranch, June 2, 1927." During subsequent reunions, Frank received other gifts, including fancy boots and a pair of leather chaps with his name and the initials "FPR," for Frank Phillips Ranch, emblazoned down each leg.

When the second annual outlaw party rolled around in October 1928, Frank and Grif had every detail organized. This time they even prepared an official invitation. From New York to Pawhuska, the invites to the F.P. Ranch became coveted items.

INVITIN'
yu an yer wimmin folks to
Second Annual

COW THIEVES AND OUTLAWS
REUNION
at F.P. Ranch
Saturday, Oct. 6, 1928

Aims to throw chuck about noon, if the
Boss can borry a side of meat and some flour.

No guns er store cloze is purmitted
er no golf breeches.

Show this here invite to the Brand
Inspector feller at the big gate, cause
he wont pass yu thru without none.

Hopin' to meet yu all
at the F.P., we begs to remain

THE COMMITTY
P.S. The Boss wants yu all to be at the wagon
at 10 o'clock forenoon.

2nd P.S. Leve yer nives an guns with the Boss at the gate,
cause we aint allowin' no shootin'.

The comical invitation, which included an illustration of
Frank dressed in western clothes, was sent to hundreds of cattlemen, peace officers, known outlaws, Indians, bankers, and business executives.

Not everyone could make the reunion, but if they couldn't
come they were quick to send word so they wouldn't get bumped
from the invitation list for the following year.

Frank's ground rules for the celebrations, held in the picnic
area near Clyde Lake, were simple. Any wanted desperadoes
would be granted a day of grace for the reunion. If there was an
outstanding warrant, the law officers in attendance would have
to wait for another time and place to make their moves. Frank
wanted to be sure all of his guests had ample time to sleep off
their hangovers and get a few miles' head start. All guns and
grudges had to be checked at the main gate.

There were some who swore the story was true that Frank
arranged for a few of the outlaws serving time to be released from
jail for the day so they could come to the reunion, and that Frank
posted his own personal bond guaranteeing their return. More
than likely that was one of the many tales cooked up and perpetu-
ated by R. C. Jopling, called "Jop," Frank's ace public relations
man. Besides insisting that all lawbreakers and law enforcers abide
by his one-day moratorium, Frank left instructions at the main
gate to "admit any cowboy with a saddle horse, admit any American Legion boys in uniform and all Spanish-American War veterans in uniform; also any full-blood Indians in costume."

It was never really clear just how many bona fide outlaws
actually showed up at the ranch, but a good number of question-

able characters always appeared, such as Henry Wells, who had served five years and one day of a prison sentence for bank robbery before winning his release in the early 1920s. Within a week of getting out of prison, Wells robbed another bank just to see if he had lost any of his criminal prowess while he cooled his heels in the "cross bar hotel."

Frank liked Wells, and from time to time the two men played poker at Okesa with a few of the outlaw's shady friends. Wells added an air of authenticity to the reunions and other ranch functions. Frank put the outlaw on the ranch payroll whenever there were guests—especially eastern guests—coming out for a visit, and Henry, an imposing six-footer who stood straight as an arrow, called on Frank at his office in downtown Bartlesville to confer about ranch matters.

On one occasion, Frank arranged for Henry and a few of his boys to have some fun at the expense of some unsuspecting easterners invited to spend the day at Woolaroc. Frank's guests wanted to experience the Old West, so he had them brought out to the ranch in an authentic stagecoach built in 1869. Shortly after the half dozen horses pulling the stage made the steep climb up "44 Hill," a gang of outlaws, wearing bandannas over their faces and with six-shooters drawn, rode out of nowhere and halted the stage. In a flash, the startled passengers were relieved of their wallets and jewelry and the stage was sent on its way. Several of the victims figured the holdup was Frank's doing, but then again they had also heard his stories about outlaws operating in the Osage. There was always the chance that the bandits were for real. When the stage pulled up in front of Woolaroc and the excited guests were greeted at the lodge, all of their belongings— down to every penny and watch fob—were laid out waiting to be claimed on a table inside the door. Out back, Henry Wells and his cronies were laughing in their beer and barbecue, their pockets filled with pay from Uncle Frank.

As gutsy as a bull buffalo in rut, Wells was proud of the fact that many bankers closed their doors and declared a holiday if they learned he was in the vicinity—something, Henry was quick to point out, that bankers usually did only for George Washington or Abe Lincoln.

Word around the Osage was that Wells was actually the bankers' best customer, and that many times they exaggerated their losses after a holdup and made more money from the robbery than Wells did. Some bankers thought so kindly of the Osage bandit that they reportedly sent Wells Christmas cards each year without fail.

At one gathering of bankers at the F.P. Ranch, the wily outlaw sidled up to a cluster of distinguished gentlemen sipping highballs and puffing on Frank's best cigars.

"Henry robbed me once," bragged one of the bankers.

"Say, I've been meaning to ask you something," Henry shot back. "What did you ever do with that $22,000? You told the bank examiners I got $25,000, but I just counted $3,000. Where's the rest?"

The banker choked on his drink and dropped his cigar as Henry walked away laughing without waiting for an answer.

To make certain his guests—especially the renegades—were content and didn't take it upon themselves to swipe one of his prized animals, Frank had his Woolaroc staff lay out an enormous feast. There was always enough to feed an army, but it was far from normal picnic fixings. For example, at the 1929 reunion it took two grown buffalo alone to make a dent in the crowd's appetite. The menu included slabs of barbecued buffalo, beef, and pork; platters of pickled buffalo; mounds of boiled potatoes, baked beans, and cabbage slaw; hundreds of hard-boiled eggs and ice-cream cones; and plenty of bourbon and draft beer.

To the delight of the guests, more than three hundred old-time range riders came from Oklahoma, Texas, New Mexico, Colorado, Kansas, and California. Local wranglers showed up from Bartlesville, Okesa, Dewey, Ramona, Pawhuska, Nowata, Copan, and Ochelata. Hamp Scudder and Joe Bartles came. Jop Jopling mugged for photographers with Doc Hammond and Henry Wells. The kangaroo court did a brisk business.

Grif Graham, wearing a new flaming-red shirt, served as the master of ceremonies and supervised the trick-riding and roping exhibitions. One of the judges was Pawnee Bill, who came, as usual, with a full complement of Pawnee Indian dancers. Chuck wagons and pack outfits competed for prizes, and there were fiddlers and square dancing and Indian stomp dancers all dressed up in feathers and paint.

At one point, Frank, wearing his cowboy best—big hat and high-top boots with fancy tooled designs—walked into the midst of the throng and bawled out: "I can outrun any man or woman in this crowd half my age!"

Quick as a flash, Grif shouted: "That's seventy-three, folks!" The crowd roared and so did Frank.

But sometimes incidents occurred at the ranch that were not laughing matters. In 1927, just a month before he hosted the first annual Cow Thieves and Outlaws Reunion, Frank put on a big barbecue feed to honor Chief Baconrind, the Osage tribal leader who had been friendly with Frank ever since the early days when the Phillips boys came to town and opened their first bank. Through the years, Frank had great success drilling for oil on Osage tribal land and as a result both the Osage and Frank Phillips prospered. It was important for Frank to maintain goodwill with the Osage Nation and he wanted the dinner at his ranch to go off without a hitch.

Boots Adams, the aggressive young Kansan who had played basketball for a few years for Phillips Petroleum while quickly working his way through the corporate ranks, was assigned the important task of checking names off a master invitation list as people arrived at the front gate of the ranch.

"At one point," Adams recalled years later, "I was in the middle of a mass of people at the entrance, busy with a hundred details, when I noticed an elegant touring car draw up with a number of persons in it. Because there were so many cars already at the gate, this new arrival had to wait."

But after idling for several minutes, with only a glance from the young man at the gate, the big automobile maneuvered out of line, turned, and sped away. Boots was sorry he hadn't been able to get to the car to check off the occupants' names, but there was nothing he could do. He forgot the entire episode until about an hour later when Frank Phillips appeared.

Frank had seen young Adams playing basketball and he was aware of his steady climb through the various departments at Phillips, but that meeting at the ranch gate was the first time that Boots Adams and Frank Phillips ever spoke to one another. It was a conversation neither man would soon forget.

Frank, his face creased with frowns, said he was worried because the party was ready to start at the lodge and the guests of honor had not yet arrived. He asked Boots if he had seen anything of Chief Baconrind and his entourage.

"No, I haven't, sir," answered Boots.

"Didn't you see a group of Osage in a large car?" Frank asked.

As Boots tells it: " 'Oh, those,' I said, with a sudden sinking feeling. 'There was a Pierce-Arrow with a chauffeur and a group of Indians in it. They drove up, but they had to wait a couple of minutes because there were other cars ahead of them, so they drove away.' Mr. Phillips looked at me for a moment as if he were about to take my head off. Then he growled, 'Those were my guests of honor—you idiot!' ''

Frank was so mad he couldn't even fire Boots—at least for the moment. Instead he jumped in his waiting car and ordered the driver to go straight to Pawhuska so he could personally apologize to Chief Baconrind, who was sulking at his home, angry at "the young upstart" who wouldn't let him in to his own party. Frank rode back to Woolaroc with the chief, more apologies were offered, and the barbecue continued with no further mishaps.

The next morning Frank summoned young Mr. Adams to his office and proceeded to give him a ten-minute ass chewing. Boots was also ordered to write a detailed explanation of the incident and a formal apology to the chief.

"That was the first time I had ever met Frank Phillips, the first time I came to his personal attention—and I made some impression," said Boots.

The timing of his faux pas couldn't have been worse. Only two weeks after he snubbed the Osage chief at the ranch gate, Boots was the subject of a memo drafted by his immediate boss— O. K. Wing, the secretary-treasurer of Phillips Petroleum. Handwritten on the company's official blue memorandum paper, the single paragraph from Obie Wing was a recommendation about Boots for Frank Phillips to consider.

> K. S. Adams has been with the company about eight years. He is now my chief assistant looking after credits, etc. He has had a fairly good education and has good potential possibilities. Has been receiving $350 per month since 1926 (Sept.) and I now recommend that his salary be increased to $400 and that he be elected to the office of Assistant Secretary and Treasurer.

Although his temper had cooled by the time Wing's memo reached his desk, Frank had not yet forgotten Boot's blunder at the ranch. He stewed over the recommendation for a while and wondered how a young man who wasn't able to recognize a guest of honor when he saw one could possibly handle the responsibilities of an executive position. Fortunately for Adams, the respect and confidence Frank had in Obie Wing prevailed. The memo was returned to Wing with "O.K., Ex. Comm., F.P.," and a few changes. The words *and Treasurer* were crossed out and the suggested salary of $400 was cut to $375.

Less than a year later, Adams was also given the assistant treasurer title and another raise. Only a few months after that promotion he was again called to Frank's attention. This time the results were better for Boots. In an effort to build up a loyal following at the Phillips 66 filling stations, Boots had started selling coupon books, good for discount purchases of gas and oil at the Phillips stations, to various business people he encountered during the course of his workday. The campaign was successful and many of those Boots reached remained Phillips customers long after the coupons were gone. When he heard about Boots going out and selling up a storm, it struck a chord, and reminded Frank of himself when he was a young barber in Iowa trying to become a master salesman.

Frank was touched by Boots's effort and he sat down and wrote Adams a note of thanks:

> I am taking this opportunity to express to you my appreciation of the spirit and initiative that has led you to go beyond your regular duties to further the interests of our company. Such a spirit throughout our organization could not help but insure for us a tremendous success in any field we choose to enter.

Boots saved the note from Frank Phillips and kept it tucked away. It took the sting out of the reprimand he had received the year before for his blunder at the ranch. Boots felt that he had finally been redeemed, but whenever he drove under the big arched gate at the F.P. Ranch, he still thought about the night he was in charge of the guest list and the first time he came face to face with Uncle Frank. Now the memories would be sweeter and Woolaroc would always be special for Boots Adams.

Even before he built the lodge, Frank invited thousands of Phillips employees out to his place in the Osage to swim and picnic, and the grassy grounds and the dance pavilion next to Clyde Lake became a favorite site for company outings for many years. Although he believed in hard work—and lots of it—Frank also saw the value in good, hard play.

In July 1928, when he perceived the summer doldrums were beginning to set in, Frank drafted what at first glance appeared to be a stern message for his employees. It was circulated on Frank's letterhead for all hands to read.

BULLETIN

Very seldom do I have an opportunity to take an hour off and visit the various offices. A few days ago, however, I visited most of the floors and my impression was that the oldtime pep which dominated this organization in the past was not in evidence. Spirits seemed to be lagging and in many rooms it occurred to me that there was about fifty per cent efficiency, with fifty per cent of the employees doing most of the work. The conditions which I met up with disturbed me very much. An office is a place for work only; if you cannot find something to do probably we do not need you.

Perhaps I am to blame, or maybe I do not understand and all of you are already overworked and need an outing. In any event, let's all go out to my ranch next Saturday afternoon and jump in the lake. I have appointed J. S. Dewar chairman of a committee on arrangements. A later bulletin will announce to you plans for next Saturday afternoon and evening.

More than seven hundred took Frank up on his offer. They not only jumped in the lake, but they ate, drank, and danced until long after the moon rose over the ranch. The following Monday, Frank noticed a decided improvement in everyone's spirits.

But Frank used his ranch for much more than employee outings and outlaw reunions. Early on in the life of the F.P. Ranch, Frank hosted a variety of groups, organizations, and individuals, ranging from Scout troops, classes of schoolchildren, and ladies' clubs to delegations of Catholic bishops and the directors of major railroad lines and well-established banks and corporations. If there were no conflicts with family or company activities, Frank was usually amenable to allowing outside groups use of the ranch. He'd arrange for the lodge to be open at a designated hour so the visitors could look at the animal heads mounted on the walls, and he even provided a Victrola they could use for dancing in the pavilion next to Clyde Lake.

Fern Butler, acting on Frank's orders, went to Abercrombie & Fitch—"the Greatest Sporting Goods Store in the World"—on Madison Avenue and ordered a diving board for the lake and dozens of bows and arrows and all the accessories, including an instructional book about archery, for ranch guests to use.

In 1928, Frank was elected as a director of the Chatham Phenix Bank in New York, one of the largest banking institutions in the nation. He also served on the board of the First National Bank of St. Louis, along with Charles Lemp, a Phillips director. Officers and fellow board members from both of these banks were frequent guests at Woolaroc, and for one of the dinners he held for the First National board at the lodge, Frank arranged for Jack "Backlash" Lamb, the champion angler from Fort Worth, to give a fly- and bait-casting demonstration.

Lamb had caught more than twelve thousand bass during his career and could fill a washtub with bass in less than three hours. Frank's guests, all dressed in suits and ties, stood with their mouths agape as Lamb quietly cast a fly one hundred feet across Clyde Lake with pinpoint accuracy.

When he entertained fifty of the nation's top railroad executives at Woolaroc, Frank seated them at a huge U-shaped table set up around an electric train representing the crack Overland Limited. The train blew its whistle and puffed tiny clouds of smoke as it raced around the guests, who were enjoying a breakfast of oatmeal, eggs, sausage, and buffalo and elk steaks. Afterward, Grif Graham initiated everyone into the "Woolaroc Klan" and sent them on their way.

A group of veterinarians was given a more animal-oriented tour of the ranch when Frank invited thirty-nine carloads of vets and their families to spend two days as his guests at the ranch. There was the usual barbecue and dance, but Frank also took the animal doctors on a close-up inspection of his huge buffalo herd and the other wild critters. Later, two of Frank's cowboys gave an exhibition in riding bucking horses and mules and several guests took camel rides. For all his trouble, Frank received plenty of free advice and tips about animal care, something he was constantly seeking.

Not only large groups visited the ranch, such as the bankers or the veterinarians or the eight hundred members of the Izaak Walton League who came for a barbecue in the spring of 1927. Many well-known individuals also came—actors and actresses from New York and Hollywood, authors, politicians, religious leaders, and other celebrities.

One weekend in May 1928, Frank and Jane hosted not one,

but two Pulitzer Prize–winning writers—Edna Ferber and William Allen White.

White, the popular editor and author from Kansas who was known as the "Sage of Emporia," brought his wife and son to the ranch. The spokesman for grass-roots and small-town America and an influential figure in Republican politics, White had won the Pulitzer for editorial writing in 1923 and later ran unsuccessfully for governor of Kansas on an anti–Ku Klux Klan plank. Frank and his guest had more in common than their political party affiliation. Both men were blunt but humane and had risen from virtual obscurity to national prominence. All afternoon while they toured the ranch and later at the lodge, they sized up each other. After dinner, while their wives and the other guests visited, Frank and the gregarious White found comfortable chairs on the front porch and talked long into the night about world affairs, White's campaign to discredit the Klan, and the merits of Herbert Hoover, only a month away from winning the Republican nomination for President.

Edna Ferber, unfortunately, did not find her stay at Woolaroc nearly as stimulating or pleasant. The popular novelist and playwright's best-seller, *So Big,* won the Pulitzer Prize in 1925, and her romantic *Show Boat,* published in 1926, had just been transformed by Jerome Kern and Oscar Hammerstein into the perennially appealing operetta. Ferber was interested in developing yet another romantic novel, this one with a western theme, which would focus on life in territorial Oklahoma through statehood. It would be called *Cimarron.* For picking up the flavor of the land and the people, Ferber couldn't have picked more inspiring subjects than Frank Phillips and his Osage ranch.

She made it through the first day and was ready for bed when the trouble started. The writer's peace of mind and train of thought were shattered. It wasn't all the political talk between White and Frank that drove her off. It was another sort of racket and it came from Jane's peacocks. The birds' plumage was handsome but their voices were loud. Very loud. The first night at the lodge, the big birds perched near the windows of the guest room where Ferber was trying to sleep. Their shrieking was constant and not even two feather pillows over her head could give Ferber any peace. Either everyone else was used to peacocks or they were sound sleepers, because the next morning only Ferber complained.

The second night Ferber could hardly keep her face from

falling into her plate of buffalo steak and potatoes, she was so weary. As soon as she ate her last bite of pie, she excused herself and retired to her room. It was as quiet as a graveyard outside. She slipped into bed and was on the edge of slumber when the high-pitched screams of the peacocks started again. Their cries were louder than ever and twice as shrill. Before daybreak, Ferber had her bags packed, and as soon as breakfast was over she bid hasty good-byes to the Phillipses, told them what she thought of their noisy peacocks, and left in search of some peace and quiet. Edna Ferber never returned to Woolaroc, which was just fine as far as Jane was concerned. Anyone who insulted her peacocks, as Ferber had done, wasn't welcome.

But Frank and Jane hosted other guests who didn't mind the peacocks and weren't afraid of the rattlesnakes sunning on the rocks leading down to Clyde Lake or the wild animals sniffing around in the pastures and pens.

In the summer of 1929, Tom Mix, now a big movie star and on tour with the Sells-Floto Circus, came back to Oklahoma after a fifteen-year absence and was the guest of honor at a dinner party at Woolaroc hosted by Jane. With Frank in New York, John Phillips was quickly recruited to stand in for his father. Jane found the reckless Mix attractive and was entertained by his stories about his wonder horse, Tony, and life in Hollywood. John remained reasonably sober and Grif Graham initiated Mix into the "Woolaroc Klan." Mix sent Jane an autographed photo of himself as a token of his esteem. He had seen many ranches, lodges, and resorts, but Mix was especially impressed with Woolaroc and the collection of wild and domestic animals roaming the ranch.

Will Rogers, another guest, made his first visit to Woolaroc just a few weeks after Mix. "Thought I'd just drop in and be neighborly while I'm back home," said Rogers.

After he toured the ranch, inspected Frank's horses and wild beasts, and gawked at the growing collection of paintings, Indian blankets, and animal trophies in the lodge, Rogers turned to the rest of the party and declared: "Well, boys, she's a success—there ain't no doubt about it." A few years later, in his autobiography, Rogers had more to say about the F.P. Ranch: "When you are visiting the beauty spots of this country, don't overlook Frank Phillips' ranch and game preserve at Bartlesville, Oklahoma. It's the most unique place in this country." Strong praise from a country boy who had seen more than his share of the world.

As the years went by, the compliments about the beauty of

the lodge and the lakes and the land continued and the flow of guests to the F.P. Ranch never slackened.

Jane hosted summer parties at Woolaroc for her circle of friends—Winnie Clark, Noretta Low, and others from Bartlesville. Minnie Hall, her old chum from Creston, Iowa, and close friends from out of town also came for visits. Jane's daughters, Mary, or Mary Frank as she preferred, and Sara Jane, or Jane as she preferred, began spending more time at the ranch.

The two teenagers were only a grade apart when they went to Garfield School in Bartlesville, just a couple of blocks from the town house on Cherokee Avenue. But in the late 1920s, both girls were sent to the Ogontz School outside Philadelphia, and by attending a few summer sessions, the sisters managed to end up in the same class. Ogontz was a girls' school founded in 1850. The students there wore military-style uniforms, drilled with wooden rifles, and were required to spend long hours with their noses in books in order to obtain a classical, and expensive, education.

At Thanksgiving and most other holidays, Mary Frank and Jane went to New York and joined their parents at the family suite at the Ambassador. But at Christmas break or after classes ended in the summer, they headed straight for Bartlesville and the ranch. Out at the ranch, everyone, including Frank, seemed to let down his guard when only family and close friends were out for the weekend or a holiday visit.

"Our parents were very strict with us," recalled Jane. "They weren't when John was growing up, but they made up for it with us. Especially Father. He was very strict." Jane would stay up late chatting with her daughters or friends. They'd sit in her bedroom, with the great animal-skin rugs and noble dog, Fidac, to keep watch, and talk the night away. Jane, with her deep voice—the voice that was full of money—would sit on her bed and take long, almost regal, drags from her cigarette holder as she told stories to her girls.

Frank, usually in bed hours before the others, would rise early and go for a horseback ride. He'd ride again in the afternoons before cocktails and dinner. "I loved to go riding with Father, but it was always the same—he didn't even know I was along," said Jane. "His mind was on something else and he didn't talk. Finally, I'd just give up and go back to the barn and he wouldn't even miss me. He'd be thinking about business. But I kept on riding with him. He loved it so much. We rode every day we were out at the ranch."

Jane arranged for the two Seaton sisters—Elisabeth and Elise, the magician's twins—to give Mary Frank and Jane dancing lessons during the summer vacations. A driver picked up the Seatons at their home in Bartlesville and brought them out to Woolaroc for the Phillips girls' daily lessons.

Elise was still aware of Uncle Frank's fondness for her and was always on her guard. One night, after a party at the ranch, Frank caught a ride back to town with the Seatons, who had driven out to Woolaroc in their father's Buick. Frank insisted that Elise sit in the backseat with him while Elisabeth drove and chatted with a Tulsa banker up front. It was a harrowing ride for Elise. She had to wrestle Frank off all the way from the ranch until they dropped him off at the town house.

Although he always paid close attention to the ladies—especially pretty ones—Frank still didn't hold a candle to the antics of his son, whose womanizing increased in direct proportion to his drinking.

"There were always stories about John Phillips and the ladies," said Tom Sears, a caddy at Hillcrest Country Club from 1928 through 1933. "The caddies would hear all the locker-room talk. The members would get in there and start drinking and we'd wait around to collect our tips and we'd hear all these wild stories. A lot of them were about the Phillipses. Frank had a real reputation for liking women, and there was even talk about Aunt Jane. But I think much of that was just jealous talk. Now, John Phillips was another question. We knew he had some real problems. Most of the time I saw him he was dazed. He'd strut around the club, looking like he was in a trance."

The alcoholic antics—skirt chasing, drinking sessions, gambling—were all taking their toll on John's marriage to Mildred. Frank was also growing more disgusted with his son's behavior. By 1929, John's alcohol problem was severe. He found plenty of company for his bouts with some of the other members of the Halcyons. Art Goebel, under contract with Frank to barnstorm the Phillips marketing territory with his skywriting plane, also served as a drinking companion for John.

One of their more infamous escapades occurred when John was flying back to Bartlesville from Dallas with Goebel in a two-seat, open-cockpit airplane. As they flew over the Red River, Goebel and his passenger developed a thirst and broke out a fresh bottle of whiskey to help wash some of the dust from their throats. They passed the bottle back and forth, and by the time they approached Tulsa, neither of them was feeling any pain. Just on the other side of Tulsa, they spied a herd of goats grazing in a field, and in a flash, the plane dove from the clouds and landed in the pasture. Goebel leaped from the plane, ran into the midst of the bewildered goats, grabbed one, and threw it into John's arms in the rear cockpit. Then they were off again in a cloud of smoke and dust, John grasping their reluctant cargo with all the strength he could muster and still hold the bottle.

Thinking some of the whiskey might calm the goat, they poured generous swigs of the stuff down the animal's throat, and by the time Goebel made his rather wobbly landing at Bartlesville, all three of them were thoroughly soused. The sun was setting when John, Goebel, and the pickled goat piled into an automobile left waiting for them at the airport. They drove directly to the residence of O. K. Wing, where John remembered Obie and his wife, Oral, were hosting a fancy dinner party. The auto screeched to a halt at the curb just as the Wings began seating their twenty guests at the dining-room table. Included among those invited was Mildred Phillips.

The china and silver sparkled in the light of the blazing candelabra, and Obie, his glass raised high, was about to deliver a toast when the doors swung open and in burst Goebel and John bearing the bleating, bellowing, burping billy goat, which they proceeded to dump square in the center of the dining-room table.

Dinner was over before it could even be served. Platters of food, broken glass, and shrieking guests went every which way. Mildred was so embarrassed she felt like plunging into the Caney River. She was also angry, very angry, but as she had done for years, Mildred eventually gave in and forgave her wayward husband and the reckless, but repentant, Goebel.

Goebel injured his knee in an aircraft accident in Kansas City a few weeks later, and when he was able to hobble from the hospital, he promptly took a taxi to the airport and chartered a plane to Bartlesville to be close to his friends. Goebel spent six weeks convalescing in the children's nursery at the John Phillips residence on Cherokee.

Mildred tended to the crippled pilot while his leg mended, and Goebel, who had a schoolboy crush on Mildred, whiled away the hours entertaining young Betty and Johnny with stories of his flying exploits. As soon as his injuries were healed, Goebel departed. Mildred, who was pregnant, had plans to put the nursery to better use than housing a handsome rascal whose wings were temporarily clipped.

On December 23, 1929—a cold Sunday morning—Mildred

gave birth to twin sons at St. John Hospital in Tulsa. She and John decided to name the boys for their grandfathers—the late Robert Beattie and Frank Phillips. The babies weighed only between four and five pounds each at birth, so the physicians attending Mildred told her and John that the boys would have to spend at least a month in a hospital incubator. When news of the twins' arrival reached Bartlesville, the family was delighted. Especially Frank. There were twins in the clan once more— Phillips twins, and one of them bore his name.

Frank's joy lasted but a couple of days. On Christmas Eve, his namesake—Frank Phillips II—tiny and weak, died. Frank went to Tulsa to see his daughter-in-law and returned to Bartlesville that evening with his dead grandson. Jane, John, Bertha Gibson, and Mildred's mother stayed with Mildred and the surviving twin.

Frank hosted a dinner on Christmas Day at the town house for part of L.E.'s family, Betty and Johnny, and the two foster daughters. It was a quiet meal, and that afternoon, instead of singing around the piano or calling on friends and neighbors, Frank faced a solemn chore at the White Rose Cemetery. Back in New York, Fern faithfully recorded Frank's movements in his daily business diary: "Mr. Phillips took baby Frank II corpse to cemetery, where simple service was held in the mausoleum." At White Rose, a chill wind stirred the cedars and the naked branches of the catalpa trees. After the brief service, Frank, wrapped in his overcoat and grief, read the inscriptions chiseled on the front of the mausoleum:

> "There is no death! What seems so is transition. This life of mortal breath is but a suburb of the life elysian whose portal we call death."
>
> —Longfellow

> "Some evening when the sky is gold I'll follow day into the west nor pause, nor heed, till I behold the happy, happy hills of rest."
>
> —Paine

Frank returned to Tulsa the next morning because baby Robert, or Bobby as the family called him, appeared to be weakening. By noon, when he was assured his grandson was out of danger, Frank came back to Bartlesville and met for several hours with his security chief and two Tulsa police officers. Frank was very conscious of his family's high profile and didn't want to take any chances. His namesake was gone, but Frank was determined that no kidnapper looking for a fortune in ransom money would snatch Bobby from the hospital nursery.

Between Christmas and New Year's, Frank stayed busy with duties at the office, executive committee meetings, and year-end strategy sessions with L.E., Kane, Wing, Alexander, Parker, and others. Work was always the best therapy for Frank, and now more than ever it helped take away the sting of the loss of his grandson.

On New Year's Eve, Frank reached the office by midmorning, in time for several conferences and a final executive committee meeting—the last of the year and the decade. By four o'clock he had concluded his business day and left for the ranch.

Out at Woolaroc, surrounded by family and friends, Frank nursed a strong Scotch and water carefully prepared by Dan. A chill winter wind swept across Clyde Lake, and from the windows of the lodge Frank watched the waters ruffle like a field of prairie grass in spring. Flames crackled and danced in every fireplace, and there was a tall fir dressed in bright lights and garlands. Bunches of mistletoe with fat waxy berries the color of ivory that ranch hands had cut from trees near the lodge were tacked above the doors and mixed with the boughs of holly spread across the mantles.

Frank called for another whiskey and reviewed in his mind events and situations from the past decade. It was a time for reflection—a bittersweet moment for Frank Phillips and all the world. The Roaring Twenties were about to vanish. There was much to consider and recall. A new decade, a new age was about to dawn.

Dan brought a fresh drink and Frank took a deep sip and saved the rest for a final toast. The whiskey and the wind and the smell of evergreen were good medicine. Frank kissed Jane and his daughters and bid everyone a Happy New Year and then he quietly disappeared and went upstairs to his room and the narrow cowboy bunk. He finished his drink in the darkness listening to the wind, and then he closed his eyes and waited for his thoughts to turn into dreams.

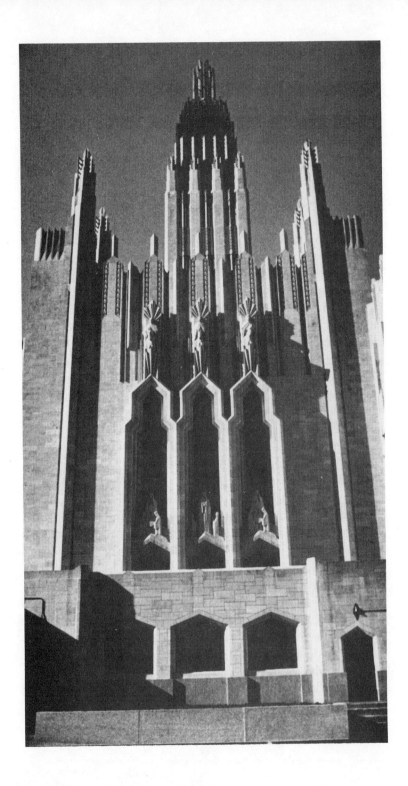

OKIE DECO

Architecture is life, or at least it
is life itself taking form and
therefore it is the truest record of
life as it was lived in the world
yesterday, as it is lived today or
ever will be lived.

—Frank Lloyd Wright

In northeastern Oklahoma—a land of lakes, hardwood forests, and lush quarter horse ranches—there's an oasis of culture and commerce named Tulsa. Forget the stereotypes of tornadoes, dust, and broken oil-patch dreams. In truth, Tulsa is a thriving metropolis that combines the hospitality of the South and the charm of the Southwest with eastern sophistication and midwestern values.

In the late 1800s Tulsa grew from a Creek Indian settlement on the banks of the Arkansas River into a prairie town with dirt streets and false-front frame buildings. But shortly after the turn of the century, that all changed when oil was discovered in nearby Red Fork and Glenn Pool. The boom was on. Promoters championed Tulsa as the proper headquarters for oil captains to conduct financial business and establish their offices and homes. The lure of "black gold" brought oil men and their families to "The Oil Capital of the World."

The excitement of oil discoveries in the region quickly gave birth to a movement of community pride and spirit in Tulsa. Oil barons such as the Phillips brothers, Getty, Skelly, Cosden, Sinclair, and others came to the area and left their marks. Shortly after World War I, as the Roaring Twenties began, residents were filled with a sense of purpose that they committed to civic and cultural development. It was a time for elegance, mischief, and magic. America was between wars and ready for something new. Flappers, bootleggers, and risk takers were de rigueur—especially in a city with as much moxie as Tulsa.

Tulsans prospered while Fred Astaire and F. Scott Fitzgerald led charmed lives and Cole Porter kept everyone in tune. Will Rogers held court in New York as the rest of the nation flocked to the movies to gaze at Swanson, Valentino, and Garbo.

By the time the 1920s really started to roar, Tulsa was sure of its future, and nowhere was the city's optimism more apparent than in a downtown building boom. Tulsa's prosperity and the need to erect corporate palaces and grand homes coincided with the birth of a distinctive style of architecture and design that impacted not only the twenties but pervaded the Great Depression years and the New Deal before colliding head-on with World War II. It was a fresh, sassy, and daring approach, and today it is fondly called Art Deco.

Art Deco's roots came from many sources. Influences ranged from the Latin and Mayan designs brought to light during the Mexican Revolution to Egyptian motifs that became popular in the 1920s following the opening of Tutankhamen's tomb. These designs, and others, inspired the monumental bas-relief figures, stylized lightning bolts, fan patterns, polychrome terra-cotta panels, and the geometric light fixtures found in many Art Deco structures.

But the true launching point for the Art Deco movement, which swept the nation and blessed Tulsa with an abundance of stunning architecture, can be traced to Paris and the 1925 *Exposition Internationale des Arts Decoratifs et Industriels Modernes*. This key event, well-attended by American architects and craftspersons, was also covered extensively by the American press, who compared it to the initiation of the Italian Renaissance. Although the term "Art Deco" was not popularized until the late 1960s when there was a significant revival in the style, Art Deco's name and very existence are derived from this important exposition, where designers and architects were urged to submit entries that would help create a new and modern architectural style.

And nowhere were those striking Art Deco lines and curves more prevalent than in many of the buildings of Tulsa.

The city became a perfect setting for the new Deco form. Thriving during this period of opulence, experimentation, and flamboyance, Tulsa attracted some of the nation's most talented architects, including Bruce Goff, Barry Byrne, and Frank Lloyd Wright. In their commercial buildings, churches, and residences, they left an Art Deco legacy that was never surpassed anywhere else in the nation, with the exceptions of New York and Miami Beach. For although many styles of architecture can be found in Tulsa, including Gothic and Tudor office buildings and homes as well as International Style steel-

and-glass towers, it is Art Deco that remains the prevailing architectural theme.

Tulsa's Art Deco period—from approximately 1925 to 1942—is made up of three phases: Zigzag, PWA (for the New Deal's Public Works Administration), and Streamline. Each phase makes up a distinctive chapter in the city's architectural story and each is represented by fine examples that survive today.

▼▼▼

Zigzag, the first of the three styles, blossomed in Tulsa in the late 1920s. By that time, the optimism that came with the oil boom and the excitement of the Jazz Age was evident throughout downtown Tulsa, where more than a million dollars a month was being spent on new construction. As one observer of the day put it: "Tulsans erected skyscrapers not so much because ground space was at a premium, but because they like to see them rise."

Often called Skyscraper Style because of the emphasis on soaring buildings, the colorful Zigzag Deco buildings employed a lot of ornamentation and intricate design made possible by using terra-cotta (Latin for "burnt earth") as a sheathing material. Architects found terra-cotta light and durable—perfect for the highly decorative high rises they wished to create. The use of terra-cotta for the "modern" buildings of Tulsa became so popular during this period that Tulsa was dubbed Terra-Cotta City.

By the start of the thirties, Tulsa boasted more skyscrapers—most of them Art Deco—than any other city of its size in the world. The skyline appeared to spring out of the prairie in what one writer described as "a rhapsody of terra-cotta." Today, in several prominent downtown office towers, the carefully chiseled designs and patterns—zigzags, spirals, and fronds incorporated in glazed and unglazed terra-cotta, stone, tile, metal, and glass—can still be appreciated.

The city's two major public utility firms—Oklahoma Natural Gas (ONG) and Public Service Company of Oklahoma (PSO)—chose to invest in Tulsa's future and erected downtown buildings that are now used for commercial offices but remain prime examples of Zigzag Art Deco. When both of these conservative firms decided to turn to the flashy new Deco style, it was heralded as a major breakthrough for the modern architectural movement.

The ten-story Oklahoma Natural Gas Building, built in 1928 at a cost of $600,000, was constructed of reinforced concrete, enclosed with buff tapestry brick, and trimmed with tile and Indiana limestone.

The Public Service Company Building, built a year later for $425,000, was only five stories tall but was given a foundation stout enough to support another three floors. (Two more stories were added in 1961.) This building is also constructed of reinforced concrete, but instead of brick facing, the architect used buff Bedford stone. PSO has since forsaken the building and established its headquarters in the renovated Central High School, several blocks away. But the original PSO building remains an active place of business and a popular stop on Art Deco tours.

A building that one architect claimed would have been "the crowning glory of early Art Deco in Tulsa" was a casualty of the times. The Gillette-Tyrrell Building, now named the Pythian Building, was built in 1930 by a pair of local oil tycoons. Originally designed as a thirteen-story hotel, the Depression forced the owners to change their plans and to sell the building to the Knights of Pythias soon after the first three floors were completed.

The Pythian's facade—a mixture of multicolored terra-cotta, marble, and granite—is striking, but the L-shaped lobby remains the most notable feature. Along with a floor design taken straight from Native American motifs, the lobby features include "dancing zigzags" (diamond patterns repeated from the exterior), colorful tiles, custom iron railings, etched-glass windows, and classic Deco light fixtures.

The nine-story Philcade was built by Waite Phillips, a quietly aggressive oil tycoon and brother of Frank Phillips, the founder of Phillips Petroleum Company. Completed in 1930, Philcade was constructed to complement the twenty-four-story Philtower (called "The Queen of the Tulsa Skyline"), another Waite Phillips office building of Gothic design with some Deco influences, which was erected in 1927 on the opposite corner. Because of the tremendous family fortune, Phillips was able to ignore the Depression and leave behind some of the city's finest architectural treasures. Today Philtower, with its polychromed tile roof, is still a skyline landmark and Philcade remains a center of commercial activity.

In the Philcade, prime examples of Art Deco appear everywhere from the zigzag motifs in the light fixtures to the ornate grillwork over the windows. With its ground-floor arcade designed in the shape of a T, for Tulsa, the Philcade is cherished by Deco lovers for its eleven custom-made bronze chandeliers with amber glass, marbled hallways, and gold-leaf ceiling. The brick building is a favorite for those on walking tours who delight in spotting the reptiles, birds, and mammals hidden in the stylized foliage above the windows. Only a few visitors are aware that an eighty-foot tunnel, made of brick and arched to carry the load of the street above, connects the Philtower and Philcade. The tunnel was dug by miners imported to Tulsa by Phillips in order to provide for the transportation of supplies from one building to another. Also, Phillips was alarmed by the rash of kidnappings of wealthy oil men and he wished to be able to move secretly and in relative safety if he desired.

Security was never a problem at another prominent zigzag building, the Warehouse Market, also known as the Farmers' Market or, simply, the Market. It was built in 1929 on the site of an athletic stadium. The park had also served as a shelter for black families during the city's bloody 1921 race riot. Eight years later a developer transformed the park into a public market and erected the huge Deco building, designed by B. Gaylord Noftsger, an Oklahoma City architect. A tower with brilliant polychrome terra-cotta ornaments acted as a beacon to attract people to the market. Two huge medallions on the building depict a goddess holding a sheaf of wheat and cornucopia, and a god wearing a winged helmet with an oil derrick in one hand and a train engine in the other. The Depression closed the Market, but a few years later it reopened as the Club Lido, where patrons danced to the music of Cab Calloway, Benny Goodman, Duke Ellington, and other touring performers. In 1938, it became the Warehouse Market and operated as a grocery store until 1978. Since that time, the building has been used by several firms for groceries or general merchandise sales.

Every Art Deco tour of Tulsa has to include the city's two splendid Deco churches—Christ the King and Boston Avenue Methodist. Situated in the historic Swan Lake neighborhood,

Christ the King Church is a combination of Gothic and Byzantine architecture with ample Art Deco styling, which includes the extensive use of terra-cotta in the lofty church spires. Francis Barry Byrne—the prominent Chicago modernist known for his imaginative ecclesiastical buildings, a former apprentice of Frank Lloyd Wright, and one of the few Prairie School architects who studied abroad—was commissioned to create the Christ the King building. Completed in 1927, it was considered the first modern design church in Tulsa. Many critics declared the design innovative; some thought it was radical.

Nevertheless, the dominant Art Deco church in Tulsa remains the highly acclaimed Boston Avenue Methodist Church, built in 1929 just blocks from the downtown Deco buildings that highlight the city skyline. When this $1.5 million edifice, which features a 225-foot pleated tower and exterior terra-cotta sculptures, was completed, it marked the first time a church building had departed from traditional styles of architecture and used contemporary symbolism and design. The church—an elegant Art Deco finger pointing toward heaven—is recognized as one of the most architecturally significant buildings in the world.

Bruce Goff, at the time a young apprentice, was given the nod to carry out the architectural planning for this grand monument to the Art Deco movement. Goff's participation came courtesy of Adah Robinson, his former art teacher and a consultant to the church building committee. Although controversy surrounds the question of who actually designed the church, records clearly indicate Robinson was the true inspiration for the building and that Goff simply executed her designs.

Goff, who became Tulsa's premier architect, was a boy genius who had designed the mosaics on the side altars in Christ the King Church. His architectural career was launched when he was eleven years old and his father, weary of his son sitting in school drawing sketches of buildings, marched the youngster into the offices of Rush, Endacott & Rush and asked the architects to put the lad to work.

One of Goff's first design projects was the Adah Robinson residence, a studio-house built for the noteworthy art teacher and designer. Robinson, a Quaker, was born in Richmond, Indiana, and attended the Chicago Art Institute and West End School of Art in Provincetown. She taught for several years in Oklahoma City and at the University of Oklahoma before moving to Tulsa to teach art at Central High School. Later "Miss Bobbie," as her friends called her, headed up the art department at the University of Tulsa and in 1945 she moved to San Antonio to become a professor of art at Trinity University. To this day the Robinson house remains a private residence and a Zigzag gem.

Besides the Robinson residence and the Boston Avenue Methodist Church, Goff was responsible for designing several other Zigzag buildings, including the Tulsa Club, 1927; Guaranty Laundry, 1928; Riverside Studio, 1929; and Merchants' Exhibit Building (Tulsa State Fairgrounds), 1930.

Beyond the array of Goff-designed buildings and the many splendid Zigzag structures located within easy walking distance of one another in the downtown area, a particularly fine example of this style is the highly acclaimed Westhope, a Tulsa residence designed and built in 1929 by Frank Lloyd Wright. Idolized by Goff and many of the other outstanding architects of the period, Wright came to Tulsa to build the striking residence for his cousin, Richard Lloyd Jones, a local newspaper publisher. Although no longer owned by the Jones family, Westhope continues to attract the attention of passersby who seek a glimpse of this sprawling home built of concrete blocks, molded on the site, and of the vertically stacked windows that caused Wright himself to admit that "the damn thing is more beautiful than I ever expected."

▼▼▼

The solid PWA-style Art Deco buildings in Tulsa provided a logical transition between the Zigzag of the 1920s and the Streamline of the next decade. Most of Tulsa's PWA structures were government buildings or institutions of monumental size and dimension. Their bulk conveyed images of permanence and strength—reassuring signs for a nation dealing with economic collapse.

Sadly, some of the best examples of the PWA style have been demolished, such as the original Tulsa Municipal Airport Administration Building. In the 1980s, the Union Bus Depot, a PWA treasure built by Waite Phillips in 1935, was unceremoniously leveled to make way for a downtown church parking lot.

Fortunately, a few of the best PWA buildings have been

saved. Several are still in use and others have been earmarked for restoration. The Fairgrounds Pavilion (Tulsa State Fairgrounds), built in 1932, as well as Will Rogers High School and Daniel Webster High School—both built in 1938—are superb studies in this genre.

One of the most prominent of the PWA buildings is the Tulsa Fire Alarm Building, with its gargoyles and stylized fire-breathing dragons that adorn the roofline and embellish the blond brick exterior. Built in 1931, the building stood idle for several years but was recently purchased by members of Tulsa Firefighters Local 176, who plan to restore the building to its former glory and transform it into a firefighter museum and union office complex.

But the single best PWA symbol of hope for economic recovery during the bleak days of the Depression was the Tulsa Union Depot, built in 1931. More than sixty thousand people jammed the area for the opening of "Tulsa's important front door." Through the years, generations of Tulsans and tourists passed through the depot, which at one time accommodated as many as thirty-six trains a day. But after almost four decades of service to the city, the massive depot, resplendent with its Deco sunbursts, chevrons, and winged wheels, fell victim to the decline in rail travel. In 1967 the great doors were closed and locked. For many years the station stood rotting in pigeon dung, a haven for winos and weeds.

All that changed in 1980 when the depot was purchased and two Tulsa-based firms—Urban Design Group and Manhattan Construction—were selected as the lead architects and contractors for the renovation of the forlorn structure. The results are magnificent. The Tulsa Union Depot is a recycled Art Deco office complex serving as the headquarters for both Urban Design Group and Manhattan Construction, the firm that constructed the depot so many years before. At the reopening ceremonies in 1983, Barbara Baer Capitman, the "First Lady of Art Deco" and founder of the prestigious Miami Design Preservation League, declared: "The restored Tulsa Union Depot represents the most significant renovation of its kind in the United States."

▼▼▼

A growing fascination with machines—especially the automobile—and the influence of transportation in general ignited the third Art Deco style: Streamline. With its curving lines representing speed, the Streamline movement offered Tulsans escape from the drudgeries of the Depression. Designs became more horizontal and simplified with circular windows and carved corners appearing as the principal building features.

Unlike the previous Deco styles, the Streamline elements were not created for behemoth buildings or public institutions but for the nation's emerging roadside architecture: small shops, movie theaters, sleek diners, and curvy gas stations.

Streamline became almost a household word as Tulsans, proud that their city was perched on Route 66, grew enamored of fast cars and smooth lines.

Many of Tulsa's best Streamline gas stations, restaurants, and movie theaters have been obliterated or destroyed, including the Will Rogers Theater, built in 1941 on 11th Street and torn down in the 1980s to make room for yet another church parking lot. Some of the best Streamline buildings that remain are People's State Bank, City Veterinary Clinic, and the Tulsa Monument Company.

Although some Streamline houses, such as the irreplacable John L. Shakely Residence, have been destroyed by uncaring owners, there is still enough interest in the unusual style to ensure a select company of Streamline homes will always remain in the city's substantial Deco inventory. In 1985, for example, the John Duncan Forsyth residence, a two-story, flat-roofed house built in 1937, was renovated and restored to its original glory.

Tulsa's Art Deco architectural treasures, both large and small, are a tribute to a fabulous era that lives on in more than fifty solid examples. The Deco of Tulsa, or "Okie Deco," as it's been called, is even more significant today since it has provided a revival of interest in the downtown area and is helping rejuvenate the city and keep the fires of commerce burning.

"Tulsa truly is a marvelous and unusual Art Deco city, and no one really realizes that outside of the area," says Capitman. "I have seen some of the best—absolutely best—examples of Deco buildings anywhere within a few blocks of downtown Tulsa. It's all over the city!"

The city's renewed interest in Deco architecture and treasures prompted Wolf Von Eckardt, the well-known design and architecture critic, to describe Tulsa as having "the finest Art Deco buildings in the country. People here are discovering their Art

Deco buildings and are treasuring them. That is very impressive. You can sense the pride, the love in the restorations."

A fitting tribute for a city with a legacy of architecture that endures. For although the history of Tulsa may be brief compared to other places, the city's Art Deco homes, office buildings, and churches provide a rare and rich heritage.

9

TEXHOMA:
THE LIVES AND TIMES
OF A BORDER TOWN

*Way out West in
No Man's Land.*

—*From a pioneer poem*

It's a fresh day—a Panhandle Sabbath. Out on U.S. 54 next to the old Rock Island tracks, a visitor digs a coyote fang from the dirt with a rusty railroad spike. Mindful that the coyote was once called "God's dog" by the Indians, the man rubs the tooth shiny clean on his blue jeans and slips it into a pocket. It will serve as a lucky charm during his stay in this land and will help fend off the ghosts of the desperadoes and warriors who still lurk here.

As he walks along the tracks picking up more discarded rail spikes for friends back home, the stranger notices the rising sun has melted like a slab of butter over the endless fields. A warm breeze stirs the grasses and tousles the man's hair. Cameras click and he turns in time to see his companions—a man and a woman who earn their living as photographers—carefully record the sun's movement. He watches them aim and focus and at that moment he realizes that they are all outlanders visiting this place that will always be a long way from anywhere.

Moments later the trio returns to the car and the highway where truckers and tourists are making time. The three visitors head southwest toward the Texas line. A Thermos of coffee is passed, and they tie "cowboy air conditioners"—bandannas soaked in water from the ice chest—around their necks. A blend of lukewarm air and homemade tape music, featuring the best cowboy crooners, pours from the vents and speakers on the dashboard.

Soon the lyrics of the songs mix with dreams and images in the stranger's mind. He recalls schoolboy yarns about buffalo hunters and Indian scouts and tales of sodbusters and trail bosses and other gypsy-footed souls who traveled the High Plains to forget their past. Then the stranger remembers a verse from a pioneer poem he read long ago.

> Pickin' up bones to keep from starving,
> Pickin' up chips to keep from freezing,
> Pickin' up courage to keep from leaving,
> Way out West in No Man's Land.

The stranger chants the words over and over to himself for the rest of the morning while the car tracks the sun and heads for twilight shade.

▼▼▼

Most of the day before had been spent just getting this far. The outlanders followed U.S. 270 and turned westward at Fort Supply, where the highway gently bends, then flattens out in a straight shot across this land that time forgot. It was a drive requiring several sacks of ice, lots of cold drinks and ice-cream bars, and plenty of Haggard and Hank Williams.

The outlanders had read their history books and listened to many of the stories. They decided to come to No Man's Land and look for themselves. They sped across Beaver County, through the towns of Slapout and Elmwood, crossed into Texas County, and stopped in Guymon ("Home of the Most Lied About Weather in the U.S.") long enough to get gasoline and directions from a crusty cowpoke with a complexion like a baseball glove.

They took the southwest cut—U.S. 54—and didn't stop again until they came to the spot along the train tracks where the stranger found the lucky coyote tooth and the photographers found rich sunlight filtering through mashed-potato clouds in a sky the color of blue amber.

Now, at last, they've come to the town they heard so much about. A sign planted on the highway shoulder states the name. TEXHOMA. That's all. No population, no elevation listed. Just TEXHOMA. A name created from the town's unusual location—nestled between two states. It's a classic border town with citizens living and working in both Texas and Oklahoma in a state of happy limbo.

The outlanders reconnoiter both sides of the border. They drive past the empty storefronts and those stores still in business, they look at the stucco homes, the churches, the corrals and sheds, the schools and the graveyard. It takes ten minutes. Then they head for the Golden Spur Motel. There is no clerk to greet them, only a guest book, an alarm clock, and a note that tells them to sign their names, pick out an empty room, and get a good night's sleep. They oblige.

Just before he drifts off, tucked beneath cool sheets, the stranger glances at the table next to his bed and spies the coyote tooth mixed with a pile of pocket change. Over the hum of the air conditioner, there is the sound of trucks shifting gears at the highway crossroads as they head into the night towards the outside world.

At 5 A.M. it's still pitch black, and the sky is loaded with stars. The stranger leaves his sleeping companions and goes to the cafe at the junction of U.S. 54 and Oklahoma 95. A half dozen pickup trucks are parked outside. Inside, all forks stop in mid-bite, and every eye stays on the stranger until he finds a stool at the counter. Only after he is served a glass of water and a steaming mug of coffee does conversation resume.

Most of the talk is about the wheat harvest, cattle prices, and the milo crop. Weather is a constant topic of conversation. In these parts, weather has a nasty habit of turning on those who talk about it. There is either too much wind, dust, or drought. There is always plenty of uncertainty.

Just by listening to the locals over breakfast, it's apparent that the distinctive character of Texhoma comes not only from the extremes in weather but from the town's location.

"It's always been sorta crazy around here beings we're where two states come together," explains a hired hand who works in Texas and lives in Oklahoma, but who is planning to move to the Texas side and get an Oklahoma job. "I kinda like it here. It makes us different. We're not Oklahomans or Texans. We're all our own—we're Texhomans."

This spirit of duality has existed in Texhoma ever since the town was created. That was right after the turn of the century. March 18, 1902, to be exact, after the Rock Island completed its main line across the Panhandle. Before that, the closest thing to a town was a post office station named Loretta that served cowboys and a few hardy settlers who made the long trek to No Man's Land and set up housekeeping in dugouts on the prairie, on one of the last frontiers in America.

In less than a year after the founding of Texhoma, more and

more families arrived and picked out homesites on both sides of what ended up the Texas-Oklahoma border. The following year the town was platted, streets and alleys laid out, and school land designated. By 1906, Texhoma was supporting a church, a bank, and even had telephone service. A year later there were three banks.

Although most of the twelve hundred or so residents in Texhoma today choose the Oklahoma side to live, there is an attempt to keep life balanced in this town with a split personality. For instance, the grain elevators—the dominant architecture for miles around—tower over the border with huge doors available to farmers from both states. Texhoma also maintains two distinct sets of municipal officials, and before the state line was shifted 473 feet south in 1934, the boundary actually went through the train depot. This meant passengers purchasing tickets stood in Texas and handed their money to an agent standing in Oklahoma. The same held true for the old post office, and there are still a few Texhomans who live in residences that are situated in both states. "They live in the best of both worlds" is how one town sage puts it.

When it comes to the schools, it finally took special acts of the Oklahoma and Texas legislatures in 1975 to combine the districts from both sides of the border. Today there are separate school boards to administer each side. All the children come to the Texas side for kindergarten, then to the Oklahoma side for first through fourth grades, go back to Texas for fifth through eighth grades and, finally, return once more to Oklahoma for ninth through twelfth grades.

By the time the sun is up, the stranger has received his own Texhoma education and managed to meet a sizable portion of the town's population without having to leave his stool at the cafe.

Across the street, the stranger finds his friends are up and about and are busy photographing a large painted sign that tells the passing world that Texhoma has 1,277 nice people and one stinker. During the rest of their stay, the outlanders will ask nearly every person they meet to reveal the stinker's name. In response, they get nothing but laughter and the promise that the varmint has fled to parts unknown.

The nice people are easy to find. They're on both sides of the state line. They're the hard-core Texhomans, tempered from generations of Panhandle life. Resilient people with both a keen sense of humor and a real sense of survival. People who can recall the prosperous years but aren't afraid to bring up the lean times. People who talk about hardships without complaining and savor the worthwhile moments from everyday life.

Many are veterans of the Dust Bowl years—the "Dirty Thirties"—when black blizzards rolled over the ranches and farms and down the streets of town. These were years when the skies were darkened for days at a time, and people died of dust pneumonia. Many believed the end of the world had arrived. But some faced the wind and held on.

Sometimes, a few of those Dust Bowl survivors can be found down at Crismon's Drug Store, just a block off Main Street.

The drugstore is the domain of William Owen Crismon— better known as Slats. "Got the name *Slats* in high school back in 1918. I was only twenty-nine around the waist and skinny as a switch. The name stuck. If you write me a letter today and put 'Slats, Texhoma, Oklahoma' on the envelope, I'll get it."

One of nine children, Slats was born in Rogers, Arkansas, in 1901. Four years later his family came to the Panhandle in a covered wagon pulled by a team of mules. Their first home was a twelve-by-fourteen dugout with dirt floors. "I recall in 1907 my father added another room on the back of our dugout, and Mother ripped gunny sacks and sewed them together to make a carpet. We thought we were really living then."

In 1928, Slats opened his drugstore. He paid $1,200 for the stock and fixtures. In 1933, he married Grace McQuitty from Welch, Oklahoma. Together they raised four children, ran the drugstore and the movie theater, and managed to farm four and a half sections of land. "My wife died several years ago, but I keep this old drugstore going just so there will be one open in town. Gotta always have a drugstore."

Most days, Slats keeps the lights off to conserve electricity, and during the summer it helps keep the store cool. He fills a prescription or two, sells shoe polish and chewing gum, and sits in the shadows kibitzing with old pals like Bill Hollis, a retired wheat farmer. "The true center of the 'Dust Bowl' was really Boise City, up in Cimarron County," Hollis tells the three outlanders scrunched in one of Slats' booths with their cherry Cokes. "Some say that was the worst of it up in those parts, but I'll tell you it was plenty bad down here." Hollis lights a Lucky Strike and lets his words sink in.

"Well, it's sure going to rain today," says Slats. "Just look at my soda fountain." Big dollops of moisture are running down the stainless steel. "See that fountain? Every time it sweats that way, it's a sure sign that rain is on its way. My fountain always tells the truth."

That's good news to Hollis, who snuffs out his cigarette and the Dust Bowl memories in the ashtray and heads for home.

A few blocks from the drugstore, the visitors come across Wynnie Carol Beck, a Texhoma native. In 1979, Wynnie, a farm wife and mother of two married daughters, became the first woman ever elected to the Texhoma city council.

"Texhoma is a good place to live and raise kids," says Wynnie, who also does volunteer work for the chamber of commerce. "These days we've got a decent medical clinic with a hard-working doctor, our schools are in shape on both sides of the line, and everyone seems to be looking out for each other. This is the way it should be."

One of Wynnie's pet projects is the Okie Relays, a May event that features hundreds of runners racing in relay teams from the Kansas state line at Elkhart across the width of the Panhandle to Texhoma. "We've been running the relay since 1967. It's a wild three-state race, and it draws men, women, children, seniors— all types of runners from a five-state region."

Then, after she's warmed to the questions, Wynnie reveals a Panhandle-sized portion of spirit and pride when she learns that two of her visitors—the pair of photographers—have decided to get married, and they believe a No Man's Land border town would make a fitting place to tie the knot. Wynnie couldn't agree more. She quickly establishes that they've already taken care of the required blood tests days before in Oklahoma City. Next she offers detailed instructions about getting a marriage license in Guymon and finally she suggests they contact Brother James, a blind Baptist preacher who, Wynnie says, can provide a Panhandle-style wedding. The two agree, and they set sunset for their nuptial date.

While his friends seek the counsel of Brother James and then race to Guymon before the courthouse closes, the stranger continues his rounds. There are more Texhomans to meet, and now there is a wedding to prepare for.

He spends time with Hallie Mai Krull and her sister-in-law, Sidna Krull. Driving forces and charter members of the Texhoma

Genealogical and Historical Society as well as keepers of the keys to the town's museum, the Krull ladies guard Texhoma's heritage like a pair of zealous U.S. marshals.

"We saw that people were passing on and that when they died the history of this place was leaving with them," says Sidna.

"We just couldn't let that happen," says Hallie Mai.

The stranger considers offering the ladies his lucky coyote tooth for the tiny museum filled with artifacts and vintage clothing, but he remembers he has another day left in No Man's Land. The tooth may come in handy. Instead, he buys an armful of booklets filled with photographs and diaries of Panhandle pioneers.

He takes his leave and catches up with a young man he met over morning coffee. David Stanhope is his name, and his occupation was once as rare in this part of the country as a debutante ball. Stanhope is the law. He became town marshal in 1984 after serving as a Texas County deputy and working as a city policeman in Guymon. He's a big man, and he looks even bigger wearing his cowboy hat, boots, badge, and pistol. He explains that most of the problems he deals with concern the traffic or a teenager tangling with a six-pack of beer. There is always the chance that trouble might be imported thanks to the highways that crisscross Texhoma, but fortunately most of those problems just keep heading down the road without stopping.

"My jurisdiction is the Oklahoma side," says Stanhope. "The Texas side of town is really under the jurisdiction of the Sherman County sheriff, but remember, those patrols have to come twenty miles or better, so if things get serious enough I need to be prepared to cross into Texas."

During the afternoon patrol, Stanhope pauses at the Texas Grocery, which, true to its name, is located on the Texas side of town. As he heads for the door, Stanhope glances at the bulletin board covered with notices about employment, auctions, town meetings, and baby showers. He goes inside and grabs a cold soda pop from the antique icebox.

"Since we don't have a town newspaper anymore, that bulletin board sure comes in handy for folks," says Les Ellis, who along with his wife, Nanell, owns and operates the store. "We're going to keep everything old-fashioned in here. We want this place to remain a good ol' country store. They're the best kind."

Stanhope and the stranger part company in front of the cafe

at the livestock yards. The cafe is packed with workingmen taking an afternoon break. Every chair and booth appears occupied, and the stranger sees that, besides the waitress, he's the only person not wearing a cowboy hat. He's about to turn and leave when a cowhand gets up and brushes past. In an instant the stranger is whisked to the booth and given a belt of coffee stout enough to raise the dead. When he discovers he's been seated across from Tom Pugh—one of three brothers who became legendary Panhandle cowboys—the stranger gives the coyote tooth a pat of thanks.

"I gave up on school," Pugh tells him. "Quit when I was a boy, and I went to work. I worked cattle. I broke horses, and I spent some time with the railroad, and I worked on a mule ranch, too. I traded livestock, and I did lots of other things. But mostly, I stayed with cattle. I chased them, roped them, branded them. I am a cowboy."

Born near Danville, Arkansas, in 1893, Pugh and his brothers, Bill, John, and Fred, come from the ranks of a legion of cowboys who helped tame No Man's Land. There will always be cowboys here, but none quite like these. Men like the Pughs and the Hamiltons (Rentie, Jean, Charlie, and Percy), Nat Young, Ike Record, Bill Crabtree, Ray Dooley, Price Brown, Pablo Trujillo, Max Miller, and many more. Their ranks are thinning fast.

Pugh, who clearly recalls shaking hands with Teddy Roosevelt in 1912, depends on a pacemaker, his third, and a lifetime of memories, both bitter and sweet, to get him through.

"It was back years and years ago when God was still a boy that my old buddy and me got some literature from Montana telling about how you could get yourself a section of land. We climbed into a boxcar down in eastern Oklahoma and headed up that way. It was St. Patrick's Day 1913."

There were many distractions along the way, including plenty of good cattle country. Pugh never made it to Montana. Instead, he worked on ranches near Dalhart and Amarillo and finally leased a spread of his own on the Beaver River in No Man's Land. Except for an all-expense-paid trip to France as a World War I doughboy and an expedition to southern California in a stripped-down Model T Ford, Pugh has stayed put.

"This is good country. Good for cows and cowboys, that is. But a person has to stay with it. You've got to stick it out. I recall during those bad times when the dusters came that I could take a 30-30 rifle and shoot in any direction and that bullet would pass over land not fit for anything or anyone. But we knew it would get better. It had to. It did."

Filled up with coffee, the stranger and Pugh stand in the dusty parking lot and finish their discussion of the way things used to be. When the photographers pull up armed with fresh film and a marriage license, Tom Pugh brightens. He shakes their hands and wishes them well. "This is a hell of a good place to get married and start your life together," he tells them. "Lots of folks have started out here." Tom's wife, Eula, is dead, and he lives alone only a short distance from where the faded yellow stripe is painted across the highway marking the state line. In his backyard are the trees and flower beds his wife loved, and in the garage next to the house are an old saddle, bridle, and blankets, and a pair of cowboy boots that Tom Pugh wore when he rode the range.

After they take his official portrait, Pugh offers one more bit of advice: "You take care of each other and stick it out."

On the way back to the Golden Spur, big drops of rain splash on the car. It's a rare summer treat, and it lasts just long enough to wash the air and cool the land. The outlanders look at each other and smile. Slats's sweating soda fountain never lies.

The stranger leaves his companions so they can don their wedding duds—fresh blue jeans and new western shirts. He returns to the stockyards to pick up a coconut-cream pie he had the cook bake for his friends. Then he drives to the edge of town. Mourning doves are starting to settle in the elm trees and lilac bushes that edge the Texhoma cemetery, and, nearby, the stranger cuts a double handful of black-eyed Susans. Every bride must have her bouquet.

As promised, Brother James is waiting at his church just as the last rays of the sun flicker over the ranch lands. The preacher, blinded years back during a farming accident, wears a Western-cut suit and dark glasses. He carries a silver-headed cane.

The four of them drive out of town on a two-lane blacktop and turn down a dirt ranch road that seems to go on forever. They stop on a rise and take their places.

Crickets are chirping, and there is a red glow on the horizon. As they stand there—not sure if they're in Texas or Oklahoma—and face each other in a tight circle, the outlanders see Venus and a sliver of new moon appear behind Brother James. They describe the scene to him and he tells them he sees it all in his mind.

"Are you thoroughly convinced that she's the right woman?"

"Yes, sir."

"And are you thoroughly convinced that he's the right man?"

"I am."

The ceremony is simple and brief. It's Bible verses and common sense—down-home Texhoma.

Afterward there are kisses all around, and as they drive off, the stranger is certain he hears a pair of God's dogs serenading from the darkness.

They leave Brother James at his home and head for the public telephone in front of the all-night convenience store to call friends and family. The coconut-cream pie is washed down with warm champagne and makes a fine wedding feast.

The next morning on the highway near the state line, in the shadows of the grain elevator, the outlanders stop for gasoline. They look up and see Brother James and his wife. The preacher gives each one a ripe peach and asks them to stop and visit if they pass this way again.

Then they leave. They head north toward the Beaver River, where dark clouds are brewing. They eat their peaches in silence and move toward the eye of the storm, way out West in No Man's Land.

10

THE WAY THINGS USED TO BE

Cowboys are romantics, extreme romantics and ninety-nine out of a hundred of them are sentimental to the core. They are oriented toward the past and face the present only under duress, and then with extreme reluctance.

—Larry McMurtry,
In a Narrow Grave

 A guardian of the Old West endures. His name is Jim Jordan, and he can be found at Four Corners, a cluster of wind-beaten buildings smack in the middle of the Oklahoma Panhandle.

As unpredictable as a cyclone, fierce as a blue norther, and wily as a prairie wolf, Jim Jordan has been a cowboy and trader for most of his years. He's a combination of Judge Roy Bean and Buffalo Bill, with a generous dose of saddle tramp mixed in for good measure.

In his time, Jordan broke horses, ran cattle, led a caravan down the Santa Fe Trail, trained buffalos for the rodeo, and put in a stint as a cowboy stunt rider in Hollywood. In the early 1950s Jordan and Bill John Pugh, an old cowboy running mate, even staged their own buffalo hunt, complete with war paint, Indians, bows, and arrows.

Jordan was always conspicuously different from others. Nothing has changed. He is still as ornery and independent as the country he calls home.

"This is open and free land up here, or at least about as close as you'll find anywhere to being that way. To me it's all one place with no state lines, no borders, no boundaries. It's the way the world used to be, up here in the Panhandle."

Jim Jordan's Panhandle is made up of three counties—Beaver, Texas, and Cimarron. The flags of five nations—France, Mexico, Spain, Texas, and the United States—have flown over this real estate. Known by different names, including the Neutral Strip, the Public Land Strip, Robber's Roost, and Cimarron Territory, this 34-mile-wide, 168-mile-long ribbon of land—a 5,738-square-mile rectangle—remains a geographic orphan best described as "No Man's Land." And that's the name Jordan prefers.

It is a region so isolated, and some feel neglected, that old-time Panhandlers still enjoy boasting that they are surrounded by five states—Texas to the south, Kansas and Colorado to the north, New Mexico to the west, and Oklahoma to the east. No Man's Land is full of silence and long horizons. Nothing that lives here finds life easy. Until the late 1880s, white settlers wrote it off as uninhabitable because of the frigid winters and scalding summers.

For many years, since it didn't belong to any state or territory, there was no law enforcement in No Man's Land. The only law was the Colt and the carbine. It was an outlaw haven, and the lonely landscape became famous throughout the West as a sanctuary fit only for the fiercest killers, rustlers, marauders, and thieves. Those with a price on their heads could roam here nameless. It's a no-holds-barred country. One old trail boss described it as "a place where the kids teethed on .45-caliber cartridges."

The stories of the outlaw gangs and desperate men who fled to this bandit territory are still told. Their names are indelibly carved in Panhandle history: Blackjack Ketchum, Tug Toland, Steven "Bugs" Yancy, Buford "Buster" Waldman, Cyrus Coe. There are those who say the Doolins, the Daltons, the James Brothers, and Billy the Kid also took advantage of the hideouts available in No Man's Land.

During the 1880s cattlemen and nesters began arriving. Vigilante committees were organized, and finally law officers began to earn their wages. Scores of towns grew on the cattle trails and next to the railroad tracks. By the time the turn of the century arrived, there was a feeling that the Wild West, including No Man's Land, was on the verge of being tamed. At least almost tamed.

But even though the bands of outlaws may have ridden into the eternal sunset, there are still those who claim that, to this day, the unbridled spirit that set No Man's Land apart from the rest of the country still exists. For them, the Panhandle remains a stretch of unbroken land and promises where people may live with one foot in the past and one in the present and get away with it.

That's the value of Jim Jordan. He's part of that vanishing

breed of individuals who have lived Panhandle history, enduring the hardships, the Dust Bowl, and the growing pains. Jordan rides the fence line of history and, without even knowing it, keeps everything mended and whole. He does a good job considering he doesn't like fences.

"I still feel like it's No Man's Land up here. Of course, I can remember when none of this was fenced. Still, right here is the only place I know where I can hunt with my dogs all winter and not be worried about crossin' lines and fences and such. There are still wide stretches of land, and you can drive out on another man's land to chase your game. So you see, in that way it still ain't fenced in. In that way it's still open. Every gate was made to be opened."

It was 1904—the year after Calamity Jane died, the month after Butch Cassidy and the Sundance Kid robbed the train at Parachute, Colorado, and three years before Oklahoma joined the Union—when Jim Jordan squalled into life. He was born in the ranching country of south-central Oklahoma just above the Red River. His birthday fell on the cusp of August 18 and 19— a midnight child.

"My daddy used to run a ferry boat down on the Red River. He carted whiskey across to the Indians." Jordan opted for a fast pony and a life on the open range. He cowboyed all over the West. He moved into No Man's Land and set up at Four Corners in 1924. He's there today, dug in like an angry badger.

"People in this country like to take care of their own business. These desperadoes come foolin' around a man that owns his own place, and I'll tell ya, they're taken care of. Always been that way. Always should be that way. Out here we still take care of the West."

Four Corners is situated between Guymon and Boise City, just to the east of where the famed Santa Fe Trail cut across the Panhandle. To Jordan, the old trail represents the best of all western highways: "The Santa Fe Trail was really something. They had all kinds of freight and people going back and forth from Independence, Missouri, to Santa Fe itself. You can keep all them superhighways. They haven't built a road yet that equaled that one."

Located at the point where two modern roads meet—Oklahoma 95 and U.S. 64—Four Corners is dominated by a rambling fortress Jim Jordan calls home. Nearby, Jordan runs a few buffalo and some beefalo stock and occasionally takes in a dollar when he permits a chosen few to cross his threshold and see his monumental collection of history. Although the Jim Jordan Frontier Museum is heralded in some tourist brochures, Jordan doesn't encourage visitors. The fact is, for the most part, he would rather be left alone.

The entire ramshackle spread is well protected by some of the wildest junkyard dogs imaginable. "I got me a pack of good ones—they're hippie dogs. Meanest dogs in the world. I trade for 'em. Anybody that's got a mean old dog they want to get rid of comes to see me. I can tell by them dogs when anybody comes around here, and that gives me a chance to go get my shotgun."

Pure cowboy—more than once Jim Jordan has been ridden hard and hung up wet to dry. Decades of riding through trail dust and stinging winds have tattooed his hide. It shows in his eyes as he sits in the relentless sun, his faded blue jeans stuffed into his boot tops, with three days of growth bristling on his khaki-colored face. His voice is like barbed wire, and he's oblivious to a fat caterpillar crawling around on his neck and shoulders. Jordan is just as much a part of nature as any critter in these parts.

The "Museum" building itself, surrounded by elaborate dog runs and walls of sunflowers, cattle skulls, and rusty farm equipment, is filled from floor to ceiling. There are more than fifty sets of longhorn horns alone—some with six-foot spans. Inventory chores could keep a platoon of curators busy for a month. There are chaps, lariats, whiskey bottles, cash registers, feathers, steel traps, pistols, rifles, shotguns, knives, hatchets, barbed wire, bows and arrows, baby carriages, saddles, army helmets, guitars, cowboy boots, stuffed birds, railroad lanterns, high-button shoes, a mummified stingray, sandals, a ceramic bullfrog, clay pipes, a javelina head, stuffed bobcats, raccoon pelts, handcuffs, horse and cow skulls, pinecones, Stetson hats, coolie hats, felt hats, straw hats, sombreros, hand grenades, ice picks, old books, political campaign buttons, an array of antique vehicles including Model T Fords and fire trucks, license plates, chairs, bighorn sheep skulls, gas pumps, sunbonnets, bullwhips, flags, catalogs, skillets, iron pots, buckets, a threshing machine, stumps, candleholders, lead pipes, balls of twine, brass beds, a Wells Fargo chest, human skulls, seashells, Jesse James's buggy, Abe Lincoln's carriage, reward posters, velvet paintings, oil portraits, newspapers, typewriters, lamps, and upright pianos. There's absolutely no rhyme or reason to the collection. It's all just there.

"I like to trade, swap, or buy. If I've got a little money and somebody happens along with something I like, well, I sure as hell attempt to get it. Right now I ain't lookin' for nothin'. I figure I've got everything."

It took Jordan many years to amass his collection. He came across much of it while working as a cowboy and a guide. "I've spent most of my life out in this neck of the woods. But I did go out to California and worked in the motion pictures for a time. I worked with Tom Mix and William S. Hart. Knew all of them old boys. A bunch of us fellas did the rough stuff for 'em like turning flips in the saddle and such. But when it all got to be more and more sissy, well sir, I left."

No Man's Land remains Jim Jordan's idea of heaven on earth.

"I put up the first building here back in '24. I started this thing." A couple of years later, Jim hitched up with Ruby, a soft-spoken lady who Jordan says "knows more about the state of Oklahoma than the guy who built it."

Says the genteel Ruby: "We don't like cities anymore. We don't like what they've become."

Jordan says he stays fit by shunning all strong drink and tobacco. He can cuss better than a fallen bronc rider when he needs to, but around Ruby, he's as gentle as a colt. "She's always been my wife. Why would I need another? Hell, if I want to know somethin' I just go ask her. I don't need to look nothin' up. I go and ask Ruby, and she knows. I don't need no computer. I married one!"

Photographs of Jordan, including one that shows him young and black bearded, are tacked to the walls in a cluttered room where the couple sometimes receives visitors.

Some people say that all the cowboy heroes are gone. They say they've gone the way of the bison and the Plains Indian warriors. All extinct. All faded memories. But maybe not.

Out in No Man's Land—where the prairie stretches like an

ocean of earth, brush, and grass—at a place called Four Corners, there are still those old buildings full of six-guns and cobwebs, and those wild-eyed dogs. Out there in No Man's Land, there's still Jim and Ruby Jordan. They're there today. And when they're gone, there will be no more.

PRETTY BOY

*Alongside every outlaw who
survives beyond days hover this
nameless legion whom the law
does not know or may not touch.
Call them his protective angels
if you like.*

—Emmett Dalton,
When the Daltons Rode

 The first time anyone ever caught him stealing, Charley Floyd was not even ten years old. A box of fancy iced cookies was his downfall. Although Mamie Floyd regularly baked enough sugar and oatmeal cookies to overflow a big dishpan, there was always something special about getting store-bought treats. Later on, as a grown man, Charley was not able to remember exactly how old he had been at the time he stole those cookies, but he damn sure never forgot getting nailed red-handed.

That first incident took place in Sallisaw at a grocery store owned and operated by J. H. Harkrider, a respectable fox hunter and merchant who came to Indian Territory from Arkansas in 1899. Harkrider was not just another middle-aged shop clerk with an apron tied around his soft belly. He could take care of himself. He had the ability to talk drunken Indians into surrendering their gun belts and sometimes their whiskey. When he was a younger man running a shoe and harness business, Harkrider had repaired a saddle for Henry Starr, one of the territory's most notorious outlaws. He remembered that Starr was "in every way a perfect gentleman." When the storekeeper heard people "talking about how mean and ugly" Starr was, Harkrider "just told them that they didn't know what they were talking about for that was all lies."

In the decade after Oklahoma's statehood, Sallisaw was still as wild and woolly as an unbroken mustang. According to an old account, there were so many gun battles in the streets on a single afternoon that Harkrider had to dive headlong into his bathtub three different times in order to stay clear of stray bullets whistling through the windows. With all the troublesome cowboys and tough farmhands he dealt with through the years, Harkrider did not even think that the Floyd boy he caught snitching sweets from his store would one day be branded as America's public enemy number one.

        MICHAEL WALLIS

"I had some little cakes and cookies in boxes and they kept disappearing," Harkrider remembered many years later. "I marked some of the boxes and watched to see where they went."

Soon enough, Charley Floyd rambled into the store. He was all alone. The youngster stood around for a few minutes, perused the neat rows of canned goods and bins of dried beans, ran his fingers over the counter tops, and then left. As soon as Charley slipped out the door, Harkrider, who had been watching the lad like a hawk, swooped down on the cookie boxes and found that one was missing from the shelf.

"I got an officer and we went around to the alley and there was Charley Floyd eating some cookies. I asked him where he got the cookies and he admitted getting them out of my store after I showed him the mark. We tried to scare him up some and show him he shouldn't steal, and then we let him go."

As far as Harkrider was concerned, Charley had learned his lesson. The boy never stole anything else from him. At least, he was never caught again stealing in the store.

Charley tried to learn from mistakes and always did his level best to escape parental discipline, especially the wrath of his father. He wanted to keep his nose clean enough to stay on Walter Floyd's friendly side. That was no easy task. Walter could be stern and unbending. Even so, when his father was in a good mood, Charley liked to be in his company. The hunting and fishing outings with his father did not happen nearly often enough for the boy, however. Charley soon discovered that there was more to life in Oklahoma than summertime baptism celebrations, berry-picking parties, or pie suppers.

Work always came first. People cherished their share of good times, but the everyday rural experience was not always idyllic—far from it. Charley quickly figured that out, too. There was an abundance of bitterness that mingled with the sweetness. For every teaspoon of honey, there was a tablespoon of castor oil—sometimes a double dose. There were endless prayer meetings and monotonous school lessons for every snowball fight or game of marbles. Charley knew he would have to invest long hours sweating in the fields to make up for his more frivolous moments.

To be properly enjoyed, pleasure had to be earned. Before sitting down to a fine squirrel dinner, there needed to be a hunt. Sweet milk to wash down the slabs of hot gingerbread resulted from a trip to a barn in the early-morning darkness. Thick molasses did not just appear in the can by magic. That took some effort, too.

Community events such as quilting bees, hog slaughters, and barn raisings, were associated with struggle and strain. Dances and play parties came at the end of a strenuous week of work. Oklahomans at this time played hard but had to work even harder.

Out in the country, where the majority of people lived, the hands of the women and children were as calloused and rough as the men's. Farm life was harsh and demanding. There was nothing easy about it. Most families had to toil like peasants from sunrise to dusk in order to keep the wolf from the door. Among honest people, nobody was exempt from labor. If a youngster showed any promise or ambition, his elders said it was because the child had grit or spunk. There was no tolerance of sissies or malingerers, and no such thing as being allergic to hard work. Everyone was expected to pull together and do his or her share.

It was certain as sunup that nothing was free. That became clear to Charley when old man Harkrider and the town policeman caught him in the alley with the cookies. Likewise, it was true that a stolen watermelon could be sweet and juicy enough to risk a load of bird shot in the butt and legs, but before a boy slipped beneath a fence with a melon tucked under his arm, at least for an instant, he weighed the consequences of getting caught in the act. Playing hooky from school, skinny-dipping at the creek, or laying up in the woods with cohorts to smoke corn silks usually resulted in extra hours spent cutting kindling, scrubbing chalkboards, and a good country whipping to boot.

Charley and the other rough-and-tumble farm youngsters were raised with an old saying: One had to pay for the piper if one wanted to dance. That single maxim was ingrained in them as much as all four Gospels and the Ten Commandments combined.

However, some of the boys of Charley's generation, like others before them, soon discovered that when it came to earning a living, not everyone chose to go to the cotton field or on cattle roundups—not by a long shot. The promise of slopping hogs was not enough to keep everybody on the farm. There were those who believed that they simply were not suited to honest labor. They stayed alive by operating on the other side of the law. They took up arms in order to steal from people, to rob banks, trains, and stores. Cattle and horses were routinely stolen. Sometimes during the perpetration of a crime, innocents were shot and even killed. Illegal whiskey was made and sold in the same deep woods where these fugitives hid. Some of these lawless people lived on the fringes. A few were able to keep a foot on both sides of the law. It was a difficult balancing act, though, and most of them eventually toppled and fell.

Folks who lived in Oklahoma recognized that it was a land conceived in violence, the last frontier of the outlaw. This was particularly true in eastern Oklahoma, called Indian Territory until statehood came in 1907. Even more than Oklahoma Territory to the west or the narrow panhandle strip known as No Man's Land, the eastern half of the Twin Territories acted as a true refuge for the lawless and untamed. These seemed to thrive there in great numbers.

When Charley and his family first came to Oklahoma, some of those old-school desperadoes, including that infamous bank robber Henry Starr, were still in business. Stories of hidden loot, gun battles, heroic deputy sheriffs turned outlaws, vigilante justice, and ruthless villains who met their Maker at the business end of a hemp rope fueled the imagination of Charley and his chums.

Most of these outlaw stories had been tampered with over the years. Lots of spice and garnish had been added. What had once been reasonably sound historic accounts were now seasoned with ample portions of hearsay and exaggeration and twisted into tall tales. Some were nothing more than pure country bunk. Bandits and outlaws were mythologized beyond recognition by dime novelists or by grandfathers who embellished their fireside yarns with each telling. Newspapers did little to help. Publishers and their reporters were not as concerned with accuracy as they were with selling papers. One day, the accused could be indicted in headlines, while the next day, the same ordinary thief might be made into an overnight celebrity. The public was confused. Fact and fiction merged uneasily. Reality was often as elusive as smoke.

In truth, outlaws had presented problems in Indian Territory from the very beginning. This was clear even in Georgia prior to the Indians' removal from their ancestral lands in the late 1830s. While still back in Georgia, the Cherokees were forced to employ a band of armed riders called regulators, whose mission, according to the tribal council, was "to suppress horse stealing and robbery, to protect the widows and orphans, and kill any accused person resisting their authority." Once the Cherokees and the four other so-called Civilized Tribes were forcibly moved to Indian Territory, similar groups called lighthorse companies were formed to preserve the peace and act as a shield against fugitives from justice who wandered into the lands.

Some of the Indians' lighthorsemen guarded the territorial

borders against the importation of diseased cattle, while others helped put down tribal insurrections. Almost all of them were particularly effective when it came to terrorizing white whiskey peddlers who crept into Indian Territory with their barrels of hooch. Among the Indian tribes, justice was sure and punishment swift. For example, those who were found guilty of stealing a horse or mule knew they would receive one hundred lashes on their bare backs. If they repeated their crime and were found guilty again, they also understood that they would go the way of convicted killers and rapists. That meant taking the long walk to the nearest gallows or a hanging tree.

For the most part, the members of the Five Tribes became prosperous farmers during the long period between their eviction from Georgia and other southern states and the outbreak of the Civil War. When the war came, however, it took its toll on the residents of Indian Territory. Although there was a definite division of allegiance among the Indian Nations, old blood ties made the southern influence strong. Many Indian slaveholders knew that they faced substantial investment loss if the Yankees won out. As a result, regiments of full and mixed bloods were mustered. They proudly carried the Confederate Stars and Bars into battle. Guerrilla bands also operated in the territory, including Colonel William Quantrill's dreaded raiders. Local renegades stole livestock and burned both Union and Confederate Indian villages, and pro-Confederate Cherokees destroyed military targets as well as the homes and barns of civilians who billeted enemy troops and stored their supplies.

After the war, there was not much improvement of conditions for the Indians. Punitive treaties schemed up in Washington during the period of Reconstruction diminished the holdings of the various tribal properties. The federal government transformed much of the land forcibly taken back from the Five Tribes into a dumping ground for other Indians, who were moved into the Twin Territories. Former slaves and vagabonds from Arkansas, Texas, and Missouri immigrated to Indian Territory and squatted on tribal lands. Many of these people raided the Indians' smokehouses and corncribs. Vigilante groups were formed to halt the rise in crime.

Besides the addition of more Indian residents and freedmen, white newcomers also entered the Indian Nations via a network of cattle trails, stage routes, and railroad tracks that crisscrossed the land. As postwar problems mounted, the Indian governments were left without adequate funds to maintain their law-enforcement efforts. Federal troops were too busy policing the western frontier to help out. Indian courts that had once been so effective were now in utter chaos and had no jurisdiction over the tidal wave of misfits who poured into Indian Territory.

The brush-covered hills, hidden caves etched in the river bluffs, and the chain of secluded towns all acted as meccas for criminals. Along with the droves of drifters, gamblers, and whores came murderers, rapists, and rustlers. If a man or woman was wanted by the authorities in his or her own state, all he or she had to do was mount up and "light out for the Nations." No questions were asked of strangers and there were no white man's courts to extradite the outlaws. The authority of the various tribes' light-horse forces applied only to Indian citizens. Indian Territory became known as a "robbers' roost," and its sinister reputation spread faster than fresh gossip at a church supper. A popular saying sprang up that fit the situation perfectly: "There's no Sunday west of St. Louis—no God west of Fort Smith." Tribal leaders and decent citizens could not agree more. They cried out for help.

Finally, in 1871, the federal government responded to these pleas by moving the Western Arkansas Federal District Court from Van Buren to Fort Smith, just one hundred yards east of the Indian Territory boundary line. A series of federal judges was brought in and charged with protecting the public by cleaning up the nearby breeding grounds of some of the most evil felons ever to pack a six-gun. However, most of the judges were either incompetent, corrupt, or inefficient. The situation did not improve in Indian Territory. A Fort Smith newspaper editorial, published in 1873, came right to the point: "It is sickening to the heart to contemplate the increase of crime in the Indian country . . . if crime continues to increase there so fast, a regiment of deputy marshals cannot arrest all the murderers."

Within two years, however, some changes for the better were made. The major adjustment came in 1875 when Isaac Charles Parker was named presiding judge at the burgeoning river town of Fort Smith. Parker was only thirty-six years old when he arrived at the courtroom, but he had a strong background in law and politics. He had been city attorney, district prosecutor, and district judge in St. Joseph, Missouri, and had put in two terms in Congress, representing a district in western Missouri that knew only too well the guerrilla escapades of Quantrill, Bloody Bill Anderson, and the James-Younger gangs.

A big, broad-shouldered man with piercing blue eyes, a

mustache, and a goatee, Parker was the youngest judge on the federal bench when he got the nod from President Ulysses S. Grant to rule the troubled court. Parker was an ardent Republican, a strict Methodist, and a careful student of the Bible. He believed that without exception the wicked should be punished to the letter of the law. On May 10, 1875, only eight days after he and his family arrived by steamboat at Fort Smith, the judge opened his first term of court. Out of eighteen persons brought before him on murder charges during that initial session, fifteen were convicted. Eight of them were given death sentences.

The very first murder trial he presided over ended in a swift conviction. Parker delivered a lengthy condemnation of the prisoner, but instead of telling the man he would be hanged "until dead," the judge emphasized the convict's fate by declaring, "I sentence you to hang by the neck until you are dead, dead, dead!" Parker did not hesitate in doling out death sentences, and more often than not, the condemned also received Scripture lessons, long lectures, and was urged to repent before he met his Maker. Parker's closing words to each sentenced prisoner were the same: "Farewell forever until the court and you and all here today shall meet together in the general resurrection."

Parker's draconian style won him national acclaim. Newspaper reporters came from all over the country to see Parker in action and hear his pronouncements. The law-abiding citizens and outlaws alike soon dubbed him "the Hanging Judge," a nickname he despised. Others called him "Bloody" Parker and "Butcher" Parker. Actually, the execution chores were left to George Maledon, a capable hangman with long whiskers and deep-set eyes who took great pride in his work. Maledon became a familiar sight on the streets of Fort Smith, usually carrying a basket that contained the handwoven hemp rope he so deftly used at the gallows. Each rope was handwoven in St. Louis and was soaked with a pitchy oil to prevent the hangman's knot, with its thirteen wraps, from slipping. This ensured a quick death for the black-hooded convicts. Of the seventy-nine criminals who swung limply from the Fort Smith gallows, Maledon's handiwork sent sixty of them to eternity. This number included the first six-man hanging ever, considered his masterpiece. When he finally retired as a hangman, Maledon toured country towns and cities with one of his treasured ropes and lectured about the lives and consequent deaths of many of the culprits he had executed in the name of law and order.

"I've never hanged a man who came back to have the job done over," Maledon quipped without the hint of a smile. "The ghosts of men hanged at Fort Smith never hang around the old gibbet." Like the judge he served, Maledon earned a sobriquet all his own. The severe Bavarian native was called the Prince of Hangmen. Posted over his well-used scaffold was a sign that read THE GATES OF HELL.

In order to mete out his brand of punishment and to restore peace and tranquillity to Indian Territory, Parker appointed two hundred deputy marshals to ride for him. They were to bring all wrongdoers to the dungeons at Fort Smith, which became known as "Hell on the Border." Certainly not all those who served Parker and the court were angels. Several of them had been either brigands themselves or would later resort to the life of an outlaw. The righteous Parker had to swallow hard and sometimes even turn the other way. As he put it, he was "obliged to take such material for deputies as proved efficient in serving the process of this court." Although Parker had to permit some rascals and questionable characters to represent him in the field, there was one kind of man he could never tolerate. No marshal who was a coward was allowed to venture out into the Indian country.

The tough lawmen who rode west out of Fort Smith had to cover more than 74,000 square miles, an area about the size of New England. It was at best a difficult assignment. Nonetheless, Judge Parker required that his men risk their lives to patrol the Nations and serve arrest warrants. "Bring them in alive or dead" was the standing order, but the officers tried their damnedest to return with live prisoners in order to collect all the mileage expenses and fees due them. Deputies were paid no salaries but received six cents a mile travel pay while on official business and a flat fee of two dollars a head for every criminal brought in alive. They depended for the balance of their income on rewards offered for the most sought-after felons.

Courageous deputies such as Paden Tolbert, David Rusk, Willard Ayers, Dave Layman, and many others took an oath to serve Parker and his court. At least one-third of Parker's total force of lawmen died in the line of duty. The best-known of Parker's deputies were Bill Tilghman, a former buffalo hunter and Dodge City marshal; Heck Thomas, a Confederate veteran who was twelve when he fought under Robert E. Lee; and Chris Madsen, a Dane who had served with the French Foreign Legion in Africa and the U.S. Cavalry in the far West. This intrepid trio was called the

Three Guardsmen. They were the top guns of all "the Men Who Rode for Parker," as the deputies called themselves.

During the late 1880s and early 1890s, new federal laws were passed that stripped away large portions of Parker's jurisdiction. As the Indian Territory's population increased, more courts were needed to meet the demands. The judge's critics, including the eastern press, which called him "harsh, cruel, and tyrannical," also helped bring about the end of his long legal career. Finally, in September 1896, after the balance of his jurisdiction was taken from him, Parker retired. It had been twenty-one years since he had first come to Fort Smith. His dark hair and beard were now totally white, and although he was only a month shy of turning fifty-eight, he looked like a man of at least seventy. He died two months later on November 17, 1896, from a heart attack, and was buried at the national cemetery at Fort Smith, just a few blocks from his courtroom and gallows.

Like most other country boys of his day, Charley Floyd was well acquainted with the story of "Hanging Judge" Parker and his band of deputy sheriffs. Charley was mesmerized with the old Indian Territory legends of the pursued and those who chased them. Charley especially liked hearing about the ones on the other side of the law.

He knew by heart the escapades of Jesse and Frank James, Belle Starr—"the Bandit Queen"—the Daltons, the Youngers, Bill Doolin, and all the other desperate men and women who had operated for many years in and around the Oklahoma hills where the Floyds grew cotton and corn. Those old desperadoes, shrouded in cobwebs and fantasy, made potent dreams for the young cookie thief. They became Charley's legacy.

▼▼▼

It never ceased to amaze Charley Floyd how only a swig of moonshine whiskey—clear as a newborn baby's piss—could loosen the tongue of any storyteller. Just a touch of corn liquor did the trick. It generally improved the telling of an outlaw tale, an Indian myth, or the high times of a fox hunt.

A good dose of home-brewed whiskey made the story—whether it was an escape by Jesse James or the flight of a white-tailed deer—much richer. Invariably, the stolen loot hidden in a cave doubled, the hanged man at the end of the rope twitched longer, and the painted whores of Fort Smith and Tulsa were prettier. A few more sips and the fighting cock that killed all the other roosters turned meaner; the catfish that managed to slip off the hook grew larger. And, upon reflection, the last batch of whiskey cooked up in the woods was the smoothest by a country mile.

Making corn whiskey was one of Walter Floyd's favorite pursuits. Drinking it was another. Like his neighbors and friends with ties to the Old South, Walter knew how to turn out decent sipping liquor. So did his brothers and their father before them and both of their grandfathers and their uncles and cousins. So did Walter's sons. He taught them about distilling whiskey just as he showed them how to shoot and fish, read signs in the woods, and track game. It was part of their way of life.

Whiskey resulted from the distillation of fermented grain mash. It originated in twelfth-century Ireland, where it was considered the "water of life." The early Floyds back in Wales discovered not a small amount of pleasure in a dram of whiskey aged in wooden barrels. No doubt they brought the distiller's art with them when they sailed to America. In Britain, King Charles II was the first to impose a tax on distilled spirits back in the 1600s. That action eventually resulted in the word *moonshiner* entering the language as a term for those who smuggled liquor past the tax collectors under the cover of darkness. In time, the whiskey smugglers became known as bootleggers, since they literally tucked small bottles of whiskey in their boot tops. Moonshining was then understood to be the act of distilling illicit whiskey.

Many early Scotch-Irish immigrants who came to America and settled in the southern Appalachian Mountains spent hours perfecting the practice of making whiskey. Various grains, including rye, wheat, and barley, could be used to produce whiskey, but in the mountains of Georgia and throughout most of southern Appalachia and the Ozarks, corn was the preferred ingredient. To avoid paying an excise tax on the whiskey, distillers operated on the sly. The timeless secrets for making Georgia Moon—also known as "white lightning," "panther's breath," "old bust head," "tiger's sweat," "woods whiskey," "rotgut," "mountain dew," "blue ruin," "ruckus juice," and "stump likker"—were passed down from father to son. Boys learned the three basic whiskey-making steps—mashing, fermentation, and distillation—just as the girls were taught how to make lye soap or apple butter.

There were significant differences between moonshine and quality bourbon, a type of whiskey perfected by a Baptist minister in eighteenth-century Bourbon County, Kentucky. Fancy bourbon came from a mash containing less corn, and it also had to be aged for two years in charred oak barrels. Most moonshine was, in fact, corn whiskey made from a mash that contained at least 80 percent corn. It had a sharp taste, but because there was little or no aging, there was no taste or color from a barrel. Moonshine was yellowish or white. Most of the southern moonshiners, including Georgians and their descendants mixing mash in the woods of Oklahoma, made nothing but gallon after gallon of potent corn whiskey. They left the bourbon making to their Kentucky cousins.

In the days before Oklahoma's statehood, a Whiskey Trail was created in Indian Territory complete with hideouts and grazing fields used by bandits and whiskey runners alike to pasture their horses. Whiskey stills were scattered throughout the Cookson Hills of Indian Territory. There were plenty of streams and creeks, and the bluffs and deep hollows were ideal for those who chose to "farm in the woods." Along with statehood in 1907, however, prohibition was one of the so-called reforms that was adopted. Oklahoma—the forty-sixth state—entered the Union as dry as a bone. The law forbade the manufacture, transportation, and possession of intoxicants. Despite the ban on liquor and the strength of such powerful pressure groups as the Oklahoma Anti-Saloon League and the Woman's Christian Temperance Union, the dry state of Oklahoma remained moist, and even sopping wet in some quarters, thanks to the diligent efforts of moonshiners and bootleggers.

Making whiskey was not merely illegal as far as the government was concerned; it was a moral crime, as well. The venerable practice of producing and selling corn liquor continued despite protestations from those with temperance on their minds, who claimed strong drink would prove to be the country's downfall. They scowled and thrust accusatory fingers at those who made the prohibited whiskey and beer or patronized the bootleggers. They pitied the wife and prayed for the children who noticed that their father's personality was slightly altered after he paid a visit to the outhouse and stopped along the way to nip at the jar of homemade liquor stashed in the barn. They considered strong drink to be the telltale sign of a malignant society. They suggested that as long as bootleg whiskey was readily available, and those who drank it went to dances, school, and church, there would be trouble. Nothing was better than a whiff of whiskey to get tongues clucking. To the righteous and the zealous, all strong drink—including blackberry brandy, grape wine, and homemade beer—were the devil's brew. Along with dancing and card playing, alcohol was to blame for the corruption of their sons and daughters. It was the very manifestation of evil.

Despite such harsh sentiments, even some of the strictest of Baptists and Methodists found a way to justify the distilling and consumption of spirits. Some of them pointed out that strong drink was mentioned throughout the Bible. Noah carried wine aboard the ark, and according to the Good Book, one of his first acts after the floodwaters subsided was to plant a vineyard, make some wine, and get good and pickled. Psalm 104:15 spoke of essentials such as oil for light, bread for strength, and "wine that maketh glad the heart of man." A little nip now and then never hurt anybody. After all, some reasoned, had not St. Paul prodded Timothy to "drink no longer water, but use a little wine for thy stomach's sake and thine own infirmities"? Jesus himself turned cold water into wine at a wedding party and he also served it at his last meal the evening before he was crucified. A few wet proponents even ventured that the Lord might have offered his disciples some moonshine had the divine beverage been in existence in those days.

Whiskey surely served as a balm that helped restore a working man's spirit after a crop failed or a child died. It was a salve for troubled souls. It was also a hair shirt for the penitent. Getting drunk on Saturday night provided the wayward with a cathartic experience for the Sabbath. Standing there before God and his neighbors in a hot church with the windows raised, a man with a pounding head and a soul riddled with guilt could let the lyrics of the hymn written by a reformed eighteenth-century slave trader wash his sins away.

> Amazing grace! how sweet the sound,
> that saved a wretch like me!
> I once was lost but now am found,
> was blind but now I see.

It was a song with no guile, and became the basis for all southern folk music. It was a song that was at once joyful and melancholy. It was a song that brought smiles and tears. At least twenty minutes were required to get through the entire hymn. By the time all five verses had been sung, the burden of sin and sorrow was lifted from the shoulders of even the most profane.

Through many dangers, toils, and snares,
I have already come;
'tis grace that brought me safe thus far,
and grace will lead me home.

Afterward, the repentant sinner, with wet eyes and the re-newed love of Jesus in his heart, could look forward to the Wednesday-evening prayer meeting as well as the Saturday card game, or an evening coon hunt, when he would once again tumble off the wagon.

All religious implications and powers of reconciliation aside, whiskey acted as an economic commodity for many country peo-ple. It had a definite practical value. Those farmers who boot-legged and sold or traded corn liquor by the gallon considered their whiskey production to be another cash crop. Selling jars of moonshine helped keep oil in the lamps and food in the pantry. Many rural citizens thought of moonshining and bootlegging as respectable businesses.

A clay jug, or at least a quart-size fruit jar or two brimming with fresh whiskey, was standard fare at many social events such as weddings, political rallies, hog butcherings, or even funerals. For dances held at homes back in the hills, fiddlers in clean overalls, arriving on horseback and with the promise of a free supper on their minds, knew they would also get a few snorts of corn liquor out in the dark. A drink or two enabled them to rasp out one tune after another that kept folks dancing until the wee hours. Whiskey was also doled out as medicine to break fevers. Mixed with honey, hot water, and tea to make a toddy, whiskey brought relief from pesty chest colds. Mothers rubbed it on the gums of teething babies to ease their pain. A dash of the stuff settled nerves, fought off chills, brought relief to aching bones, and allowed a good night's rest for the elderly.

Most of all, whiskey was an essential ingredient at all fall and winter hunts. Corn whiskey was as important as the pack of dogs, as necessary as the guns and the bright hunter's moon lighting the night sky. Moonshine was as comforting as the bonfire the hunters stoked with squaw wood and half-truths while their hounds chased coons and 'possums to the tops of sycamores and oaks. When the wild geese passed high in the heavens and the air was cold enough for a hunter to see his own breath, a spot of strong drink went a long way.

Folks said that whiskey "helps to kill the poison in the night air." Some geezers out cutting timbers for railroad ties took drinks from a freshly made batch and explained that the whiskey protected them from snakebites. They would wink and take another long tug, even though they knew that if they were ever bitten by a cottonmouth moccasin or a rattlesnake, the alcohol would cause the venom to surge through their system faster than ever.

There were probably more recipes and techniques for cooking whiskey than there were for making peach pie or cream gravy. Although the basic steps were always the same, each moonshiner had his own special and mostly secret method for producing corn whiskey. No two men distilled white liquor in quite the same way. Each one was proud of his own particular formula. Whenever an especially mellow batch was distilled, even the most discriminating drinkers would not turn up their noses at a jigger of 'shine. "If it's older than a year, the mellowness will make you breathe deep and happily" is how one master moonshiner explained it. "If it's stilled less than a month, there's a zip that curls around your neck when you sniff it."

When he was still a boy, Charley Floyd became familiar with the smell of cooking mash on the breeze. He knew that only a novice at whiskey sniffing would place his nose closer than two inches from the mouth of a jug or jar when trying to determine the age and quality of some moonshine. Walter taught him to select the best corn and to cull out the rotten and discolored grains. He learned how to turn out the corn malt that came from changing the starch of the corn into sugar and he found out about hurrying the process by burying sacks of unground corn in the manure pile, where it was always good and warm. Once the corn sprouted, it was dried and ground into a coarse meal called corn grits, or "chop." Water and sugar were added, and the mixture was made into a mush called sweet mash. The mash was allowed to stand in a barrel in a warm place for several days and ferment, and then it was thinned out with more water. Again the concoction was covered and ripened some more until the sweet mash soured as the sugar changed to alcohol. Now the time was right to distill.

Out in the Oklahoma hills, it was said that an experienced moonshiner actually listened to the mash. He knew it was ripe and time to cook in the still when it sounded like side pork in a pan. Farmers had no way actually to test the strength or the proof of their whiskey, and so in order to measure the alcoholic content, they relied on their own judgment, years of experience, and a simple procedure. When a moonshiner shook a jar of fresh whiskey and the foam, or the "bead," rose in small bubbles about the size of number-five bird shot, the proof was just right. "This stuff holds a purty good bead," a moonshiner would tell his friends. If instead the bead would not stand up and remained full of big, loose bubbles that looked like bulging frog eyes, the moonshiner knew he had whiskey that was unworthy of putting in a clean fruit jar. "I don't believe this here beads so good," a moonshiner would then say.

While the old Georgia-bred moonshiners religiously went through the time-tested steps for making corn whiskey, some of the younger bucks thought that process was slow and too much trouble. This younger generation born with the new century looked for a shortcut. Some did not even use corn, and few, if any, used corn chops. Instead, they made powerful alcohol that had the kick of a mule by using only water, yeast cakes, and plenty of sugar and bran. They could turn out a fresh batch every few days. A handful of oak chips thrown in provided a little odor and gave the liquor an aged look. Some of the country folks called this one-hundred-proof whiskey, made with only a small amount of corn to start fermentation, "sugar liquor" or "sugar jack." It may not have tasted quite like Georgia Moon, but the end result after consumption was the same. The fiddle music whined just as sweetly, the girls appeared just as comely, and the headache was every bit as mean. And the morning after a jar of that stepped-up moonshine was drained, the poetry of "Amazing Grace" would still make a band of angels weep.

After the first batch of bran or corn whiskey was run off, any respectable moonshiner knew that the "singlings," a cloudy liquid corrupted with pollutants, had to be purified and the still pot thoroughly cleaned before a second run could be made. Spent mash, or the slop, was thrown out in the barnyard and emptied into feed troughs. It often made roosters that imbibed it fall down dead drunk. Likewise, it soothed cattle that managed to get a snootful. Once the slop was pitched, the pot was washed out with some of the unstrained sour beer, or the "choc," that was left in the mash barrel. A good many folks were satisfied by just drinking the murky choc. It was considered a neighborly gesture to put some in a jar and offer it to thirsty friends who came calling.

The word *choc* no doubt came from Choctaw beer, originally a synthetic drink made of barley, hops, tobacco, fishberries, and a small amount of alcohol, which had been schemed up in the old days of the Choctaw Nation. For many years, the law had made it illegal to sell or manufacture choc beer, but the prohibition statutes were often ignored. Wives from the mining communities that dotted Oklahoma supplemented their husbands' wages by selling the beer. It seemed miners especially enjoyed sipping choc. They swore by the renegade brew and insisted it was an essential tonic for their good health. In the oil-field camps—frequented by bootleggers, gamblers, and two-bit whores—a basic 120-proof alcoholic drink that was colored with tobacco juice or creosote was a favorite. Choc beer and "Jamaican" gin—nothing but raw alcohol flavored with gingerroot or bitters—were also much-sought-after intoxicants. Those who invested their paychecks at the saloons and barrelhouses or with the local bootlegger often were stricken with "jake leg," a paralysis caused by the consumption of too much strong liquor. Men with muscles hard as walnuts shrugged it off as an occupational hazard.

When Charley visited his mother's kinfolk in the mining district around McCurtain, Oklahoma, he watched the men guzzle choc beer after they had scrubbed the coal dust from their hands and faces. They claimed the brew was better for them than the drinking water available in the area. Sometimes they gave the growing boy sips from their jars. Back home in Sequoyah County, out among the post oaks and brush, Charley developed a taste for this cloudy ferment that was found in the bottom of the mash barrel. He dipped out cups of choc and slurped it down every chance he got.

One afternoon when Charley and his big brother, Bradley, were tending their father's still, they noticed that a stud horse was having a difficult time breeding with a young mare in a nearby pasture. Charley watched for a few minutes and came up with a clever solution. He reached into the bottom of the choc barrel, whistled the mare to him, and slapped a handful of the mash on the skittish horse's rear end. In an instant, the frustrated stallion mounted the ripe mare and, with the help of the lubricant, drove it home as smooth as satin. The sight of the big stallion snorting over the filly made Charley grin, and Bradley saw to it that the story of his brother helping the horses get together spread faster than heat lightning.

Charley Floyd's taste for wild beer, along with his ingenuity at playing Cupid with a pair of amorous horses, created a nickname for the farm boy that some people, mostly his running buddies, called him from his early teens until his death.

Choc Floyd is what they would say when they saw him riding lickety-split on a hell-bent horse down a dirt farm road with the wind at his back: "Here comes Choc Floyd."

NEAR CLARKSON, OHIO
OCTOBER 22, 1934

Charley Floyd ran for the trees and the freedom that lay beyond. If he could just get across the field of corn stubble to the tree line, he would be safe. The weeds and the wild grapevines, the honeysuckle and the brambles would grant him yet another reprieve. He would race into the woods and down the slopes, up the steep hills and across the crumbling masonry of abandoned canal locks filled with water from the recent autumn rain.

He was known to some as the Sagebrush Robin Hood, to others as the Phantom Terror. But he was most commonly called Pretty Boy Floyd—public enemy number one. He was invincible, and he always got away.

The weather was warm on this October afternoon. Charley's white shirt and silk underwear were soiled and sweaty, and he needed a shave and bath. His dark blue suit was stained and covered with hundreds of tiny thistles, Spanish needles, which ran the length of his sleeves and trousers. He was a country boy dressed in a city slicker's clothes. A farmer's wife had given him ginger cookies and apples that morning, and he stuffed them in his suit coat pockets. He grasped a .45 pistol in one hand, while his other pistol was tucked in the top of his trousers.

Just moments before, he had chatted with Stewart Dyke and his wife, Florence. The farm couple had kindly agreed to give him a lift up the road a ways in their automobile, away from the farm owned by Dyke's sister, Ellen Conkle. Charley had passed an hour with Mrs. Conkle. She had just fed him a hot meal. Inside the farmhouse, she still held the dollar bill the stranger had insisted she take in exchange for the plate of spareribs. Ellen Conkle watched him wolf down the dinner she had prepared. He sat in a rocking chair on her porch and ate in silence. Afterward, she saw him pacing around, waiting for Stewart and his wife to finish with their cornhusking. Charley fingered the keys in the car's ignition, deciding not to steal the machine. He waited for the farmer to come along.

MICHAEL WALLIS

Just before the Dykes walked out of the cornfields, Charley pulled out his pocket watch. It was almost four o'clock in the afternoon. Sunset was about an hour and a half away. He stared at the fifty-cent piece attached to the watch fob. Ellen recalled that he smiled when he rubbed some dirt off the cameo ring he wore. No one knows, but perhaps he thought about Ruby, or Dempsey, or the cotton fields of Oklahoma and the times before he went on the scout.

An airplane, an unusual sight in those parts in 1934, droned overhead. Charley turned his face toward the cloudy sky. The rains of the past few days had disappeared, and even though it was deep into autumn, there were smells of new life in the woods where the maples showed their true colors. Soon, killing frosts would give way to snow that would enrich the land.

Ellen Conkle watched as the stranger climbed into the backseat. Her sister-in-law got up front as Ellen's brother started his automobile. They waved good-bye, and she went back to the kitchen chores. Suddenly, she heard machines driving up to the front of her house and the sound of car doors slamming shut. When she looked out the window again, she saw a band of men in suits, carrying guns. They began fanning out over her property. The stranger jumped from her brother's car behind the corncrib and began his run across the field toward the trees.

The run only lasted a few seconds. It must have seemed forever to Charley. Maybe it was like one of those dreams, filled with monsters, that seem to last forever in slow motion. Many years later, a federal agent remembered that Charley ran like an athlete, that he cut and dodged in a broken field sprint. Cookies and apples fell from his pockets and bounced on the ground. Someone yelled for him to halt. Then gunfire erupted and the bullets bounced up puffs of dust around his feet. He ran on toward the trees.

He gulped in mouthfuls of freedom as he ran.

Chester Smith, a policeman from East Liverpool and a sharpshooter who had proudly fought in France and Belgium, knew the man running away was Charley. There was no doubt in his mind.

It was now ten minutes past four. Smith shouldered his .32–20 Winchester rifle. He took aim at the man running in zigzags across the field. When he had Charley in his sights, Smith wrapped his finger around the trigger. He took a breath and held it. He slowly squeezed.

12

AN ALL-AMERICAN
SPIRITUAL WARRIOR

*The fear of death follows from
the fear of life. A man who lives
fully is prepared to die at any
time.*

—Edward Abbey,
A Voice Crying in
the Wilderness

 Joe Don Looney died on a gentle curve. Nobody could figure out just how the accident happened. He was on his motorcycle riding full tilt into the wild west Texas wind on Highway 118, a two-lane ribbon of asphalt that stretches due south across an ageless land toward the Big Bend country and the Rio Grande. He had already passed through the most dangerous portion of the route when he lost control. The big motorcycle left the road, raced down the soft shoulder, and crashed through a barbed-wire fence, snapping cedar posts like they were twigs. Joe Don was hurled through time and space.

They found him when the dust had settled and everything was still. He was lying face up beneath a mesquite tree. Arms at his side, legs straight out, he looked as if he were catnapping. But Joe Don was stone dead. His trachea was crushed, his head at an odd angle. There were no disfiguring wounds and no witnesses except for silent desert creatures. There was hardly a trace of blood.

Maybe a flight of doves caught his eye. Maybe he pulled over to let a pickup truck pass. Maybe it was the sun or the wind. No matter about the maybes. Whatever caused him to run off the road, Joe Don didn't fight it. He didn't try to lay down the powerful machine. He squared off with death just as he faced every moment of life—head-on and no pulled punches. He ended his time on earth at peace with himself and all those whose lives he touched. The undertaker said there was the start of a smile on his face. "I know what Joe Don said at that exact moment when it was clear he was going to die," said Dorothy Looney, his mother. "He just looked up at the sky and said, 'Is this it? Is this what it's like? God, I'm ready.' "

The news flashed around the country: Joe Don Looney, the former great college and professional football halfback and punter whose exploits on and off the gridiron were legend, was no more. Football's "Marvelous Misfit" had finally met his match. "I was very shocked and felt his life might have been a little better," said Bud Wilkinson, who tried to coach Looney at the University of Oklahoma. "He was an unusual person."

Unusual but never ordinary. In a two-year span in the 1960s, Joe Don was an all-American at the University of Oklahoma and a number-one NFL draft choice. In 1973 the *New York Times* called him "a handsome devil with Arrow collar features. . . . He threw a block like a house falling down. He could catch passes. He was a superb punter. He had it all—from the neck down."

For his obituary the sports scribes dredged up the countless Looney stunts and escapades. They wrote of the doors he kicked in and recounted the brawls. They talked about his scrapes with the law and years spent wandering the world. They interviewed old coaches who claimed they had tried but failed to control him. Most of them shook their heads and said it was too bad Joe Don had wasted his great athletic talent and ruined his life. They figured they knew the man so well. They said he was a maniac, an eccentric who searched but never found himself. None of them realized they missed the mark by a country mile.

When family and friends gathered for Joe Don's funeral in Alpine, the closest town to the remote retreat he called home, there was much sorrow. But the grieving there wasn't for the dead. Tears flowed for the living. The void Joe Don left behind was bigger than all of the great outdoors.

For Joe Don Looney was more than a rampaging jock from the tumultuous 1960s plagued by a "bad boy" image. Like Diogenes, the Greek philosopher who scorned convention as he searched for honesty, Joe Don was a truth seeker unable to abide the hypocrisy he encountered both in big-time sports and the world at large. "People say he was a Jekyll and Hyde type," said Janine Sagert, Looney's best friend. "He wasn't that at all. Joe Don was always Joe Don. There was no split personality. He was just painfully honest. So many people never did realize that simple fact."

Born October 10, 1942, in San Angelo, Texas, Joe Don was a pure Libra child. Independent and sensitive, even as a boy he treasured truth and justice more than profit, happiness more than fame. His mother, Dorothy, was a Texas beauty from an old ranching clan. His father, Don, the son of a poor dirt farmer, was a football star at Texas Christian University in the 1930s. Don Looney went on to play with the Philadelphia Eagles and became an NFL official for twelve years while building a prosperous oil business. The Looneys were a blend of quintessential western breeding, good looks, physical prowess, and money. Joe Don was their only child. "My son was no angel—he was a real boy," said Don Looney, "but he always had so much to offer, so much to give. He was different. A lot of folks just didn't understand him."

It was clear early in Joe Don's life that misunderstanding was to follow him wherever he went. Caught in a cross fire between a daddy who wanted his son to excel at football and a mama who didn't want her boy's natural good looks marred, Joe Don developed what some folks termed an "attitude problem" toward authority figures while still an undersized school kid. "Joe Don could never stand a phony," said Dorothy Looney. "Even though he was a child, he had the ability to see right through people who didn't deal in the truth."

While his parents argued about his playing football, Joe Don began working out with weights. By the time he was ready for high school, his body and his speed were both well developed. But instead of pulling on a jersey and pads, Joe Don was chosen to be a cheerleader, a job most macho westerners figured to be girl's work. "Somebody has to do it," he told his disappointed father. To ease the sting, Joe Don made the track team and played baseball.

After a brief stint at a Florida military academy, Joe Don returned to Fort Worth and Paschal High School where in his senior year he gained a reputation as a star running back and a hothead. Once Joe Don supposedly chased a Golden Gloves boxer who became so terrorized that he locked himself in a car trunk to escape. In one version of the story, Joe Don's fury burned so hot that he bought a quart of beer from a convenience store, splashed it on the car, then leaned over the trunk and told the cowering pugilist inside that it was gasoline.

Joe Don came by his combative spirit naturally. The Looney family had had its share of contrary ancestors. Great-grandfather Looney down in Alabama had been so opposed to slavery that he fought with the Union during the Civil War, and Joe Don's grandfather was a spry ninety-five when he knocked the hell out of a man during a nursing-home fistfight.

When Joe Don was ready for college, the long hours spent with barbells and slamming his fists into punching bags had paid off: He was in superb physical condition. Joe Don marched off to the University of Texas in Austin and promptly decided to try out for the track team. He also took time to flirt with fraternity life, make lousy grades, watch soap operas, swig beer, and break many a coed's heart with his Hollywood good looks. Looney lasted a semester. He never ran a lap. "Joe Don really wanted to run track at the University of Texas, but he found out he didn't like it there," said Don Looney. "So then he came home to go to Texas Christian and discovered he was ineligible and was going to have to sit out of sports for a while. That upset him."

Obsessed with physical fitness, Joe Don continued his regimen of marathon workouts and weight training. After a semester, he was ready to move on. That's when Joe Don met Leroy Montgomery, a straight shooter who treated his players fairly and like adults. He would be the only coach Looney ever really respected.

In September 1961, Montgomery—a native Okie who invested most of his life in the game as a player, coach, and professional scout—was running the football program at Cameron Junior College in Lawton, when he first heard Joe Don Looney's name. "I was in my office at Cameron, and I got a call from a guy down in Texas who told me he had a new player for my team," recalled Montgomery. "He said this Looney kid punted the hell out of the ball and ran like a deer. I told him to forget it, I already had enough talent. Then a half hour later, the phone rings again and it was Don Looney. He told me all about his son. He said he understood I had a full squad but he really wanted his boy to play for me. All I had to do was to give him a chance. He said he'd pick up the tab if the kid couldn't earn a scholarship. Couldn't refuse that offer. I told him to send Joe Don to me."

Joe Don was ecstatic about the prospect of playing for Cameron even though his initial meeting with Montgomery was less than cordial. "The evening Joe Don reported, it was raining and we moved practice inside the field house," said Montgomery. "He didn't show up on time, so I sent a boy to fetch him. When Joe Don finally walked in, I proceeded to chew on his ass for ten minutes—really ate him out. When I finished, I stuck out my hand and introduced myself. After that, I never had a bit of trouble with Joe Don. It was always 'Yes, sir' and 'No, sir.' I was honest with him and fair, and that's what I got back. That's all he ever wanted. My door was always open for Joe Don. He was as good a kid as I ever coached."

Don Looney never received a bill for his son's tuition. Joe Don became the school's leading runner and punter and led the team to an undefeated season and a 28-20 triumph over Bakersfield Junior College in the Little Rose Bowl in Pasadena. "He played in that game with a hurt knee that was so swollen he could only fit into practice pants," said Montgomery. "It looked funny in the game, but did that kid ever put out! He averaged more than forty yards a punt, including a fifty-two-yarder, made maybe a half-dozen saving tackles, and swept over Bakersfield's end for the winning touchdown. It was a tremendous effort on his part, but that's what I always got from Looney."

A shoo-in for junior college all-American, Joe Don—despite his reputation for being a nonconformist—found an abundance of major college recruiters sniffing around his door. But the one school that appealed to Joe Don above all the rest was Oklahoma, where Bud Wilkinson had built a football dynasty. Montgomery, aware that Looney would be the first junior college transfer to join the Sooners, strongly advised against Joe Don going to the big state university in Norman. "I told him those people weren't used to junior college players and that those boys had been playing together for a couple of years and he wouldn't fit in. But Joe Don was determined to go to Oklahoma. He had his mind made up, and that was that."

Joe Don appeared at Oklahoma's fall practice in 1962 and immediately got off to a poor start by refusing to pose for team photographs. He also avoided treatment in the training room and often arrived late to practice. But the strapping 207-pound halfback with blinding speed also turned heads whenever he came near a football.

The first game of the season established the Looney legend. Down three to zip against a tough Syracuse team with 2:57 left on the clock, Oklahoma was on the brink of defeat. Near the Sooner bench, Joe Don paced the sideline like a caged wolf. When he could stand it no longer, he walked up to Wilkinson and said, "Bud, put me in there, and I'll win this [game] for you."

Amazed that anyone, especially a newcomer, would talk to him in such a manner, much less call him by his first name, Wilkinson did as he was told. Looney, eyes glazed over, ran to the huddle. "Gimme that damned ball!" he ordered the quarterback. "I'm gonna score a touchdown." "I knew what play I was going to call when I went into the huddle," quarterback Monte Deere later said in the locker room, but "I just gave him the ball." On the next play from scrimmage, Joe Don delivered. He broke through the line, stumbled, and recovered, then turned on his speed and tore down the sideline. With the Sooner fans screaming their approval, Joe Don never looked back. He raced sixty yards for the winning touchdown. There was still 2:07 left to play.

Things were never quite the same at Oklahoma. For every big play made by Looney, there was a story. He finished the season leading the country in punting and gained 852 yards rushing to rank fifth nationally. He made all-conference and was selected for one all-America team. But even though he was a catalyst in the Sooners' drive to win Wilkinson his final Big Eight championship and a trip to the Orange Bowl, Looney's theatrics also caused him grief. He was a nonconformist in the days before it was fashionable. Just as Leroy Montgomery had predicted, Joe Don never meshed with most of the members of the Sooner team.

In *When All the Laughter Died in Sorrow*, his best-seller about the strange world of football, Lance Rentzel, another member of that Sooner team, talks about his friendship with Looney and the drudgery of playing for Wilkinson. "Practice was a series of drills that were as much fun as boot camp in the Marines," wrote Rentzel. "Wilkinson had a regimen that made us think we were prisoners on Devil's Island."

It was no place for a free spirit like Joe Don. Eventually, Looney found a pal in John Flynn, a 225-pound bad boy who some say egged Looney on from bad to worse. Rentzel, however, remembers it differently. "They were really tremendous," Rentzel said of Flynn and Looney. "They didn't give a damn about what others said or thought or pretended to think. They were completely themselves. They were very talented and tough."

That wouldn't, however, be enough to keep Joe Don at Oklahoma. For the 1963 season—Wilkinson's swan song at Oklahoma—Joe Don came back to campus beefed up to 227 pounds and faster than before. Word was Wilkinson didn't want Looney to return, but Joe Don told his coach that he had taken his advice and seen a psychiatrist during the summer. Joe Don worked hard those first few weeks, but it wasn't long before the coaches claimed they found Joe Don more independent and obstinate than ever. They said he'd become bored at practice and would skip workouts if he felt too tired. Joe Don countered that he knew his body better than the coaches. "Why run during the day when it's so hot?" questioned Looney. "I like to run early in the morning when it's dark and cool. It's much better for your body."

Despite the conflicts, Joe Don was wearing his familiar "33" when the season got under way that September. After rallying from behind to subdue Clemson 31-14 in the opener, Oklahoma took on defending NCAA champion and number-one-ranked Southern California. It was a sweltering afternoon in Los Angeles, and Joe Don sped into the end zone on a picture-perfect, nineteen-yard double reverse for the game's first TD. "There wasn't anybody around," Joe Don said after the 17-12 Oklahoma victory, which vaulted the Sooners into the number-one spot. "Everybody was layin' down."

The future finally appeared bright for Looney, but it only took a few days for Joe Don's star to turn into a comet. It came after the third game of the season—a 28-7 loss to arch rival and number-two-ranked Texas. That's when Wilkinson finally gave him the boot. The popular story was that Joe Don had punched out an assistant coach during an argument on the practice field. "Looney has been dismissed from the squad for disciplinary reasons," was Wilkinson's official comment on the matter. "It was just something that had to be done." Others disagreed.

"People are always talking about that punching business," said Don Looney. "First of all, it was during a scrimmage, and it was a student assistant coach who was holding a blocking dummy. This fella grabbed Joe Don by the face mask, and that's when Joe Don knocked him loose. He was provoked. You never ever grab a guy's face mask unless you want to get knocked on your ass."

Joe Don himself said that Wilkinson, his mind already on leaving the coaching profession to run for the Senate the next year, was upset about not winning a national championship following the humiliating Texas defeat, his sixth straight loss to Texas and its rising star of a coach, Darrell Royal. It was Royal, a former Sooner, who later won the 1963 national championship. Said Joe Don: "After he [Wilkinson] screwed that up, he needed a quick scapegoat, and the logical person was me. I punched that assistant before the Texas game. I think Wilkinson resented me being on the team from the start. I hadn't come up through the indoctrination program like the other guys. This made me an outsider."

Lance Rentzel backed up Joe Don's story. "He just didn't

have the patience to be a disciplined part of a team. If he didn't feel like it, he simply didn't work. Early in the season, before the Texas game, he was fooling around at practice and Coach Wilkinson said if he wasn't going to put out, he could just go on in. Joe Don looked at him and then called his bluff, I guess; he picked up his helmet and left. Wilkinson gestured for him to come back. . . . The other guys didn't appreciate the way Looney had defied the coach and gotten away with it. Wilkinson recognized this and kicked him off the squad a week later."

Joe Don's career at Oklahoma had lasted only fourteen games—longer than some of his critics had predicted. College days were over, but pro ball beckoned. Looney was a first-round draft pick by the New York Giants in 1964. Allie Sherman, the Giants' coach, was convinced he and veteran players like Y. A. Tittle and Frank Gifford could make Looney a team player. Dead wrong. At the Giants' training camp, Joe Don drew a quick fine when he refused to have his ankles taped before scrimmages. "I know my ankles better than you do," he told the amazed coaches. "It's better for them not to be taped. If you want to fine me, go ahead and fine me."

When Joe Don thought a meeting was unnecessary, he skipped it. He also cut practices without permission. Fined for missing curfew by ten minutes, Joe Don protested that he had checked in an hour earlier the previous night. "You owe me fifty minutes," he protested.

Don Chandler, then a veteran punter with the Giants, was Looney's roommate at camp. "They knew he was going to be a problem, so they put Joe Don with me because I was from Oklahoma. It was obvious that he was a young man with great physical talent who was not ready mentally to play the game—and not because he was dumb. He was anything but stupid. I found him quiet, and he kept to himself. But he just wouldn't conform to the rules. Playing games wasn't important to him, money wasn't important to him. Being himself was important to Joe Don."

Chandler remembers the day Y. A. Tittle, the Giants' star quarterback, tried to reason with Looney. "Tittle was practically old enough to be Joe Don's dad. He went in the room and closed the door, and we all waited outside. They were in there for a long time, and finally Tittle comes out shaking his head and smiling. He just looked at us and said, 'You know, I went in there to sway that kid, but I think he ended up swaying me.' "

Joe Don couldn't sway management. They soon grew weary of

him missing practices, ignoring the coaches, and refusing to learn the playbook. He was a loner and preferred reading Ayn Rand and listening to his stereo. "You felt like you were working with an unfinished song," said Allie Sherman. Joe Don lasted twenty-eight days with the Giants. Before the season even started, they traded him to the Baltimore Colts, where Looney went on to help Don Shula win the 1964 Western Conference championship.

But, like the others, Shula never got a handle on the unpredictable Joe Don. "I was afraid to put Looney in the game to punt," Shula later admitted to reporters, "because I didn't know if he would punt. He might do anything."

One afternoon during warm-ups, Looney showed his defiant side when he took a snap and kicked the football as high as he could straight up in the air. As he stood there, hands on his hips, watching the ball soar into the heavens, Joe Don yelled, "How do you like that, God?"

The *Saturday Evening Post* that year said Joe Don "runs like a wild horse, blocks like a marble tombstone, and punts with the power of a bazooka. The only trouble is, nobody knows for sure whether he's going to play the game or start throwing punches."

The Colts failed to break Looney's spirit. They shipped him off to the Detroit Lions, where coach Harry Gilmer predicted Looney would "save the franchise." The honeymoon was short-lived. During a heated contest with the Atlanta Falcons, Looney refused to carry a play to the Lions' huddle. "If you want a messenger," he told Gilmer, "then call Western Union." Joe Don was history in Detroit.

Next stop: Washington, D.C. Joe Don fared no better with the Redskins and coach Otto Graham. "He didn't know what he wanted," Looney said of Graham. "I could organize a practice better than he could." Joe Don's playing days were numbered.

Leon Cross, a Sooner cocaptain during Joe Don's OU days who still lives in Norman and works with the team, believes Looney was a casualty of his time. "In those days football was more of a team sport. You were taught the team always came first, and an individualist couldn't really fit in that model," says Cross. "Joe Don was one of the most talented athletes of his day, and that's why all the pro teams took chances on him. It's why they all tried. Every coach thought, 'I can handle him,' but none of them could.

"Joe Don was one of football's first rebels. He'd fit in very well today."

In 1968, Looney was told to report to a different kind of team—Uncle Sam's. Joe Don's Army Reserve unit was activated, and he received orders to go to Vietnam. Furious, he sued the federal government for breach of contract. To his mind, the government had the right to call men to active duty only in a war or national emergency. Vietnam didn't fit either definition. "In a national emergency," Looney said, "they wouldn't have to call me. I would be down there and ready to go. All we want to point out is that if the government can do this to us, think what it can do to the individual citizen. It takes a lot of guts to stand up for your rights in the Army. A lot of guys try to bribe the draft board or leave the country. . . . I said to myself, 'Joe, if you do that, then you're going to be just like all the people you don't like.' "

He finally reported for duty and promptly went AWOL for twenty-five days before reluctantly serving nine months in Vietnam guarding a fuel depot near the DMZ. Looney, like thousands of others, opposed the war. Vietnam was the last place he wanted to be. "In the Army he still looked out for the little guy," said his father. "He was like that all his life—always for the underdog." When another soldier was bullied by a bunch of GIs, Joe Don intervened. "He made an announcement in front of the whole bunch," said Don Looney, "if they wanted to whip up on the little fella, that was fine, but they were going to have to come through Joe Don first. The guy had no problems after that."

Joe Don's situation, however, got worse, and his refusal to carry a rifle didn't help matters. "What are you going to do, send me to Vietnam?" he asked his incredulous superiors.

When he came home, it was clear that more than the war was over for Joe Don. He felt disoriented and lost. "Joe Don was different when he got back from Vietnam," said Don Looney. "It was a long time before he could sleep at night." Joe Don played a final season with the New Orleans Saints before retiring because of a nagging injury. He also divorced his wife, Peggy, and left her and their daughter, Tara, on an east Texas farm. He was ready to launch an around-the-globe odyssey in order to restore his faith in the world.

He went to Hong Kong with a boyhood friend and bought a sailboat. He experimented with drugs and investigated a variety of religions. He fasted for forty days. He lived in South America for a while. He was jailed for possession of marijuana. He was implicated but cleared in a plot to murder a Texas judge. He became a vegetarian, gave himself enemas, and dropped seventy pounds. He began to read Nietzsche and Hesse as well as Spinoza and John Milton and Ganai Yoga. He kept looking for the truth.

After years of wandering and self-examination, Joe Don was at the end of his rope. His search for truth seemed hopeless. He could find no remedy for his anger, brought on by the dishonesty he encountered everywhere.

Then in 1975 Joe Don met Swami Muktananda at the Houston airport. The sage from India was touring the states, and Joe Don understood that Muktananda taught that inner peace comes through meditation. Looney went to hear the simple message and was immediately mesmerized. The reception room at the airport was filled with people bearing gifts for Baba, as his followers called Muktananda. Looney had nothing. "All I have for you is the love from my heart," said Joe Don. The Indian holy man nodded, and Joe Don turned to leave. Then Baba spoke. "The heart is the most valuable possession," he said. Joe Don stopped and whirled around. He knew he had found at last an honest man whose love and acceptance of other people were unconditional.

Baba was the best experience for Joe Don since he was a kid playing his heart out for Leroy Montgomery. Sitting with Baba and watching him, Joe Don began to at last comprehend the full range of human potentiality. He gave up drugs and became a devotee. Like Joe Don, Baba possessed the spontaneity of a child as well as the wisdom of a man who had found the answers to all his questions. "There was always an emptiness in me until I met Baba," said Joe Don. "He tells you to love yourself and see God in each other. I had everything, but I just wasn't happy until I found Baba."

Joe Don followed Muktananda on a spiritual journey to India. There Joe Don was given the job of caring for Vijay, a rogue elephant. It was a humbling and often dangerous assignment—cleaning up giant piles of elephant dung and washing a beast as headstrong as its keeper. Baba knew just what he was doing. Joe Don tried to work with the temperamental elephant, but the animal was as mean as a big-time linebacker. Looney would become frustrated and slam his fist into the obstinate animal's side. It was like hitting a concrete wall. But through Baba, Looney learned there were easier ways to get along with both people and beasts. At last he learned how to deal with raw power. "I realized that you can win anything with love," said Joe Don. He and Vijay learned to respect one another.

Baba gave his star pupil the spiritual name Hanumanji. In Hindu myth, Hanuman—son of the god of wind—was a monkey warrior tall as a tower who could leap so high he seized the clouds. In one courageous deed he helped Ram, a human form of the god Vishnu, rescue his wife, Sita, who had been kidnapped by a demon-king. The name acknowledged just how far Joe Don had come. "It doesn't matter if he didn't make it in pro football," said Baba. "He made it here. He's a champion."

In 1982, Muktananda was seventy-four years old when he had a heart attack and died. Joe Don was devastated, but his faith pulled him through. He celebrated the time he had spent with his beloved Baba. He went to Thailand and Tahiti, and then Joe Don came home.

He tried Austin, and stayed at his family's farm in east Texas. In 1984 he ventured to Alpine, near the Davis Mountains in far west Texas. The chamber of commerce likes to brag that Alpine is "where the rainbows wait for the rain." It's the Texas many people expect the whole state to look like—sprawling ranches and wide-open spaces, rugged mountains and cowboys tending cattle. Stories abound of Apache and Comanche warriors, outlaws and Pancho Villa. There are tales of buried treasure and desert ghosts. The movie *Giant* was filmed nearby. Independent-minded people live in this country and still depend mostly on themselves. At night the moon rises out of Mexico like a ball of white fire, and town lights are visible for forty miles. It is the wildest and most primitive part of the state, a land full of silence except for the relentless wind.

As soon as he set eyes on the mountains and rolling land covered with tall grass and flowering cactus, Joe Don realized he loved the place more than anywhere he'd ever been. "If the end zone is where happiness is, I'd be living there. It's not, so I'm living here," Looney said when asked why he chose to live so far from civilization.

Thanks to some investments and a life-style that was anything but lavish, he had enough money to get by on. He bought twenty-two acres just a few miles outside Alpine, Texas. With the help of a master carpenter named Wade Copeland, he designed and built a sturdy three-level geodesic dome made of cedar. It was solar heated and as solid as granite. "He had an immense amount of energy," said Copeland. "He had learned how to use it. When we started building his house, he didn't know how to hold a hammer. It was amazing to watch him learn and grow."

An old man with a forked stick found a deep well of sweet water. Joe Don planted a vegetable garden and a grove of fruit trees. There was a separate workout room for his weights and punching bag. Inside the house were plenty of beds for guests, hundreds of philosophy and spiritual books, and a small meditation chamber permeated with the odor of incense. There was no telephone. From the redwood deck, Cathedral Mountain rising 6,800 feet into the clouds seemed close enough to touch. It was the ideal spot for a warrior.

A pack of handsome Ridgebacks, strong dogs with sleek wheaten coats, roamed the land and stayed at Joe Don's side for early-morning runs. The big male named Ram and a bitch called Sita—both capable of catching lions—led the others. They were as stubborn and loyal as the man they adored.

"All his life, Joe Don had been searching for just the right place," said Copeland. "He searched and searched and found it right here. This is where he belonged. It was a place where he could look out and see nothing and see everything at the same time."

Joe Don cherished his solitude but made many friends. No one in Alpine was a stranger. He became a familiar face in the small town, where he enjoyed helping others. "Joe Don did a lot of things people didn't know about," said Don Looney. "He'd leave groceries at the local rest home for the elderly folks, but he didn't want any credit. He just gave of himself."

The women's basketball team at Alpine's Sul Ross University was another Looney cause. He became a loyal fan and traveled with the coach and the squad on road trips. High school football was also important, especially at the small schools. During the autumn he'd go clear across Texas to cheer himself hoarse while his favorite team—usually an underdog made good—struggled on the field. For Joe Don, the innocence and courage of small-town Texas football was the purest form of sport. He and Leroy Montgomery—his link to the old days—kept in touch and planned to build a boys' camp for wayward kids who needed a boost.

"Joe Don had a soft spot in his heart for the losers of the world," said Montgomery. "He was always willing to help them out."

After four years of hard work on his land, Joe Don had finally found the way of life that best suited him. As always, he was in tremendous physical condition and was at ease with himself and the world. His parents, divorced since 1966 but still good friends, spent as much time as possible with their son. Joe Don was busy building them a residence, with separate bedrooms, just up the hill from his dome. Looney's best friend, Janine Sagert, a Ph.D. stress management consultant he had met in India in 1977, moved to Alpine to be near Joe Don.

"He was so happy out here," said Janine. "I really believe his whole purpose for being was to get that experience of God, and certainly that was what was happening the last years of his life."

Janine and many of Joe Don's other friends often gathered at the dome to work and play. It was a special place. They could chant or meditate or crank up the tape player and dance to the Pointer Sisters, the Eagles, or Joe Don's favorite—*White Winds,* the haunting music of Andreas Vollenweider.

"He was a purist regarding how he perceived life and freedom," said Harmon Lisnow, a deputy attorney general in Texas who called Joe Don a friend. "I could come away from my hectic life and have my roots watered at Joe Don's. Few of us really understand true freedom, but Joe Don did. And he had such an extreme range of passions but with absolutely no social filters. He let it all hang out. It hacked off a lot of people, but he was always honest. He forced all of us to question ourselves. And through it all, he bowed to no one. He was truly a warrior—a spiritual warrior—and I loved him for that."

September 24, 1988, was a Saturday. It was game day across the nation. Joe Don rose early, meditated, and slipped into jeans and a Windbreaker. On that day Joe Don and his friend Tom Connor, a home builder from Alpine, were going to ride their motorcycles seventy-five miles to the Rio Grande and take part in a raft race. After days of watching the Seoul Olympics on television, Joe Don was pumped up, his competitive juices flowing. The big dogs sensed his excitement as he gulped juice and herbal tea.

Tom arrived in the morning darkness and Joe Don fired up his Suzuki 850. The two friends sped off to Highway 118. Ram and Sita loped alongside, but at the top of the hill Joe Don told them to stop and they stood watching as he rode off toward the distant mountains that guard the Big Bend country. For the first time that Tom could remember, Joe Don was wearing a helmet.

They raced down the highway, crossing dry creek beds and old Indian trails, passing peaks and the ruins of homesteads. Tom pulled away from Joe Don and led the way. He soon lost sight of his friend but assumed he was close behind. "It was such a fine ride that morning," recalled Tom. "It was awfully pretty."

The sun was softening the desert landscape and all the twists and turns were behind when Joe Don came up a steep hill. He saw the road flatten out before him and bend into a gentle curve.

It took hours for Tom and law officers to find Joe Don's body. He was just a couple of weeks from his forty-sixth birthday—an age when most men are worrying about coronary disease and getting fat; the age when T. E. Lawrence, the mysterious hero of Arabia, died in a motorcycle accident.

"No one knows what caused Joe Don to crash," said Connor. "I'm sure that at the moment it happened, he was joyed. I'm certain he saw there was no use to fight it, there was no holding back."

A crowd came to the simple services at Gessling Funeral Home, a pink stucco building in Alpine. Don Looney bought his son a suit for the occasion. There were flowers from old friends, and Leroy Montgomery and several of Joe Don's teammates showed up to pay their respects. One fellow rose to sing a hymn but was so choked up he had to leave. Some of the girls from the Sul Ross basketball team were there and so was Joe Don's ex-wife and his daughter, Tara—a grown woman with her father's good looks. She visited with her grandparents and they told her stories about the father she was just beginning to know. Tara promised to come back to the land. Joe Don's friends said they would keep the orchards and garden alive and care for his faithful dogs. Dorothy and Don studied Tara closely and could see in the young woman's bright eyes that she would return.

After the funeral, Joe Don was cremated and his mother kept his ashes and the Bible she had given him years before inscribed, "I place you in God's hands." Friends and family went out to Joe Don's land and walked around and watched the Ridgeback dogs chase over the hills. Ram was restless as if he was waiting for his warrior to come riding home.

To mark his birthday, Janine and Dorothy drove down Highway 118 and went to the gentle curve where he died. Dorothy spied a snatch of her boy's jacket snagged on a branch. They found the place under the mesquite tree where his head had come to rest and they left a pile of rocks. They stood and listened to the eternal wind. When they left they were smiling.

13

OKLAHOMA'S MOST HAUNTED

Happy Halloween!

—*Prince Eletsky,*
great-nephew of Dracula

 In Tulsa, the lights still burn behind the drapes of a tidy home where a distinguished gentleman, clad in an elegant robe, wraps small stacks of shiny pennies in plastic. These will be his offerings to the legion of tiny goblins, witches, werewolves, and pirates who will trudge up his sidewalk on their annual trick-or-treat pilgrimage. Although the big event is still weeks away, the man wants to be prepared for his guests. Halloween is his favorite night of the year.

It's only fitting. After all, this man has a reputation to uphold.

A bona fide old-world prince with the official ribbons, badges, and genealogical paperwork to prove it, he answers to the name Vladimir II, Prince Eletsky.

He is none other than a descendant of the legendary Count Dracula.

As he carefully wraps the coins, Prince Eletsky stops to read aloud the typed greeting he tapes to each package: "Happy Halloween to You! May these 7 brand new coins bring good fortune in your life. Given in love from Vladimir II, Prince of Eletz, great-nephew of the real Dracula . . ."

Prince Eletsky pauses to run his fingers through his silver hair. A warm smile spreads across his face.

"On Halloween night I put on my best tuxedo with all my royal badges and sashes and I meet the children at the door with a huge bowl filled with these packets of coins," explains Eletsky. "Before they have a chance to say a word, I glare down at them and say, 'Here you are, my little monsters, I'm the big monster. Happy Halloween?' Then I give them my very best villainous laugh and stand back and watch their faces."

A pleasant man with a warm disposition and keen sense of

humor, Prince Eletsky was born in Los Angeles in 1920 and has lived all over the world. He spent more than forty years serving as a merchant marine officer and hobnobbed with royalty and the rich and famous until a heart attack in 1982 slowed his pace. He looked for a tranquil setting and decided on Tulsa. "I think that Oklahomans are about the friendliest people I've ever encountered," says the prince.

Although Dracula has become synonymous with the primary character in Bram Stoker's 1897 horror novel of the same name, Prince Eletsky is quick to point out that the book is only a fictional account of the vampire legend.

"Actually the fictitious Dracula was nothing when compared to my ancestor who lived in the 1400s," says Eletsky. "I call him Uncle Vlad but his full name was Vlad III, voivode (prince) of Wallachia. He became known as the Dracul, or the Devil, since he was an extremely ferocious man and the absolute terror of his enemies."

According to the published history texts and genealogical documentation carefully preserved by Prince Eletsky, the dreaded Vlad III had a talent for survival that helped create the vampire myths. "In one battle he was struck by four arrows and another time more than thirteen arrows pierced his body," says Eletsky. "He was left for dead on the battlefield. But in the cool of the evening as the sun set, he awakened and struggled back to camp. The arrows were removed and remarkably, he recovered.

"On another occasion Vlad was run through by an enemy lance and again was left for dead until a retainer happened by and pulled out the lance, whereupon the prince regained consciousness and again lived. These incidents were sufficient to start the legend of Dracul as a vampire."

Vlad III's son, called of course Vlad IV, added to the family reputation by subscribing to the harsh practice of driving a stake through captive enemy soldiers. He became known as the Impaler, or Dracula (son of Dracul), and after one skirmish he saw to it that twenty thousand Turks met their Maker in such a fashion. The bloodthirsty Dracula was finally decapitated by his enemies in 1476. Since that time the family lines have become much more refined.

"Our family has certainly come a long way." The prince smiles as he busily wraps more pennies and gives his visitors a sly wink.

Meanwhile, in historic Guthrie, the seat of government for Logan County, former capital of Oklahoma Territory and the capital of the state until 1910, "ghostbusters" have gathered for an evening of excitement, fine dining, and entertainment at the picturesque Stone Lion Inn, a stately three-story house that has been transformed into a popular bed-and-breakfast.

Built in 1907 by F. E. Houghton, a prosperous Guthrie businessman who came to Oklahoma during the 1889 land run, the old residence is reportedly the abode of the mischievous spirit of Augusta Houghton, the eight-year-old girl who died of accidental poisoning in one of the upper-story bedrooms more than sixty years ago. "We usually don't tell our guests about our little ghost until after they've spent the night," says Becky Luker, the woman who bought the Stone Lion in 1986 when she moved from Santa Fe to Guthrie. "But she does absolutely no harm and we've all become rather accustomed to her."

Becky and her two sons didn't realize they shared their home with the youthful ghost until a few weeks after they moved into the old place, a former funeral home, and began working to restore the building to its former glory.

"My youngest son, Ral, was seven years old at that time and he was the first one to really make contact," explains Becky. "He picked out a big closet on the third-floor ballroom to store his toys and immediately he found that during the night someone was playing with his things. The toys would be rearranged and the puzzles and games were out on the floor. Ral's a meticulous boy and this bothered him. He accused me and his brother, Grant, but we told him that we weren't the culprits. Then he put a padlock on the closet, but even then he'd find all of his things scattered about when he'd unlock the door in the morning."

It was about that time that Becky and her boys started hearing the footsteps. The soft patter of tiny feet could be heard on the back staircase in the evenings between ten o'clock and midnight. "We'd hear the footsteps and then we'd hear doors being methodically opened and closed," says Becky. "That scared us to death. We were convinced we had burglars and I called the police on several occasions. I bet they thought we were crazy because they could never find anything. Finally we became used to the noises and I told the boys it was probably the old house settling. I didn't know what else to tell them. None of us was about to say it was a ghost even though we all thought it."

Ral was the first one to use the "G" word. He came down to breakfast one morning and announced he would play with his toys later.

"She's up there now," said Ral.

"Who is 'she'?" asked a startled Becky.

"Why, the ghost," answered Ral as he dug into his cereal.

Although the boy said he couldn't see her, Ral told the rest of the family there was definitely a presence of some sort in his toy closet and he was convinced it was a little girl. "I do know the difference," he explained to his mother. "I just know it's a girl ghost."

A short time later some of the other Houghton siblings, by now elderly men and women, paid a visit to Guthrie and Stone Lion Inn in order to explain some of the history of the home to Becky. "It was a Houghton son and two of the daughters," says Becky. "They spent a great deal of time telling me about their former home. They also told me about their sister Augusta's death. They told us that she had contracted whooping cough and during the night a maid attending her gave the child the wrong kind of medicine. Augusta became violently ill and soon died from poisoning."

The trio also talked about happier times. They spoke of holidays, parties, and picnics. And they talked of nightly pilgrimages to the ballroom to play with their toys.

"They said that they'd wait until their parents had gone to bed and then they'd sneak up the back stairs and quietly continue their games," says Becky. "They said they did this between ten o'clock and midnight—the exact time that we hear the mysterious footsteps on those same stairs. They took me to the upstairs room and showed me where they kept their playthings. It was the same closet my son used—the very same one. I got a chill."

Becky Luker and her sons have learned to accept Augusta, and so have the guests who come to Stone Lion to spend the night or take part in one of Luker's "Murder Mystery Weekends," a diversion that includes a formal dinner with everyone in costume as characters in a drama scripted by Becky herself. But that tolerance could be because so far no one has actually seen the little ghost.

Still, not all Oklahoma ghosts are as shy as the beguiling Augusta Houghton. There are instances here of spirits who have been known to make appearances and not just creep up the stairs to play while one slumbers.

Tulsa has its share of ghosts, some of whom reportedly mingle with the living every chance they get. Many of the big-city ghosts are of the standard garden variety but a few are considered celebrity spirits, among them the famed virtuoso Enrico Caruso. He is said to haunt the seventy-six-year-old Brady Theater as payback for the pleurisy his managers insist the tenor contracted after an open-air ride through the cold and wet Oklahoma countryside in 1920. (He died a year later of the ailment.)

And then there's the ghost of Thomas Gilcrease, the late philanthropist responsible for the highly touted Gilcrease Museum. Gilcrease was laid to rest in a limestone mausoleum one May morning in 1962, but there are those who believe he may have been the restless type. Some say Gilcrease still patrols the manicured museum grounds. Others claim he makes occasional appearances in the museum and has been spied beside his former residence, now the home of the Tulsa Historical Society.

On a cloudless afternoon just as a hunter's moon considers an appearance and the sun disappears beyond the distant Osage hills, some after-hours guests make their way through the quiet museum. Dan McPike, a rumpled museum curator, fusses with locked doors before he allows the visitors into a windowless storage room. It's a large chamber but appears cramped, filled with shelves and display cases bearing the invaluable treasures that a few thousand years past were household items in some bygone culture's daily routine.

McPike permits his gold-framed eyeglasses to slip a bit on his nose so he can properly inspect the room and get his bearings. He is on the brink of offering a colorful account of an exquisite Carolina parakeet effigy excavated from an ancient Indian mound, when a distant tinny noise halts all conversation. He pauses and peers into the shadowy corners of the room.

"Anybody come with you?" asks McPike with a grin.

"Maybe it's a ghost," offers one of the guests.

The interruption passes with no further explanation.

Later, the behind-the-scenes museum tour completed, McPike and the others stand outside in the fading twilight and reflect on Gilcrease, the man who left a legacy of American art and history for the world to enjoy. Finally, after McPike has expounded on the usual biographical and historical anecdotes, he tells the visitors what they want to hear—more ghosts stories.

"After Mr. Gilcrease died, some folks from the museum lived next door in his residence," says McPike, pointing with his pipe toward the house, a two-story stone building with a veranda and a pagoda-style metal tile roof. "It seems they had a houseguest come see them. His very first night in the house, he came down to dinner and he asked his hosts if the other guest was going to join them. They wanted to know what other guest he meant. 'Why, the older gentleman I saw earlier on the landing of the stairs,' the man told them. He said he had bid the man good evening and the man nodded in reply and then turned and went upstairs and he heard a door slam."

McPike pauses to tap his pipe on the sole of his shoe and rub the warm bowl between his palms. "Well, let me tell you that those folks dropped their napkins and their mouths fell wide open. You see there were no other guests in the house that evening. None invited, that is."

There are plenty of stories about mysterious noises and footsteps in the museum galleries and reported sightings of a kindly old gentleman, dressed like Gilcrease, puttering in the flower beds scattered over the 115-acre museum grounds. Yet most folks willing to discuss the ghost maintain that his favorite haunt is his residence.

The most colorful Gilcrease ghost episode occurred several years ago on an Easter evening after the museum was locked and only the watchman remained to make his rounds. Suddenly, the alarm at the Gilcrease residence sounded. Police officers responded—including a canine unit boasting Baron, a 110-pound police dog. The muscular animal was extremely agitated and strained at his lead. When the officer released him, the dog made a beeline to the front door, pawing and whining to get inside. The watchman unlocked the door and Baron dashed for the stairs. But when he reached the landing, Baron came to a complete halt. Witnesses on the scene said it was as if he ran into an invisible wall. With his fur bristling and ears pinned back, the dog dropped to his belly and quivered. He finally had to be carried down the stairs by an officer and taken outside. As soon as he was placed on the ground, Baron bolted back to the police car. He wanted nothing more to do with the Gilcrease house.

Inside the residence, nothing was out of place and there was no evidence of any intruders—at least no one that the officers could see.

▼▼▼

But Tulsa doesn't have a monopoly on ghoulish yarns. In Oklahoma City, another favorite haunt for the living as well as at least one reputed ghost is the County Line, a busy barbecue restaurant situated not far from the Cowboy Hall of Fame on a hillside overlooking old Route 66. Built back in 1918 and known for many years as the Kentucky Club, this was once a busy roadhouse and a favorite hangout for none other than Charles Arthur "Pretty Boy" Floyd, the most daring of the Sooner State's Depression-era desperadoes. The bootleg booze, poker chips, and soiled doves may be long gone—replaced by platters of giant beef ribs, bowls of homemade cobbler, and patrons from across the state—but sometimes late at night, when all the customers have left and the big front door's locked tight, unexplained noises have been heard coming from the kitchen and bar area.

"I've heard the racket," admits Gene Caldwell, the restaurant owner. "There's no logical explanation. Maybe it's one of the fellows from the old days. Maybe it's 'Pretty Boy' himself hunting up some leftovers."

▼▼▼

Oklahoma's big cities provide their share of ghosts, but a good many goblins seem to favor the rural areas as well. All across the state—from the ghostly quadrangles of frontier forts and musty schoolhouses to the cavernous theaters and lonely country roads flanked by quiet thickets—restless spirits and scary creatures are on the prowl. The stories about them are as colorful as the storytellers.

Just off old Route 66, about ten miles northeast of Claremore near the tiny Rogers County community of Foyil, folks get goosebumps the size of strawberries thanks to the unearthly screams most old-timers claim come from deep in the belly of a mysterious giant panther. Tales of the huge beast roaming the hills and valleys and screaming like a woman in the darkness have been passed down from generation to generation. As early as January 11, 1908, the *Foyil Statesman* reported that just a few miles outside town, a local woman named Mary Tiger heard strange noises and piercing screams outside her house. An investigation yielded nothing. Later that same year the newspaper reported "a panther scare east of Foyil, none seen but unearthly yells and movements." Most of the panther reports came from around the Dog Creek area, so the critter came to be known as the Dog Creek Panther.

Decades later there are still occasional reports of hideous screams and even panther sightings in the area.

A few years before statehood in rural Nowata County, a young farm woman and her baby son ventured out in her horse-drawn buggy one stormy evening to visit friends. Just as they were crossing a narrow bridge over a swollen stream, rising waters swept away the buggy and the infant was lost in the raging torrent. After several minutes of battling for her own life, the dazed woman managed to drag herself up on the riverbank. She frantically scanned the dark water for any sign of her son and although she could hear the baby's screams, she never saw the baby again. Within a few minutes the screams stopped and only the raging waters could be heard. A new bridge now spans the stream, but to this day locals claim that if they stand at the center of the bridge they can hear the faint cries of a baby above the sounds of the evening breeze and chirping frogs. Most of them say the best time to hear the phantom child is around midnight after a heavy rain.

In the Yellow Hills east of Ardmore there are still a few old-timers who can recall stories of the fabled "little helper," or Kawnakuasha, the Choctaws' version of the Irish leprechaun. They speak of Uncle Billy Washington, a Choctaw herb doctor or medicine man, who came to Indian Territory from Mississippi. It's said that Uncle Billy relied on his little helper to guide him to rare herbs in the woods and to lead him to patients' homes on dark nights. The story goes that only the medicine man could actually see the Kawnakuasha and that other Indians could only see the glow of a light guiding Uncle Billy through the darkness. The good doctor died in 1930, but some people believe that the Kawnakuasha has never left. On dark nights, the full bloods say that the strange light seen in the distant hills not far from where Uncle Billy lived is actually his Kawnakuasha, still looking for another Indian to serve.

Around northeastern Oklahoma, people have swapped stories about the Spooklight or Ghostlight for more than a century. In fact, this particular legend has been known to the Quapaw Indians even longer. The mysterious light in question is described as a huge ball that bounces over the hills and through the fields. Most of the sightings have been along Devil's Promenade Road, northeast of Miami not far from the old Quapaw reservation. There are several notions about the light's origin, including marsh gas and refracted starlight. The most ballyhooed theory concerns an Indian couple who became involved in a heated dispute that ended with the wife slicing off her husband's head. Still angry, the woman then proceeded to hide the evidence. It is said that the light is actually the spirit of the decapitated Indian searching for his missing skull.

In the Osage County seat of Pawhuska, a Grecian landmark called the Constantine Theater is home to a mysterious occupant said to be Sappho Constantine Brown, the daughter of Charles A. Constantine, original owner of the property. Pawhuska Mayor Janet Holcombe, one of the leaders in the successful effort to restore the old building, has spent many hours working in the theater. She's convinced the Constantine is haunted. "I've heard the footsteps," says Holcombe. "I was working on the stairs in the foyer one night by myself and I heard what sounded like someone walking on the stage with a hard-soled shoe. I looked and nothing was there. I do think it's a friendly ghost." During the five years it took to renovate the building, others working there had similar experiences. There have been several candidates, but most believe it's the ghost of Sappho, an expert palm reader and master of tarot cards. Word has spread about the spirit in the Constantine. A pair of California men even sent a donation and asked that it be used to preserve the ghost of the Constantine. The money was used for construction materials.

Light frost blankets Oklahoma like icing on a cake. Above cities, prairie towns, oil-patch hamlets, and slumbering ranches and farms, the moon breaks through the veil of evening clouds and rules the autumn sky. Owls—silent as gargoyles—perch in catalpa trees and Chinese elms. They pay no heed to cats skulking in the shadows. By dawn these creatures of the night will have vanished, but as the witching hour draws near, they are free to bask in soft moonlight.

14

FRECKLES

And tonight bull ridin' histry's
made,
A cowboy gained a crown
his bull was called Tornado
and the cowboy,
Freckles Brown.

—Red Steagall,
For Freckles Brown

 Dawn is softly breaking over the Kelly Bend Ranch near Soper in southeastern Oklahoma. The new day comes with slow steps, and stillness blankets the pastures. Except for an occasional snort from a slumbering cow pony, everything is as peaceful as a cat asleep on a chair.

The moon drowses between the trees, and clusters of ancient stars still wink brightly. But out of the night shadows, long pink and lavender fingers of light streak the sky. A tame wind is beginning to stir, barely moving the long winter weeds hunkered along the fence line.

The Kelly Bend got its name from an Indian family which settled here long ago and from the bend in the Muddy Boggy River, which flows nearby on its way to join the Red River, that legendary stream the color of tea that keeps Oklahoma and Texas worlds apart.

By most standards, the Kelly Bend is a modest 540-acre spread with plenty of sweet water and lush grass. More than one hundred springs percolate on the ranch creeks and, where cattle now graze, Choctaws stalked game and planted their crops. It's a fit place for raising beef cattle and kids. There are good swimming holes, plenty of forage for turkeys and deer, and every October wild hog plums can be harvested and made into a superior jam that makes even the most grizzled cowpoke's mouth water. The Kelly Bend is a complete working ranch. It's also the home of Freckles Brown—a living cowboy legend.

Inside the snug ranch house he built of native stone and pine for his wife, Edith, the legend himself—Freckles Brown—parts the curtains with a mug of steaming coffee and checks in with the dawn. He pads back to the leather couch, pulls on his boots, and with two long sips finishes the coffee. For a moment, there

MICHAEL WALLIS

in the dark room, he gazes at the logs burning in the fireplace. The fire pops and crackles, and shadows dance off the furniture. There are familiar sounds coming from the kitchen where Edith faces breakfast dishes and a pail of juicy pears waiting to be canned. Suddenly, in one smooth motion, Freckles grabs up his Stetson, tosses a smile over his shoulder to Edith, and slips outside into the cool air. His face catches the full strength of the rising wind, and he smells the river-fed earth, fresh manure, and wood smoke curling from the chimney.

Pete, an Australian shepherd dog who can cut cattle with the best of them, appears at Freckles's side for his daily ration of scratches behind the ears. Together, Freckles and Pete make their rounds. Behind the ranch house a dozen Manx cats, who earn their keep by hunting gophers, nest on the woodpile. Before the bobtailed cats have time to stretch awake, Freckles has fired up the trusty pickup and, with his pal Pete riding shotgun, he heads off to feed the Kelly Bend's herd of mixed-breed cattle.

As the truck bounces and creaks down the dirt road, Freckles's mind wanders back to when he was a young man learning to ride and rope and holler like a banshee in the great American West. He recalls when he was a smooth-faced kid earning his spurs as a cowboy. But most of all, he remembers dazzling those audiences, from Calgary to Houston, from New York City to Mexico City and the capitals of Europe, as a GI in China, and in the countless arenas and stadiums around the world as he rode bucking Brahma bulls and made rodeo history.

"I always wanted to be a cowboy. That was my main desire ever since I was a little boy. I used to dream of working on a ranch. I used to dream about breaking horses and tending cattle. All I ever wanted was to be a good cowboy. I never even thought of being good enough to rodeo. Never entered my head," he says.

▼▼▼

Warren Granger Brown was born in Wheatland, Wyoming, on January 18, 1921. He was the youngest of ten brothers and sisters, all raised on the family homestead between Fort Laramie and Lingle. There the Brown family grew potatoes, alfalfa, and sugar beets. Despite the rich North Platte River soil, young Freckles realized he wasn't cut out to be a farmer. When he was still a boy, he learned to ride horses and herd cattle. By the time he was fourteen, the family left Wyoming for Arizona so the desert climate could help soothe his mother's arthritis. And it was on a dusty Arizona ranch where Warren G. Brown would become a fully brevetted cowboy and get the nickname he'd carry for the rest of his life.

"Had a bunch of freckles back then," he says. "I guess by the time I got to be eighteen or nineteen, they started dimming out. But I had plenty when I was a youngster. Anyhow, when this fella hired me on my first cowboy job, it was on a ranch near Wilcox, Arizona, and he asked me my name. I said Warren Granger Brown and he said 'Anything you say, Freckles.' Well, that name sure did stick even if my freckles didn't. You could hurt your eyes trying to find any of those freckles on me now. I reckon all those bulls I've been riding over the years just shook those freckles off."

It wasn't too long after folks started calling him Freckles that the fledgling wrangler decided to commit his life to cowboying. In the years that followed, Freckles Brown would cowboy throughout the West—from the high pastures of the Rockies to the Oklahoma plains. He'd feel the sting of blizzard snows and the scorching Panhandle sun. He'd ride endless miles in wind and rain, mending fences and searching for lost calves. He'd break ice in the thick of winter so his cattle could survive. He'd become accustomed to herding mother cows and branding dogies and spitting trail dust. He learned to enjoy bunkhouse breakfasts and look forward to warming his frozen feet by a mesquite cook fire. Years of tending stock would make Freckles Brown a man with a gift of silence, and he would also be filled with that unmistakable pride that comes with being a cowboy—the genuine article—part of a vanishing breed. And, early on, even when he was a rookie cowpuncher green as new mistletoe, he'd come to find his greatest love of all—the rodeo.

Freckles recalls, "I rode my first bull at the age of sixteen at a rodeo in Wilcox. But I won my first bull-riding trophy in 1941. I was back up in Wyoming working on a ranch in the Starlight Basin near Yellowstone National Park. I rode an ol' bronc horse fifty miles into Cody to go to the stampede. I left at eight in the morning and got to town about six o'clock, in time for supper. I got kicked by a bull during the rodeo, so after I won I had to ride back to the ranch the next day with my hurt foot outside of the stirrup. Rode all the way back like that, but I didn't care 'cause I had me a fine trophy. I was a real honest-to-goodness bull rider."

From his first wild and woolly rodeo ride in 1937 until he

hung up his chaps and spurs in 1974, Freckles Brown gave his all to the sport of rodeo. He was the professional's professional, the cowboy's cowboy. A consistent big winner in rodeo for an incredible thirty-seven-year span, Freckles rode bareback broncs, bulldogged, and did his share of team roping before he decided to concentrate on bull riding, the most exciting and dangerous of all rodeo events. He paid his dues.

The litany of injuries includes ten broken legs, two broken collar bones, countless broken ribs, and shoulder and knee injuries. His neck was broken twice, and in one thirteen-month period he broke his leg three times. A piece of his hip bone was used to replace a bone removed from his neck. There is a metal pin in his shoulder and a screw in one of his ankles. Freckles laughs off the scars and bruises and calls himself "a walking hardware store." Besides all the pain, Freckles managed to earn an honest living along with a ranch house full of trophies and honors including engraved saddles, loving cups, belt buckles, certificates, and plaques.

In 1962, at the ripe old age of forty-one, he was declared "World Champion Bull Rider." Freckles's riding boots, bull-riding spurs, rope, chaps, and some of his trophies are prominently displayed in the Pro Rodeo Hall of Champions and Museum of the American Cowboy in Oklahoma City. There has been a song written about his rodeo exploits, and plans are under way to make a motion picture about his life and times. He's been the official spokesman for a large western-wear manufacturer for many years, and there's even a line of cowboy boots bearing his name for sale in the better western stores. Not bad for a dirt farmer's kid.

"I've sure had a good life as a cowboy, and I had a good rodeo career, too." He says, "It was a swell time. I stopped rodeoing in 1974. That's when I quit. I was in Tulsa and I climbed on my last bull. I had been drawing pretty fair that year. I recall I drawed a fine ol' bull at Ardmore and then I drew a good one in Tulsa. That was my last bull ride. I was fifty-three years old."

Edith Brown, a slender woman with classic ranch-wife looks, has been Freckles's biggest fan ever since they met when he was stationed at Fort Sill during World War II. A native of Purcell, the McClain County seat nestled on the banks of the South Canadian River, Edith often served as a rodeo timekeeper in order to be near her bull-riding man. She traveled all over the globe watching "Brownie," as she calls her husband of more than four decades, ride humpback Brahma bulls. For Edith, the best rodeos of all were the ones held in small-town America. She loved it when she could actually feel the movement of the crowd in the wooden bleachers as they cheered and stomped their boots and clapped for the cowboys. She never grew weary of the travel, and to this day when she's asked which of Brownie's rides gave her the biggest thrill, she never wavers: "Every single one of them."

"I met Edith when I was in the Army down at Lawton during the war," he says. "She was working as a cashier in the dime store and I saw her. She was a pretty, black-haired gal, and we got fixed up on a date. Never forget it. Edith had laryngitis and couldn't talk. So we went to a dance and had a high ol' time. We've never quit."

Freckles married Edith the following year, and in 1944 their only child—a daughter named Donna—was born. That same year, after completing both horseshoeing and jump school and serving a hitch with a horse-drawn artillery outfit, Freckles was assigned to duty in China with the Office of Strategic Service (OSS). It was in China where Freckles would start building on his rodeo legend when he helped produce the country's first "rodeo" using army mules and native cattle. To this day, Freckles believes he was the Orient's first, and probably only, all-round champion cowboy.

"It was the first rodeo ever held in China," he explains. "I bet they ain't never had another. I went into this cafe run by the Red Cross and spotted a hand-lettered rodeo poster. Well, I got into it and competed. I won first in saddle mule riding and first in bareback mule riding. Boy, those Chinese didn't know what to make of it. At first, half of them were just dumbfounded. And the other half were laughing so hard I thought we'd need ambulances for them. It was fun and, heck, how many other cowboys can say they were 'Bareback Mule Riding Champion of China'?"

Nobody, not even Freckles, knows just how many bulls and broncs he rode during his long and colorful career. In one two-day period, Freckles climbed on forty-one bucking horses, and on more than one occasion he rode as many as twenty bulls in a single day. By his own best estimate, Freckles reckons he took on somewhere between four thousand and five thousand bulls. Many of them were highly ranked. Some were as famous as the cowboys they bucked. Among the "biggies" that Freckles rode were: 19 (also called Very Seldom), Tex M, Black Smoke, Snowman, Iceman, Troubleshooter, Eight Ball, and Big Bad John. But there is no doubt that the bull most rodeo fans remember Freckles riding and the one animal that Mr. Brown will never forget is the great snorting beast still regarded as the toughest rodeo bull that ever came out of a chute—Tornado.

He was a true bovine champion—a bull supreme, as quick, violent, and lethal as his name. With eyes as dark as pitch, this hissing, snorting beast had been to every National Finals Rodeo (NFR) since 1961 when he finally met up with Freckles Brown in 1967 in Oklahoma City. Tornado had been picked the NFR Bull of the Year in all but his rookie season, and the big bull's owner, Jim Shoulders, himself a former all-around cowboy champion, considered Tornado his pride and joy. When the 1967 NFR opened, Freckles drew Tornado, his first encounter with the infamous critter. The eleven-year-old Brahma was a mean and lean 1,800-pounder at the time and had defeated more than 220 cowboys. No one ever made the eternal eight-second ride on Tornado's back. The day he drew Tornado, Freckles was a month shy of his forty-seventh birthday.

"It was the greatest experience of my life," he recalls. "I had never drawn Tornado before. I knew him, though. I'd watched him. Saw him for the first time in Memphis and I knew I had to ride him. It took me seven years. But every rodeo where I had the chance to see him go, I'd sit up in front of his chute and watch. I studied Tornado. Sometimes he was just impossible, and on those days there wasn't a bull rider alive who could have ridden him. I had never seen Tornado have a bad day. But he was an honest bull. He always fought the clowns real good and he hardly stepped on anybody. Many a cowboy said he couldn't be rode. A lot of guys would draw him and not even try to ride him. They would walk away. But I had to give him a go. I knew he was due to be rode. I thought I could do it. I had to give it a try."

And did he ever try! Freckles Brown beat Tornado. To this day, the Freckles Brown–Tornado match-up is considered by many rodeo aficionados to be one of the finest events in modern rodeo history. Clem McSpadden, the rodeo announcer that stormy December evening, declared the ride "the greatest legend-making incident in rodeo." He gets few arguments.

"In the chutes just before we went for it, I laid my rope on him, and he was just like any other bull," Freckles says. "He was standing there relaxed. His muscles were soft. When I pushed against him there was a lot of give to him. But when we were ready to go, he was a completely different bull. He was ol' Tornado—hard as a table. His muscles were tensed like a runner in the blocks. It was then and there that it dawned on me. I knew what made Tornado different. He was an athlete. He loved the contest. He was tense with anticipation—ready for the gate to crash open. And then he came out with a big leap, made a sharp turn and went to kicking and bucking. I held on. I couldn't hear nothing. But then I saw the clowns move in and I knew I made the whistle. I got off Tornado real good—landed on my feet. The hollering wouldn't let up. I stood out there in the middle of the arena with my hat off for the longest time. The applause didn't die—it just kept going. Even the cowboys were clapping and yelling. I finally walked off, but it didn't let up any. I looked up at Clem McSpadden, and he motioned to me to go on back out. So I did. And it started up louder than ever. Never heard anything like it."

Freckles Brown could have been elected governor of Oklahoma that evening. He had ridden the unridable. He had conquered Tornado. Forever, this 5-foot-7-inch, 150-pound cowboy would serve as the symbol of the human spirit's ability to beat insurmountable odds. They say when he finally left the arena that night, hat in hand and tears in his eyes, Freckles said to no one in particular: "He was overdue."

There are many memories for Freckles to consider these days, as he feeds his cattle and watches Pete, his good cow dog, move through the meadows. Some memories are bitter, but most are sweet. A few, maybe even sacred.

Life's good at the Kelly Bend Ranch. Freckles's daughter and her husband and their two growing boys ranch the adjoining 160-acre spread, and more than enough visitors come to the Kelly Bend to see Freckles. Pete gives everybody a friendly bark, and out back the platoon of Manx cats—some calico, some striped, and a few the color of honey—stay on their gopher patrol. Edith gives all comers plenty of coffee and makes sure they sign the guest book on the kitchen table.

And every once in a while, Edith and her Brownie get in the pickup and take off for a rodeo. They see old friends and recall the days when rodeos may not have been bigger but in many ways were sure better. A lot of his rodeo mates are gone. Tornado is gone, too. The old fighting bull is buried at the Cowboy Hall of Fame in Oklahoma City.

But sometimes, in the evening after all the chores are done and he's taking one last look at the day, Freckles probably lets himself hear that chute bang open and he sees the arena dirt fly high. And there in the twilight, he's riding Tornado again. Freckles holds on tight to the braided manila rope looped around the big bull's belly, and he waves his hat in the air to a chorus of hoots from cowboy ghosts. It's an eight-second dream for a champion. It all belongs to the man called Freckles.

"All I ever wanted was to be a good cowboy."

15

HAIL TO THE CHIEF

Though the view from my door was still more contracted, I did not feel crowded or confined in the least. There was pasture enough for my imagination.

—Henry David Thoreau

Dawn arrives in the countryside of north-eastern Oklahoma, warm and familiar like an old pal who's come calling. Sunlight seeps through stands of oak, sycamore, and dogwood, then melts as slowly as country butter over thickets of sumac, sassafras, and persimmon. Stalks of soft light reach the weeds and vines clinging to the sagging wire fences. The rays inch across the garden, and finally the frame house in the clearing is streaked with gold. Inside, the aroma of coffee and biscuits mixes with radio news and morning murmurs.

Before too long the front door opens slowly and Wilma Mankiller—the woman of the house—emerges. She is barefoot and wears a brightly colored dress. Her dark hair is still damp from a morning shampoo. She sits on an old kitchen chair on the narrow front porch and sips a mug of coffee. A murder of mischievous crows, dancing like ebony marionettes, scolds from the nearby trees. In the distance, voices of jays, mockingbirds, and wrens deliver a backup chorus. Soon hawks will begin patrolling the sky.

Walkingsticks appear, seemingly from nowhere, to dine on tender leaves. The spindly insects resemble twigs as they slowly creep over the porch and the railing. Some crawl up the chair. One moves across Mankiller's legs, but she doesn't appear to notice or care. Another moves across her shoulders and starts up her hair, but Mankiller gently shakes the creature free. She knows the walkingsticks are not interested in her, but merely want to reach the redbud tree growing next to the porch.

The surrounding forests and hills conceal the animal life native to this eastern region of Oklahoma. There are a few mountain lions and bobcats and an abundance of coyotes, foxes, and many breeds of smaller animals. There are also deer. Plenty of deer. Often they appear near Mankiller's house and take their share from the garden. Every hunting season, she gets requests from sportsmen who want to stalk the land. She always tells them the same thing. They may hunt all they wish, but they may not shoot anything.

This is the place on earth that Wilma Mankiller loves best. She is surrounded by 160 acres of ancestral property, allotted to her paternal grandfather, John Mankiller, when Oklahoma became a state in 1907. The land is located in Adair County, within hollerin' distance of the Cherokee County line. Named for a prominent Cherokee family, Adair County is the heart of the area first settled by immigrant Cherokees in the late 1830s. The county still claims a higher percentage of Native American population than any other in the United States.

With the Cherokee Hills on the north and the Cookson Hills on the south, the county has a natural beauty that at least partially masks its very real poverty. Small farms and ranches, fruit or-chards, and lumbering are the economic mainstays. But the peo-ple derive only modest incomes from their hard labor. Here, a person's wealth and worth are measured in other ways besides bank accounts and worldly goods.

In generations past, the Cherokee people came to this area to rebuild their nation after the westward trek from their beloved homelands in the mountainous South. Herded by federal soldiers, the Cherokees took a path in 1838–39 that became known as the Trail of Tears.

At Tahlequah, the seat of Cherokee County in the eastern foothills of the Ozarks, where their bitter journey ended, the Cherokees built new homes and some of the first schools west of the Mississippi for the education of both men and women. They also reestablished an intricate government in Indian Territory, including a system of courts of law. Although oral historians assert that the tribe possessed a written language long before, the Cherokees put to good use the eighty-five-character syllabary developed by Sequoyah over a twelve-year period prior to the Trail of Tears, to publish Oklahoma's first newspaper in both Cherokee and English.

Many Cherokees continue to live on the hardscrabble farms dotting the region—a land of streams, cliffs, forests, and meadows that is still much the same as it was years ago when outlaw gangs fled to the dark hills to find refuge from the law in the Cherokee Nation. Colorful place names given to favorite natural haunts persist, such as Wildcat Point, Whiskey Holler, and Six-shooter Camp. It is country where conversation centers on farming, hunting, weather, football and, forever and always, politics. Not just mainstream party politics, such as candidates for county commissioner or sheriff or the U.S. Senate, but also tribal politics—the critical issue of Cherokee leadership.

Much of the talk at the gas stations, bait shops, and convenience stores scattered along the country roads is about Wilma Mankiller. This is only natural, since she serves as the principal chief of the Cherokee Nation of Oklahoma. The Cherokees represent the second-largest tribe in the United States, after the Navajo Nation. Mankiller is the first female to lead a major Native American tribe. With an enrolled tribal population worldwide of more than 140,000, an annual budget of $68 million and more than 1,200 employees spread across 7,000 square miles, her responsibilities as chief are the same as a head of state or the chief executive officer of a major corporation.

Although it is the land of rugged males who, for the most part, prefer to see fellow "good ol' boys" run for political office, it is difficult to find anyone from the Cherokee ranks, including some of Mankiller's former political foes, who can find fault with the performance of her administration. It was not always that way. In the beginning, there were many problems and obstacles. Often, those were mean times. There were some Cherokees who didn't wish to be governed by a female. Wilma Mankiller had her share of enemies. Her automobile tires were slashed. There were death threats. Chief Mankiller was admittedly an unlikely politician. But gradually she won acceptance. In time, most of her constituents became quite comfortable with her. Now when disagreements occur, they are based on issues rather than gender.

Wilma Mankiller shares her home and life with her husband, Charlie Soap, and Winter Hawk, his son from a former marriage. Her two daughters, Felicia and Gina, and their children often stop by to visit, as do other family members and friends. Mankiller's mother lives just down the road.

In the winter, Mankiller's house is warmed by a stove fed by the constant supply of firewood cut from the surrounding forest. Native American art, including masks, baskets, and pottery as well as Cherokee, Kiowa, and Sioux paintings, adorns the shelves and walls. Colorful blankets drape the chair backs and couches. Framed family photographs are scattered about tabletops, and on a living room shelf is a small bust of Sam Houston, the revered

as a predominant theme as more and more Cherokee land was taken to make room for other tribes who were also forced to leave their homes and move into Indian Territory.

By 1907, the federal government had dismantled the tribal government, discarded the Cherokee constitution, and divided up the land in individual allotments. It was at that time that Wilma Mankiller's family received its share of property in the wooded hills. In that remote setting, where she and her siblings were raised, the family grew strawberries and other crops for a living. There was no indoor plumbing, so the Mankiller children hauled water about a quarter of a mile to their home.

"I remember the hard times when we ate what we grew," she says. "But those days helped me so much. I was raised with a sense of community that extended beyond my family."

When she was ten years old, Mankiller's entire family was moved to California as participants in the federal government's relocation program. "It was part of the national Indian policy of the 1950s," she explains. "The government wanted to break up tribal communities and 'mainstream' Indians, so it relocated rural families to urban areas. One day I was living in Oklahoma, and a few days later I was living in California and trying to deal with the mysteries of television, neon lights, and elevators. It was total culture shock."

The Mankiller family eventually became acclimated to California. Mankiller attended school and met her first husband, a well-to-do Ecuadorean. They had two daughters, Felicia in 1964 and Gina in 1966. It was during the turbulent 1960s, while starting her family, that Mankiller began to raise her political consciousness. Her concern for Native American issues was fully ignited by 1969 when a band of university students and members of the American Indian Movement occupied the abandoned prison on Alcatraz Island in San Francisco Bay. They wanted to attract attention to issues affecting them and their tribes. Mankiller answered the call. Out of that historic experience, an activist was born.

"In most ways I was a typical housewife at that time," recalls Wilma, "but when Alcatraz occurred, I became aware of what needed to be done to let the rest of the world know that Indians had rights too. Alcatraz articulated my own feelings about being an Indian. It was a benchmark. After that, I became involved."

She attended sociology classes at San Francisco State College and took on Native American issues with a fervor. Mankiller worked as a volunteer for five grueling years with the Pit River Tribe in California on treaty-rights issues, helping to establish a legal defense fund for the battle to reclaim the tribe's ancestral lands. She also devoted much of her time to Native American preschool and adult education programs and directing a dropout prevention program for Native American youngsters.

In 1974, Mankiller divorced her husband of eleven years. "He wanted a traditional housewife. I had a stronger desire to do things in the community than at home." Two years later, she returned to Oklahoma with her daughters. "I was delighted to be back on our ancestral homelands," she recalls. "I wanted to come home and raise my kids and build a house on my land."

She managed all that and more. In 1979, after almost three years of helping to procure important grants and launch critical rural services for the tribe, Wilma enrolled in graduate courses at the nearby University of Arkansas. Late one afternoon in the fall of 1979, while returning home from class on a two-lane country road, Mankiller was seriously injured in a freak automobile accident which resulted in a fatality. An oncoming car which had pulled into her lane to pass collided head-on with Mankiller's station wagon. Unbelievably, the young woman driving the other vehicle, who was killed, was Mankiller's best friend. When Mankiller regained consciousness in the hospital, her face was crushed and her ribs and legs were broken. It was one of several brushes with death. After avoiding the amputation of her right leg, she endured seventeen operations and was bedridden for months. During the long healing process, Mankiller turned to the power of positive thinking, as practiced by the Cherokees.

"That accident in 1979 changed my life," she says. "I came very close to death, felt its presence and the alluring call to complete the circle of life. I always think of myself as the woman who lived before and the woman who lives afterward. I was at home recovering for almost a year, and I had time to reevaluate." For Mankiller, it proved to be a deep spiritual awakening when she adopted what she referred to as "a very Cherokee approach to life—what our tribal elders call 'being of good mind.' "

Then in November 1980, just a year after the tragic accident, Mankiller was diagnosed with myasthenia gravis, a chronic neuromuscular disease that causes varying weakness in the voluntary muscles of the body. Treatment required surgery to remove the thymus gland and a program of drug therapy. In December 1980—just barely out of the hospital—she was back on the job.

She needed only one month to recover from her illness. Although a regimen of chemotherapy followed, work seemed to be the best medicine of all.

"I thought a lot about what I wanted to do with my life during that time," says Mankiller. "The reality of how precious life is enabled me to begin projects I couldn't have otherwise tackled."

In 1981, she spearheaded the tribe's most ambitious and lauded experiment to that date—the Bell Community Project. With hundreds of thousands of dollars in federal and private funds and with their own labor, the residents of a poverty-stricken community named Bell in eastern Oklahoma remodeled dilapidated housing, constructed new homes, and laid a sixteen-mile pipeline that brought running water to many homes for the first time. Beyond the physical improvements, the volunteers from the Bell community did the work themselves, while developing a strong bond and gaining a sense of control over their own lives.

The national publicity that followed made the Bell Project a model for other Native American tribes eager for self-sufficiency. This work also established Mankiller as an expert in community development, and brought her to the attention of Cherokee Chief Ross Swimmer.

The ascension to deputy chief occurred two years later and in 1985, when Swimmer resigned from office, Mankiller became principal chief. Still, she did not feel she had a mandate until 1987 when she was elected on her own, even though from the very start she never slowed down.

"In order to understand how I operate, it is necessary to remember that I come from an activist family," says Mankiller. "My father was involved in union organizing, community service, and liked to discuss political issues. With a background like that, you naturally get involved in the community."

Her terms of office have produced countless highlights: a dramatic increase in tribal revenue and services; the attraction of new businesses to eastern Oklahoma, where many Cherokees live; the garnering of $20 million in construction projects, including new clinics; the procurement of funding for innovative programs to help Cherokee women on welfare become more self-reliant; the establishment of an $8 million Job Corps training center; and dozens of other projects, ranging from an extensive array of services for children to revitalization of the Cherokee judicial system. Other initiatives Mankiller has spearheaded include a new tribal tax commission, an energy-consulting firm, a pilot self-government agreement with the federal government, and an agreement with the Environmental Protection Agency.

In October 1986, Wilma married her old friend, Charlie Soap, a full-blooded Cherokee and the former director of the tribal development program. Mankiller and Soap met while working together on the Bell Project. Known as a quiet but effective "Cherokee powerhouse," Soap has focused his effort on development projects for several low-income Cherokee communities. He also directs a community-based program designed to assist needy children in rural areas. "Wilma's a hard worker and she is very sharp, but most of all she is a caring person," he says. "It's that quality of Wilma's that has made a real difference for the Cherokees."

When Soap recites his personal heroes, his wife tops the list. When Mankiller names her heroes, Soap is her first choice. "He is the most secure male I have ever met," says Mankiller. "On the outside, Charlie may have all the attributes of an authentic macho male, but he is not threatened by strong women. He is supportive of women, of women's causes, and of me and my work."

Mankiller's love of family and her people paid off in major dividends again, in 1990, when she was faced with yet another physical dilemma. Recurrent kidney problems resulted in the need for a kidney transplant. Her oldest brother, Don Mankiller, consented to serve as the donor, and the operation was a success. During her convalescence, she had many long talks with Charlie Soap and other members of her family before ultimately deciding to run for yet another term as chief.

"It was a big decision," says Mankiller, who admits that it finally came down to the fact that she believed too much unfinished work remained. Her mission was not completed. With her reelection in 1991, the Cherokee people returned Mankiller to office with a landslide vote.

But all the honorary degrees and successful tribal development projects do not begin to measure the influence that Mankiller has had in so many diverse circles of America. First and foremost is her stewardship of the Cherokees, and the pride she has instilled in literally hundreds of thousands of Native American people. Curiously, she has shown—in her typically ebullient and joyous way—not what Cherokees or other native people can learn from "mainstream" European Americans, but what whites need or want to learn from Native Americans. In fact, without the knowledge, spirituality, and inner peace that Native American culture so powerfully possesses, so many white Americans are learning that they are indeed the cultural pagans, for it is they who lack the balance and tranquility that are so dominant in the culture of native people. It is an odd concept to grasp, a philosophy that stands in direct counterpoint to the perception, throughout the nineteenth and twentieth centuries, of "Indians as savages," but it is a revolutionary and enlightening philosophy that has begun to take hold throughout America in the 1990s with the coming of a new millennium.

Spirituality is then key to the public and private aura of Wilma Mankiller, a leader who has indeed become known as much for her able leadership of the Cherokee Nation as for her spiritual presence among all Americans. A rabbi who serves as the head of a large synagogue in New York City commented that Mankiller was a significant spiritual force in the nation. One would imagine that a rabbi in Manhattan and an Indian chief in Oklahoma would have little in common, but it is clearly Mankiller's way of life—her religion, so to speak—that has formed bonds with spiritual leaders throughout the country.

No less significant has been Mankiller's reputation among women and women's groups. A woman who proudly describes herself as a feminist, a leader who is concerned with women's issues worldwide, Mankiller is ironically a female leader who has been as comfortably embraced by men as by women. The few attacks directed against her in those early days of campaigning because of her gender, because she threatened the male Cherokee status quo, all have subsided. She has become a leader who can play easily to a multitude of audiences—from the cover of *Ms.* to the cover of *Parade*—in an effortless way that few others have been able to duplicate. Perhaps it truly is her innate love of all people that breaks down so many doors.

16

THE REAL WILD WEST

*Mama, don't let your babies
grow up to be cowboys.*

—*Willie Nelson*

 Once upon a time, in the far reaches of north-central Oklahoma—not too far from the Kansas border—prospered a ranch empire of cattle, oil fields, and grasslands.

This remarkable spread, although now long vanished, remains the stuff of legends and dreams. Old cowboys, who paid their dues through lifetimes spent chasing calves, sleeping in drafty bunkhouses, and knocking around dusty corrals, believed the ranch would always persist as a shining icon of a time forever past. Some of them argued it was where the souls of all the sagebrush heroes and the most audacious saddle tramps were summoned to rest. Even though this mythical domain has been broken up and scattered to the winds, a few of the grizzled veterans who still draw breath contend that the ranch is a cowboy's Valhalla. Not even a chronic cynic dares dispute that at its zenith, all 110,000 acres in the Ponca Indian country embodied what had to be one of the wildest, woolliest, and most wonderful ranches in the history of the American West.

It was known far and wide as the Miller Brothers' 101 Ranch.

On this immense cattle ranch thrived a rollicking company of buckaroos, wranglers, ropers, trick shooters, and wild-horse riders. Guests from far and away who ventured into the wide meadows of tall grass could expect to see vast herds of grazing cattle and fleet cow ponies. To the visitors' surprise, they also might encounter elephants, camels, dancing mules, or other exotic creatures. Oil tycoons and cigar-chewing politicians came to the ranch to sip whiskey, munch roasted buffalo, and wager huge sums of money—not on sleek horses but on racing turtles at a gala event dubbed the National Terrapin Derby. Even stuffed-shirt easterners could not help but feel like children again when they set foot on the 101 and let down their hair.

Everything about the place was on a grand scale. The owners of the 101 operated their own trains, including a string of 150 freight cars and Pullmans. They grew all the food they needed and then some, and, after oil was discovered on the ranch in 1911, they ran every engine on the premises with fuel pumped from beneath the ranch sod. The 101's holdings included thousands of acres devoted to wheat, corn, oats, and forage. There were schools and churches and miles of roads used by both the work force and the public. A telephone system linked the ranch headquarters to every foreman out on the distant range. Mounted riders delivered daily mail to all sections of the ranch.

The 101 Ranch orchards produced countless overflowing bushels of apples, cherries, and peaches. There were grape arbors, a cider mill, both a cannery and a tannery, packing plants, poultry farms, a dude ranch, novelty shops, an electric power plant, an oil refinery, blacksmith shops, an ice plant, a dairy, machine and woodworking shops, a laundry, and a cafe. At the formidable two-story 101 Ranch Store, everything from "a needle to a Ford car" could be bought. A combination department store and trading post, it catered first to the ranch employees, but it also attracted customers from a radius of more than one hundred miles. Hired hands were paid with printed 101 folding scrip and with coins stamped out of copper and brass. The money was used to purchase clothing and groceries at the store, to buy food and drinks at the concession stands, and even to help pay off gambling debts.

Will Rogers twirled a rope and sang cowboy songs all night long when he came calling at the ranch. Geronimo, the wise Apache warrior, was brought there by soldier guards just so he could shoot and skin a buffalo for the benefit of a horde of ogling white folks. John Philip Sousa became an honorary member of the Ponca tribe during a visit. Admiral Richard Byrd rode an elephant over the 101 Ranch prairie. The nation's premier horticulturist, Luther Burbank, studied the records of the crops grown on the ranch. So did entire classes of university students, craving for agricultural knowledge they could not find anywhere else but at the 101.

William Jennings Bryan and Theodore Roosevelt were guests. So were Warren G. Harding, Jess Willard, John D. Rockefeller, General John Pershing, Pawnee Bill, and William S. Hart. Others who came to see what the 101 Ranch was all about included Mary Roberts Rinehart, Jack Dempsey, William Randolph

Hearst, Edna Ferber, and one of the most mythologized western figures of all—William F. "Buffalo Bill" Cody. Most all of them sat down to beefsteaks bigger than saddlebags that were so tender they cut easy as pie. Dinner was served at the imposing stucco ranch headquarters, dubbed the White House, built not far from the banks of the meandering Salt Fork River.

It was an uncommon place, as unusual as the people who lived, worked, and died there.

Kings and queens, matinee idols and millionaires, along with hundreds of thousands of ordinary working folks cheered themselves hoarse as the nimble 101 Ranch riders performed at rodeo grounds, stadiums, and exhibition halls across the nation and in Europe, Mexico, and Canada. All of these spectators, no matter their social standing or the size of their bank account, were adoring fans of the 101. Men and women still alive remember as kids seeing the 101's pet bear guzzle bottle after bottle of soda pop outside the ranch store. These elderly folks also can recall the striking costumed figures pictured on the 101 Ranch show posters who came to life on movie screens and during shows at hundreds of hometown arenas.

The men and women of the 101 were a flamboyant bunch. Bandits and lawmen with notched six-guns who spent most of their lives riding the range traveled the ranch's Wild West circuit. So did a multitude of Native American people. Eastern dudes and kids from all around the countryside ran away from home just to hook up with the 101 in order to fulfill their dreams of becoming genuine cowboys or cowgirls. Sometimes their timing was impeccable. A few of them managed to make the leap from real life to film just as the western motion picture business was created. Tom Mix, Hoot Gibson, and Buck Jones saddled cow ponies and drew wages from the 101 paymaster before they became moving-picture stars. Bill Pickett, the fabled black cowpoke who invented bulldogging, rode for the 101 until the day he died.

During the first three decades of the twentieth century, the 101 Real Wild West Show was known halfway round the globe. It featured as many as one thousand performers—cowboys and cowgirls, Indian warriors in bright paint and flowing headdresses, clowns, sharpshooters, bucking horses, fancy Russian cossacks, equestrian acrobats, brave bull riders, trained buffalo, and musicians. Many of the 101 Ranch alumni were rough-and-tumble stars and luminaries whose names became household words.

During the ranch's glory years, movie crews moved freely

around the property among the working cowboys. On Sundays, free rodeos were held. What was not so well known, especially abroad, was that the show and the performers originated from an authentic working ranch that truly rivaled all the other great cattle operations in the folklore of the West. On this ranch the West of imagination collided and merged with the West of reality. This made for a spectacle that will never be duplicated.

▼▼▼

It all began long ago with a shrewd Kentucky trader named G. W. Miller.

There has been much written and said about the Miller family and its lasting impact on ranching and entertainment. But in order to realize the absolute value and influence of the three Miller sons—Joe, Zack, and George—it is necessary to have a basic understanding of their father. He was the man who launched the 101 and who set the stage for the drama that his boys portrayed so well until the final curtain fell.

Born on February 22, 1842, to George and Almira Fish Miller on his father's ancestral plantation in Lincoln County, near Crab Orchard, in central Kentucky, this man who was destined to be known as the founder of the 101 Ranch was a pure child of the South. For reasons unknown, the family surname had been changed from Milner to Miller some years before his birth. The date of the baby's arrival, falling on the first president's birthday, coupled with his own father's given name, ensured that he could be named only George Washington Miller.

Soon after his birth, Miller's parents separated and divorced. The baby and his mother went to live on the nearby plantation of his maternal grandparents, John and Mary Fish. The Fish plantation in those antebellum years was an efficient operation, kept running smoothly thanks to the sweat and toil of many slaves. Young Miller's grandfather, John Fish, like other southern gentry, was a lover of livestock, especially thoroughbred horse flesh. In this atmosphere of lush bluegrass, bumper crops of burley tobacco, and genteel manners, Miller shared his grandfather's passions as he grew to manhood and helped manage the sprawling farm.

When the Civil War erupted, Kentucky was divided in its sentiments and became a true border state. Kentucky joined the Union side, although it was drawn to the South through cultural and familial ties and was represented with a star in the Confederate flag. Certainly, there was never any question about which side George Washington Miller was on. He was a die-hard rebel. During the bloody conflict, the rugged young Kentuckian made even more money by trading in mules with the Confederate government. Because of his extra earnings, Miller, who by then bore the title "Colonel," as was customary for southern men of prominence, purchased a portion of the plantation.

About this time young Miller also embarked on his courtship of Miss Mary Anne Carson, a gracious and beguiling southern belle known simply as Molly. The daughter of Judge David B. Carson, Molly was born on August 26, 1846, on her father's plantation in neighboring Rock Castle County, Kentucky. George Miller and Molly Carson recited their marriage vows in Louisville on January 9, 1866. Miller brought his bride to the family plantation where his grandfather, wishing to retire from active farm management, turned over the reins to his grandson.

Little more than nine months after their wedding, Molly gave birth to the couple's first child. The baby boy was born October 18, 1866. George Washington Miller, a proud father and always the southern maverick, insisted the baby be named Wilkes Booth Miller. The baby's name was meant to honor the late assassin of Abraham Lincoln, sixteenth president of the United States and a figure despised and vilified even in death as a tyrant throughout the defeated South. On March 12, 1868, another son, Joseph Carson Miller, was born to the Millers. But that very same day, Miller's mother died. Only a week before, his esteemed grandfather, John Fish, by then in his eighty-first year, had passed away. Joy over the birth of Joseph was mixed with sadness at the family's huge losses. Colonel Miller turned inward for solace and hoped a hectic work schedule would ease his pain.

Like other surviving gentlemen of the Confederacy who valued horsemanship and the ability to use weapons above all else, Miller also attempted to maintain a sense of honor and style while upholding the cavalier traditions of the Old South. This proved to be a most difficult task in those bleak Reconstruction years. Despite his strong convictions, Miller soon recognized that his future in Kentucky was quite grim. He finally admitted to himself that long gone were the winsome days of sipping juleps, swapping slaves at market, and breeding horses. Miller found little to gladden his heart in the Reconstruction South, where the federal government imposed severe economic restrictions on the vanquished rebels.

Economically handicapped without a reliable and cheap work force because of the freeing of slaves, Miller and his associates were left with only broken dreams and ruined countryside. The time had come for them to roll up their own sleeves and go to work for themselves. Further disgusted and bitter when his eldest son, Wilkes Booth, succumbed to illness just before the boy's fourth birthday in 1870, Miller decided to leave his Kentucky home for "greener pastures." A third son, John Fish Miller, named for Colonel Miller's deceased grandfather, was born on April 20, 1870, only a few months before Wilkes Booth died. Despite the birth of yet another son at the plantation, the hurt caused from losing his cherished firstborn was difficult for Miller to bear.

Later that same year, Miller, utterly discouraged in body and spirit, sold off his share of the family plantation. He only wished to pick up the pieces of his life and start all over again. Prepared to leave behind his precious Old South, Miller was resolved to move to the American West, where he hoped to rediscover a way of life that had been lost.

In a final visit to the family plot in the cemetery surrounded by a wrought-iron fence, Miller paid his respects to family members and put blossoms beneath the headstone where the words *Going Home* were chiseled in memory of Wilkes Booth. Then Miller packed some belongings and started overland with his wife, Molly, his two-year-old son, Joseph, and his infant son, John. The family was headed for California, where Miller hoped to find a suitable site to establish a mammoth livestock ranch. Although he had a sour taste in his mouth about any sort of future in Kentucky, none of Miller's enormous aspirations had been squelched.

By late 1870, the Millers arrived in the bustling river city of St. Louis. The colonel purchased a pair of Missouri mules and outfitted a rig to carry the family to the promised land in California. Miller's plan called for them to head southwest across the Ozark Plateau, enter Indian Territory, and then strike out on the southern route to the Pacific coast. As they bounced along the trail through Missouri, Miller, always the entrepreneur, kept his sharp speculator's eye peeled for business opportunities along the way. When the family paused to pitch camp for the winter months at the prairie village of Newtonia, deep in southwestern

Missouri, Miller found a way to bring in some income by doing what he knew best—trading.

The economy in the small frontier town of two hundred souls, mostly former citizens of the South like the Millers, was primarily based on the raising of hogs and trade with the residents of nearby Indian Territory. Miller immediately saw that although there were plenty of pigs, there were few cows. Instead of idling away his time until the warmer weather of spring returned so the family could resume its westward trek, he at once became an active force in the local hog business. The enterprising Miller spent the long autumn and winter months acquiring hogs from settlers in the area and converting the hogs into bacon and hams.

Through conversations with cowboys fresh off the Texas cattle trails, Miller learned that herds of longhorn steers could be fattened on sweet grass in Indian Territory and Kansas en route to northern markets. Before spring had a chance to return, Miller had changed his plans. He decided not to resume his journey to California. At least not for a while. On February 16, 1871—"a pretty winter day"—Colonel Miller left his family in Newtonia under the protection of some of his wife's younger brothers summoned from Kentucky. He saddled his best horse and set out for Texas.

Miller did not go alone. Included in the party was his brother-in-law, George W. Carson, along with hired hands Luke Hatcher, Frank Kellogg, and Jim Rainwater, an Arkansas youngster who marked his fifteenth birthday while on the trip and went on to ride as Miller's head cowboy for many years. Perry Britton, a local black man, was retained to drive the chuck wagon and serve as camp cook. Hearty teamsters were also enlisted. Their work was cut out for them. Miller had ten large wagons groaning under the weight of twenty thousand pounds of cured hog meat to swap for a herd of lively Texas steers once the party reached cow country. According to trail gossip, cattle were so plentiful and cheap in the Lone Star State that a full-grown steer could be had for one hundred pounds of bacon.

The trip south to Texas took the Miller bunch across the Missouri-Arkansas border, near the site of the Pea Ridge battle-ground. There the riders spied trees still standing that had been shattered from cannon fire. As they rode below the broken limbs, Colonel Miller doffed his hat. Perhaps he thought of the trees as mute remembrances of the thousands of men, especially those in gray, who nine years before had fought and died in combat on that scarred plateau in the northwestern corner of Arkansas.

The caravan continued south, fording streams and creeks and crossing the Arkansas River at Fort Smith into the wilds of southeastern Indian Territory. After many more days of travel through the rugged countryside, they crossed the Red River and pushed on deep into the heart of Texas. Finally, after what seemed like a lifetime, Miller and his men reached their destination—San Saba County. Finding themselves almost in the geographic center of Texas, they encountered hardened cowboys, many of them Confederate veterans, who carried Winchester rifles and six-guns. There were also great herds of longhorns—more than Miller had ever dreamed of seeing, so many, in fact, that the deft trader was able to swap fifty pounds of meat for every steer. He and his drovers rode off with a herd of four hundred bona fide Texas longhorns.

The return trip northward up the Eastern Trail through Indian Territory was far from uneventful. On Easter Sunday, not far from Fort Worth, the Miller herd stampeded in the face of a storm, as did most of the cow ponies. It wasn't until late that night that the cowboys were able to quiet the cattle. At dawn, they miraculously found that not a single head of beef had been lost. To reward young Jim Rainwater for his skill in helping to hold the herd together, Colonel Miller presented him with a two-year-old steer, which meant the rookie cowboy would receive the proceeds when that steer was finally sold at market. For good measure, Miller also gave the boy an overcoat and a pair of pants, which Rainwater noted "was the greatest treat of my life up to that time—first time in my life that anyone, who wasn't kin to me, had given me anything."

Perilous times lay ahead. There was potential danger when crossing the Trinity, the Red, and the North Fork of the Canadian River and while camping in the Indian Nations, where the threat of a renegade ambush was always present. In a turbulent creek in Indian Territory, Colonel Miller nearly drowned when his horse panicked in deep water. But Miller, as stubborn and tough as the mules he used to boss, refused to give up. He finally grabbed his mount by the tail and was pulled to safety.

Throughout the long ride home, the cowboys had few creature comforts other than a rare slug of strong drink or a plate of greasy bacon and beans served up around the evening campfire and washed down with gallons of bitter coffee. Except for the extremes of climate and weather and the constant risk of tangling with brigands and cutthroat thieves, life on the trail was lonely, dirty, and monotonous. There was little to recommend it.

The early trail riders, men like Colonel Miller, Jim Rainwater, and the others who prodded, cussed, and coaxed tens of thousands of cattle hundreds of miles to market, helped to shape the image of the mythical cowboy. It was their basic act of bringing longhorns from Texas through Indian Territory and to Kansas that ultimately formed the way generations of persons would imagine the American West.

Miller's first journey to Texas ended about three months after it began, when he and his men rode into the cattle town of Baxter Springs, Kansas, just above the Indian Territory boundary, with most of the herd intact. Permission was granted by the nearby Quapaw tribe to graze the longhorns on their land. Miller immediately established his first ranch a few miles south of Baxter Springs, not far from a trading post that eventually became Miami, Oklahoma.

Once the ranch was in operation, Miller mustered more cowboys, including Rainwater and some of those from the first journey. On March 6, 1872, they lit out for distant San Saba County on a second cattle-buying trip. Only five days before Miller's departure, his grandmother, Mary Fish, died back in Kentucky. Because Miller was committed to take his men to Texas and could not return to Crab Orchard for the services, he did his grieving from the saddle while she was laid to rest beside her husband.

This time, as they moved due south through Indian Territory to Texas, there was no procession of creaky wagons filled with smoked pork to fret over. Instead of hog meat, Colonel Miller carried saddlebags crammed with gold. He learned from his first visit that the Texas ranchers had no use for paper money, since most of them had been paid off in worthless Confederate scrip after the war. Gold coin of the realm was more to the Texans' liking. Miller was pleased, since gold was easier to transport than bacon. Best of all, only three dollars' worth of gold fetched a steer priced at six dollars.

Weeks later, Colonel Miller and his exhausted men finally returned home with more steers to turn loose in the ranch pastures. When he climbed off his horse, Miller was told that on March 29, just a little more than three weeks after he had left for Texas, his youngest son, John Fish Miller, had died. The boy had been a month shy of his second birthday when death came after a brief illness at the Miller home in Missouri. Molly and her brothers took his body back to Crab Orchard and buried him near Miller's grandparents and their firstborn son, Wilkes Booth. Four-year-old Joseph was the Millers' sole surviving child.

George Washington Miller again turned to work in order to lessen his sorrow. Any thoughts of going to California disappeared as he plunged into the cattle business with a vengeance. Miller's first operation below Baxter Springs was called the L K Ranch, for Lee Kokernut, his partner from Texas. The "L K" brand was burned into the hides on many of the longhorns arriving at Baxter Springs as they began their odyssey to the slaughterhouse.

Miller kept the family residence in Missouri, since it was only a little more than twenty miles from his Indian Territory ranch. Colonel Miller had built a general merchandise store at Newtonia, which his wife and her brothers operated while Miller spent months at a time on cattle-buying trips. Alma, the Millers' only daughter, was born at the Newtonia house on June 21, 1875. And on April 26, 1878, another son was born there. He was named Zachary Taylor Miller for the old Indian fighter and former president who had owned slaves and planted cotton. Family and friends called the boy Zack.

In 1880, Miller uprooted his family and moved to a new ranch headquarters at Baxter Springs. It was at this home-site on September 9, 1881—a date that fell between the shooting death of the legendary Billy the Kid and the well-known gun battle at the OK Corral in Tombstone—that the youngest Miller son was born. He was named George Lee Miller, for his father and also after Colonel Miller's business associate, Lee Kokernut.

Primed to expand the family's holdings, Miller had already turned his sights on grazing lands farther to the west. In 1879, he leased sixty thousand acres of Indian land located on the route of the Texas cattle trails in the famous Cherokee Strip. One of Miller's pastures, called Deer Creek Ranch, was situated about twenty miles south of Hunnewell, Kansas. The other pasture, located on the Salt Fork River, naturally became known as the Salt Fork Ranch. The Salt Fork operation, west of Ponca City, near the present town of Lamont, Oklahoma, became the Millers' primary headquarters. It consisted of little more than a sod-roof log cabin with a dirt floor, a horse corral, a branding pen, some storage sheds, and a barn. Miller and his cowboys were also proud that they erected the first barbed-wire fence in the Cherokee Strip. The Salt Fork Ranch was the source of what would become famous as the 101 Ranch.

In Winfield, Kansas—a town much closer to the ranching operations in the strip—Colonel Miller bought an elaborate, two-story brick residence. He moved in the family when Molly took their three sons and daughter back East for the annual pilgrimage to Kentucky. The Winfield home was a mansion compared to some of the family's previous dwellings. There were servants, fruit trees, a squawking parrot trained to make racial slurs, and a fancy carriage pulled by strutting bay horses to carry the Miller brood around town. Colonel Miller and his wife also made sure that their four children were steeped in the traditions of the Deep South. This meant that private tutors were employed, since Miller's strict southern heritage made him shudder when he thought of sending his offspring to Kansas public schools with blacks.

At about the same time that Miller established his ranches in the Cherokee Outlet, he also bought out the holdings of Lee Kokernut. That meant Miller had to choose a new brand for marking his cattle. There are varying versions of how Colonel Miller selected his particular brand. Many of the stories are at least partially correct, while some are outright lies or outrageous yarns undoubtedly dreamed up by cowpokes hunkered around an evening fire and enjoying a liquid supper provided by their local bootlegger. What is known is that as early as 1881, he had settled on the brand and had begun to use it. By the early 1880s, Miller's brand was being burned into the horns and eventually the hides of all his cattle. It was a brand that would one day become world famous—101.

Some ranchers and cowboys claimed the 101 brand was picked because the number represented the size of the ranch—101,000. But at the time, the Miller spread covered only sixty thousand acres of leased land. Others said Colonel Miller purchased the brand from another cattle company or that the 101 was an adaptation of the brand used by the Bar-O-Bar ranch, which Miller bought, with the bars turned upright so they could be more easily seen at a distance. None of these theories was nearly as vivid and colorful as the one furnished to Fred Gipson, author of *Fabulous Empire*, by one of the colonel's sons, Zack Miller, when he was an old man.

According to Zack, during the course of one of his father's

many cattle-buying trips to south Texas, the Miller cowboys got a tad out of hand when the outfit laid over at San Antonio for a night of revelry and refreshment before they tackled the long trail home through Indian Territory. It seems the boys headed out to an infamous watering hole that was dubbed, for reasons never revealed, the Hundred and One.

Before the long night was over, Colonel Miller's bunch managed to sample all the whiskey, women, and gaming tables in the joint. They participated in several big-time fistfights to boot. It supposedly took a frustrated and angry Miller four round trips and the assistance of at least half of San Antonio's finest to extricate all his drovers from the wreckage of the saloon and get them back to camp. Some of the greener cowboys were worthless for days after their misadventure at the Hundred and One. For Miller, a man never pleased with wasted time and lost money, the escapade was less than memorable.

So when the salty trail boss asked what road brand to put on the steers, Colonel Miller allegedly quipped, "We'll brand 101 this time. I aim to make this tough crew so sick of the sight of those figures, they'll ride a ten-mile circle around town to keep from reading that honky-tonk signboard." Ranch lore had it that not a single working stiff who rode for Colonel Miller and his sons ever again mentioned the name of that certain San Antonio establishment with three numerals for a name.

Soon the 101 name flashed like rolling prairie flames throughout the Indian Nations, as the Millers continued to pasture Texas cattle and sell them to northern ranches and in Kansas rail towns. Miller, joined by his trio of growing sons, continually expanded not only his herds but his leased acreage. Much of their land belonged to the Ponca Indians, a tribe with which Miller had forged a working relationship during the early years when he had set up his first cattle depot on the Quapaw lands.

In the late 1870s, the federal government had relocated the Poncas from Dakota Territory to a temporary home with the Quapaws. Many Poncas were unhappy with the move and longed to return to their native country in the North. Some Poncas led by Standing Bear left the Indian Territory to join some of their kinsmen in Nebraska. The government intervened and Standing Bear was imprisoned. Miller was sympathetic with the plight of the Poncas, but he also sensed a chance to improve his own lot.

Colonel Miller and his eldest son, Joe, became more friendly with the Poncas, especially with another tribal leader and most famous of the Ponca chiefs, White Eagle. With the Millers prodding all the way, the Poncas finally consented to be moved westward to the lands the government set aside for them on the eastern edge of the Cherokee Outlet. That was when sixty thousand acres of Ponca pastures became the grazing lands for the fledgling 101. Miller was allowed to feed his cattle on the tall bluestem grasses for an incredibly low sum. For many years, the Millers continued to provide business advice and counsel to the Poncas. And the friendship paid off in big dividends.

When the Cherokee Strip was finally opened to white settlement in 1893, the Poncas leased Colonel Miller thousands of additional acres of their tribal land. All Miller had to do was move his cattle and headquarters down the Salt Fork. Colonel Miller kept the family home in Winfield for his wife and daughter and built a new ranch headquarters on the south bank of the Salt Fork. Later in 1893, when the land lease was approved in Washington, it became official—the great 101 Ranch was established.

Besides the ranch founding at its permanent site, that year was pivotal for the Millers for yet another important reason. The devastating Panic of 1893 caused the 101 Ranch to make the critical transition from a pure cattle operation to a diversified farm. This all came about when the commission house in Kansas City, which the Millers used for cattle transactions, failed and closed its doors. The Millers immediately lost $300,000 due them for cattle already sold.

To make matters even worse, the bankers back East—their own backs against the wall—called in their notes. They demanded that Colonel Miller pay off his outstanding loans of $100,000. They wanted the money immediately. Without the cash needed to pay the loans, Miller was forced to let the bankers take all but his crippled livestock. "The eastern bankers sent in men who took all our cattle," Zack Miller said years later. "When they got through, all we had left was eighty-eight old horses and a handful of cows. We were as flat as the prairie."

But the Millers did not admit defeat. It was not in their nature. Nor was it characteristic of Colonel Miller, the patriarch of the clan. A council was called in the front parlor of the Winfield residence. The entire family, including Molly and Alma, sat down and planned the future. Finally, after much discussion, they struck upon a solution.

They would alter their approach to business and, instead of

raising just livestock, they would also become farmers and plant cash crops. It called for a roll of the dice, but the Millers had few alternatives. Because of the family's reputation in the community, local financial institutions took a chance and underwrote the Millers' purchase of plows, seed wheat, and five hundred calves to be fattened for market. Old hands, accustomed to rounding up strays and branding dogies, pretended their cow ponies were draft horses in order to plow thousands of acres of rangeland for a wheat crop. It proved to be a wise maneuver. In 1894, the Millers brought in more than seventy thousand bushels of quality wheat, which they immediately sold for a lucrative $1.20 per bushel. This gave them seed money to use for rebuilding their depleted herds of livestock and expanding their growing fields for more crops.

For the next decade, the 101 Ranch grew and prospered. All the while, Colonel Miller continued to teach his sons the fine points of entrepreneurship and risk taking. They proved to be able students. All three of them adhered to a basic business philosophy that purported: "It is just as bad to go broke in a little way as it is in a big way." These were words that the Miller brothers would live and die by over the course of the next forty years.

By 1903, after a decade of successful ranching and farming, the Millers were prepared to make a total commitment to the land they had been leasing from the Ponca tribe. This occurred as the federal government broke up various Indian lands and doled out allotments to individual tribal members. Now the tribes could sell property with federal government approval. When White Eagle received the government's permission to sell some of the Ponca land, the Millers were finally permitted to buy thousands of acres they had been leasing from the tribe. By and by, the Miller's property holdings extended throughout the lands of the Ponca, Otoe, Pawnee, and Osage Indians in four counties. No longer burdened with uncertainties, restrictions, and government red tape, the Millers at last felt comfortable about making permanent improvements on the land. They were anxious to draw up plans for a large ranch headquarters residence to take the place of the sod dugout on the bank of the Salt Fork.

Colonel Miller wanted the 101 headquarters house to be the finest in cow country. He told his family and friends that no cost would be spared. Influenced by Miller's love of the fine plantation homes from back in Kentucky, the plans called for a three-story prairie palace to be built on the north side of the Salt Fork and furnished with the best things from the house in Winfield. Work commenced at once.

Unfortunately, the elder Miller never set foot in the completed residence that came to be called the White House. That spring the old rebel was stricken with pneumonia. Almost as soon as he was diagnosed, Miller recognized that he would not recover. But his sense of manners and hospitality remained constant to the very end. Only a few hours before his death, he made sure that some friends who had ridden out to bid him "so long" were fed a proper meal. He told them that he was sorry that he could not join them at the table. Then Colonel George Washington Miller, founder of the 101 Ranch empire, quietly died inside the old dugout headquarters on the Salt Fork. He was sixty-one. It was Saturday, April 25, 1903.

Brief services were held for Miller the next day on the ranch. They washed and dressed the old man and laid him in a coffin packed with ice so the body would keep while being shipped by rail to Crab Orchard, the old family home in Kentucky. An escort of the colonel's favorite cowboys, dressed in their best hats and boots, rode beside the hearse as it rolled from the ranch headquarters toward the train depot at the nearby town of Bliss. Many Ponca Indians also accompanied the black hearse moving across part of the Millers' domain, past the wheat fields, past herds of grazing cattle.

The Ponca chief, White Eagle, and other tribal leaders paid their last respects to one of a few white men whom they considered a true friend. They viewed Miller's body at the dugout, but they did not go to the railroad station. A *Kansas City Star* reporter who was there that day heard White Eagle quietly explain, "I would not weep where men and women could see me. I must retire alone." All day and into the night, Ponca mourners wailed death chants and butchered several head of cattle for a big feast to honor their departed friend.

Colonel Miller left no last will and testament. Instead, he decreed that the 101 Ranch should remain intact and forever stay in the Miller family. His widow received $30,000 from an insurance policy her husband carried on his life. By late that year, the Miller boys saw to it that the work on the new ranch headquarters was completed and that the family place in Winfield, Kansas, was sold.

On Halloween Day of 1903, Miller family members and

friends turned out for the wedding of Alma Miller—the first official social event at the still-unfinished residence. The lone female sibling in the family, Miss Miller retained a share of the 101 Ranch estate. She wed William Henry England, a young up-and-coming lawyer from Winfield. The couple soon moved to Kansas City, where England practiced law. Later they came back to Ponca City and raised several children while England continued his practice and served as a legal adviser to the ranch until his death in 1923. On Christmas Day 1903—less than two months after Alma's wedding ceremony—Molly Miller, her three sons, her daughter, and some other guests sat down to the first meal ever served in the new house.

Following their father's death, the Miller brothers operated the ranch as a family alliance, and with the encouragement and inspiration of their mother, the enterprise grew by leaps and bounds. It was not too long before the ranch became known as the Miller Brothers' 101 Ranch, with each of the three sons focusing on a different aspect of the partnership. Joe, the eldest of the trio, purchased some of the finest breeding stock in the Southwest, and specialized in the agricultural aspects of the business, including the care and feeding of the orchards and fields. Zack was the pure cowboy who most enjoyed buying, selling, and caring for the cattle and horses. The youngest Miller brother, George, possessed the hard-nosed business talent, serving as the executive who ran the busy offices, oversaw financial operations, and negotiated contracts.

It was a formidable combination, with more still to come. The Millers were poised to take center stage under floods of public limelight. Their impressive dominion, long considered by some to be the last bastion of the "Real Wild West," was due to become one of the most significant training grounds for the motion-picture industry.

The first major event to thrust the 101 Ranch into the public eye took place in 1905 when the Millers hosted a roundup extravaganza that would ultimately evolve into the Miller brothers' famous Wild West shows. The idea for the big shindig at the 101 was sparked in 1904 when Joe Miller accompanied Frank Greer, a newspaper editor from Guthrie, to St. Louis to attend the annual meeting of the National Editorial Association. While there, Miller promised that if the association would come to the territorial capital of Guthrie the following year, he and his brothers would arrange for a Wild West show at their ranch the likes of which had never been witnessed. Association officials agreed, and the Millers immediately launched a plan of action.

A dress rehearsal was successfully staged in May 1905 at the newly constructed arena near the south bank of the Salt Fork. Months and months of careful preparation paid off by the following month, when visitors from all over the country began arriving. A literal swarm of newspaper and magazine editors, estimated at more than 65,000, came to the 101 Ranch that June to watch the Miller boys re-create the West of yesteryear. Many visitors made the trip on special trains, while others journeyed to the ranch by horseback, wagon, and buggy. Hundreds of tents were pitched along the river. Crowds milled about under the warm June sun, eating ice cream and barbecued buffalo and slurping up barrels of red soda pop.

The program included parades, rodeo events, and Indian raids on stagecoaches and wagon trains. Lucille Mulhall, billed as "America's first cowgirl," thrilled onlookers with daring stunts performed while dashing around the arena on her galloping horse. Bill Pickett, the illustrious black cowboy from Texas who was credited with "inventing" the rodeo event known as bulldogging, or steer wrestling, made a lasting impression on the audience by using his famous teeth to best a feisty steer. Pickett would go on to ride with the Miller brothers for many years before his life ended on the ranch in 1932 after being kicked by an unruly horse.

Thousands of guests also witnessed Geronimo, the aging Apache warrior brought to the 101 by a military escort from Fort Sill, shoot and kill a buffalo during a mock hunt. Publicity for the event billed the appearance as a chance to see Geronimo stalk and shoot his final buffalo. In truth, it was probably the first as well as the last buffalo that the once-proud Indian leader ever shot.

When the dust finally settled, the resulting editorial coverage, with virtually every major newspaper and magazine reporting, catapulted the 101 into the public's imagination. Encouraged by the overwhelming publicity and positive response from a cross section of society, the Miller brothers decided to put the show on the road. "Boys ten years old and younger have never seen a genuine Wild West show, and we are going to make it possible for them to see one," bragged Joe Miller, who along with his two bothers put the honorary title of "Colonel" before his name just like their father did long before them.

In the years that followed, it became a common sight to spot the Millers and their company of cowboy and Indian performers departing Oklahoma in a train of Pullmans and freight cars. They played to capacity audiences in Norfolk, Oklahoma City, Kansas City, Wichita, St. Louis, and New York. Everywhere the Millers took their show, they were greeted with eager throngs of fans and rave reviews. Even when catastrophe struck, such as the disastrous fire that destroyed the ranch headquarters in 1909, the undaunted Millers did not miss a beat. They immediately rebuilt an even bigger and better White House, complete with every known modern convenience. For the Millers and their robust outfit, there was no looking back.

Tom Mix, who first encountered the Millers years before he signed on to ride with them, when he was pushing stiff drinks across a mahogany bar in Guthrie, spent several years with the 101 Ranch. It was at the ranch on the Salt Fork where Mix learned his best cowboy stunts. He put them all to good use later as a big-shot moving-picture star in California. In 1926, many years after he left their employ, Mix recalled his time with the Millers in a feature story written for the *101 Magazine.* "In the old days, with the blue sky above me, a good horse under me, the vast acreage of the old 101 Ranch rolling green about me and a bacon-filled atmosphere from the chuck wagon calling me, I was the richest of men," wrote Mix. "To me there has always been an inspiration in the broad expanse of far-stretching prairie, the ranch houses and the low corrals of the 101."

The 101 Ranch inspired a host of others who also went on to fame and fortune as western motion-picture heroes and heroines, including Buck Jones, Mabel Normand, Neal Hart, and Hoot and Helen Gibson. The early western films shot on the 101 Ranch may have been crude compared to their modern counterparts, but they helped stir the nation's imagination and extend the concept of the Old West. Those early films featured authentic cowboys, cowgirls, and Native Americans.

W. A. Brooks, a cousin of the Millers, acted as the primary film director for the 101 Ranch when new ground was broken in California. By 1911, the Millers quartered their performers in winter not far from the resort town of Venice, on the Pacific just west of Los Angeles and the little town of Hollywood. Thomas Ince and his Bison Motion Picture Company joined forces with the Millers, and Ince went on to hire many of the men and women from the 101 to appear in his popular western films. He eventually purchased almost twenty thousand acres of land in southern California, where he built a movie studio. At first called the Miller 101 Bison Ranch, the property became known as Inceville, and remained in constant use until the early 1920s.

All the time the early film work was being produced, the 101 Real Wild West Show continued to travel through the United States, Canada, and Mexico, thrilling audiences wherever it went. In 1914, the show went abroad and played to enthusiastic crowds in Great Britain. At a memorable matinée performance in London, Queen Mary, along with the czarina of Russia and the queens of Greece, Rumania, and Spain, sat in the royal boxes applauding what was described as "the most marvelous wild west performance ever seen."

But when World War I erupted in July 1914, the British government cut short the 101's European tour by commandeering the show stock and equipment for its Army. Only some fast talking allowed the Millers to salvage their very best horses from being pressed into military service. Despite the great losses sustained, the Millers cut their losses and tried again to put fine shows on the road during the 1915 and 1916 seasons. Jess Willard, the world-champion prizefighter known as the Great White Hope, was hired to help attract crowds, and in 1916, Buffalo Bill Cody, at one time the idol of every red-blooded American boy, joined the 101 show. Although by this time he was unable to even mount his famous white stallion, Cody nonetheless rode into the arenas in a buggy drawn by a pair of matched steeds. The old showman and scout delighted his fans as a young man tossed glass balls into the air for Buffalo Bill to shatter with his rifle. Cody died a year later in Colorado in 1917.

Only a few months later, Molly Miller—the matriarch of the Miller family—passed away at the White House. Her boys laid her to rest at a cemetery in Ponca City. Shortly after that the United States entered the war. The Millers disbanded their show as many of the 101 performers went off to fight in France.

The Millers tried a comeback in 1924 under a new name— the 101 Ranch Real Wild West and Great Far East, but their time had passed. The Roaring Twenties were under way with all the trappings of modernity. It was the age of the circus, and there was serious competition from the moving pictures. The Millers relied more and more on spectacular stunts and less on the authentic western skills that had brought them riches and glory years before. Accidental fires and cyclones ravaged their tents, and train wrecks and other misfortunes added to the Millers' woes. There were also more deaths that took a serious toll and sapped much of the magic of the 101.

On October 21, 1927, Colonel Joe Miller died. His death was ruled accidental, due to carbon monoxide poisoning while he was working on an automobile in the garage at his new home, just north of the ranch. Joe's sudden passing not only stunned his brothers but undoubtedly marked the start of the downfall of the 101 empire. More bad news was soon to come in the form of severe drought and crop failures, a horrendous flood, and a sharp decline in oil royalties. Ranch finances were strained to the limit.

More tragedy visited the 101. Around midnight on February 1, 1929, George Miller was returning home when he lost control of his Lincoln roadster on an icy curve near Ponca City. The car skidded on the pavement before it overturned, pinning Miller's head beneath a front wheel. He died before reaching the hospital. The 101 Ranch had not only lost another of the Miller brothers, but the one who was the best when it came to business dealing. Of the sons, only Zack Miller survived. His back was against the wall, leaving him little or no time for sorrow over his losses.

Zack and his nephews tried their best to keep the operation afloat. But by late 1929, the bottom fell out of the stock market. The grim years of the Great Depression had begun. In little time, the once-lucrative oil business was clobbered, as were the Millers' agricultural ventures. Livestock prices dropped to the lowest on record. Zack tried to stop the bleeding by securing a new mortgage, but it did not help. No matter what he tried, the economic situation grew only worse. By the time 1930 ended, the ranch had suffered a net loss of more than $300,000 for the year.

No cash reserve remained to curb the mortgages, bank notes, and taxes. In 1931, a court-appointed receiver stepped in and liquidation was started. The Millers' beloved Wild West show was dismantled and sold off. Zack still made desperate attempts to save his family's historic ranch, but before long, much of the ranch equipment and the livestock went on the auction block. There was scant hope in sight. Even Zack's old friend Bill Pickett—the faithful bulldogger—was dead after being kicked by a horse.

Finally, over Zack's protests and his attempts with a six-shooter to halt the proceedings, everything was sold. A poignant story published on March 25, 1932, in the *Daily Oklahoman* described the scene at the 101 Ranch, where everything was up for sale: "There were sad doings here Thursday, marking the passing of a great Oklahoma institution, the 101 Ranch, internationally famous symbol of a young state that rides 'em cowboy. A picturesque crowd of more than 3000 persons turned out for the receiver's sale of all the property of the Miller Brothers' 101 Ranch Trust, a few coming to buy, but a vast majority simply to walk stolidly along the dusty lanes and watch with calm solicitude the disintegration of the greatest showplace in the West. Over in the historic White House of the ranch, Colonel Zack Miller, sole survivor of the trio of brothers which made the place famous, roared defiance to the world, threatening to blow up the mansion, and even fired a shotgun in the direction of attorneys seeking a conference with him. He termed the sale a 'legal robbery.' "

Zack, ever defiant and painfully aware of all that his father and brothers had sacrificed to make the 101 Ranch a truly remarkable empire, finally had to be hauled off to the county jail. There he remained until Oklahoma Governor William "Alfalfa Bill" Murray, through his state militia, saw to it that Zack was released.

The last of the Miller brothers still was not ready to stop his battle to save the 101. Later that year, news stories surfaced that in order to keep at least a portion of the spread going, Zack was even negotiating with Chicago gangster Al "Scar Face" Capone. The plan was for Capone and his brother Ralph to purchase several thousand acres of the 101. A Ponca City real estate broker suggested that the Capones would manage the ranch after Al gained release from the federal penitentiary. The Capones would then divide the 101 into small forty-acre and eighty-acre farms to be worked by a colony of Italian immigrant families. The scheme was short-lived.

Soon all that remained was the White House and the furnishings. Then, in 1936, the entire contents of the twenty-two-room White House were auctioned off, including antique guns, buffalo overcoats, Indian rugs, and a prized Lender portrait of White Eagle, the Ponca chief and the Millers' friend. Again, a *Daily Oklahoman* reporter at the ranch that hot July day described the occasion: "Grim, gray-haired Zack T. Miller stood in the shadows of the old White House Saturday and watched the last of his vast empire crumble under the hammer of an auctioneer. He stood without visible emotion, although his face set in hard lines as one by one his personal belongings went on the block, ending another epic of the Old West.

"The sale ended, and bargain hunters scattered. The last of three famous sons of a famous father stood on the steps of the big white mansion, and gazed over what once was a 110,000-acre ranch. Perhaps he saw another time, when 50,000 persons gathered in 1905 to cheer the first annual roundup that later grew into the wild West circus. Miller looked at deserted, fallen farm buildings that once housed the state's finest blooded cattle and hogs. He looked over weeds and disorder where once were showplace orchids [sic], wheat fields, packing houses and power plants. Miller walked slowly down the steps to the car of his sister, Mrs. Alma England, and drove toward Ponca City."

Over the years, Zack tried to make his share of comebacks by riding with Wild West shows. He even bought back the old 101 Ranch Store building and set up a curio shop, but that did not last. Ultimately he ended up in a wheelchair. He hired a young man to push him around and they made the rounds of sale barns so the old cattleman could see the livestock. Finally he went to live at his daughter's home in Waco, Texas. Zack Miller died there on January 3, 1952. He died in the state where so many years before his father had swapped hog meat for steers to start the 101 Ranch.

They brought Zack home to Oklahoma. He was buried close to the banks of the Salt Fork, on Cowboy Hill, a plot of land given by Zack to the Cherokee Strip Cowpunchers Association as a place for annual reunions of those who had ridden the range in the famed strip. Years later two old 101 veterans—Jack Webb, a trick roper and sharpshooter, and Sam Stigall, a 101 cowboy and foreman from 1902 to 1929—were laid to rest nearby. Just up the road a short distance, near the town of Marland, are the graves of White Eagle and Bill Pickett.

Hardly any physical trace of the 101 Ranch remains. The land was divided into scores of privately owned farms. Through time all the buildings, even the White House, were burned down, razed, or left to decompose.

But sometimes if the morning light is just right, or late at night when the moon is making puzzling shadows, those who know what was once there pause along the two-lane road that runs by the old spread. They let their minds play tricks. In the thistle and clumps of sumac the wind sounds like strong cow ponies on the move. Hundreds of ghosts are difficult to keep quiet. The beating drums, the solemn chants, the crack of pistols, the waves of applause cannot be stilled.

None of what happened there can ever be forgotten.

PHOTOGRAPHIC CREDITS

iv–v: Phillips Collection in the Western History Collection, University of Oklahoma Library
xx: Western History Collection, University of Oklahoma
18: Guy Logsdon
28: Terrence Moore
58: Tom Luker
72: Terrence Moore
88: Terrence Moore
98: Michael Wallis Collection
124: Suzanne Fitzgerald Wallis
136: Terrence Moore
148: Suzi Moore
156: Collection of Michael Wallis
176: Connie Harris
194: Tom Luker
206: Suzanne Fitzgerald Wallis
216: Rod Jones
228: Suzanne Fitzgerald Wallis

ABOUT THE AUTHOR

Michael Wallis is a biographer and historian of the American West. He is the author of *Pretty Boy: The Life and Times of Charles Arthur Floyd*, published by St. Martin's Press in 1992, as well as the critically acclaimed *Route 66: The Mother Road*, published by St. Martin's in 1990. In 1988, *Oil Man: The Story of Frank Phillips and the Birth of Phillips Petroleum*, another best-selling biography, was published by Doubleday.

An award-winning journalist, Michael Wallis's work has appeared in many publications, including *Time, Life, People, Smithsonian,* and *Texas Monthly*. Wallis is a contributing editor to *Oklahoma Today*. Born in Missouri, Wallis held many jobs during his early years as a writer. He worked as a bartender, hotel waiter, social worker, printer, and ranch hand, and he managed a ski lodge. He also served with the Marine Corps and was honorably discharged as a sergeant.

Wallis has lived and worked throughout the Southwest and Mexico. He and his wife, Suzanne Fitzgerald Wallis, have resided in Oklahoma since 1982.